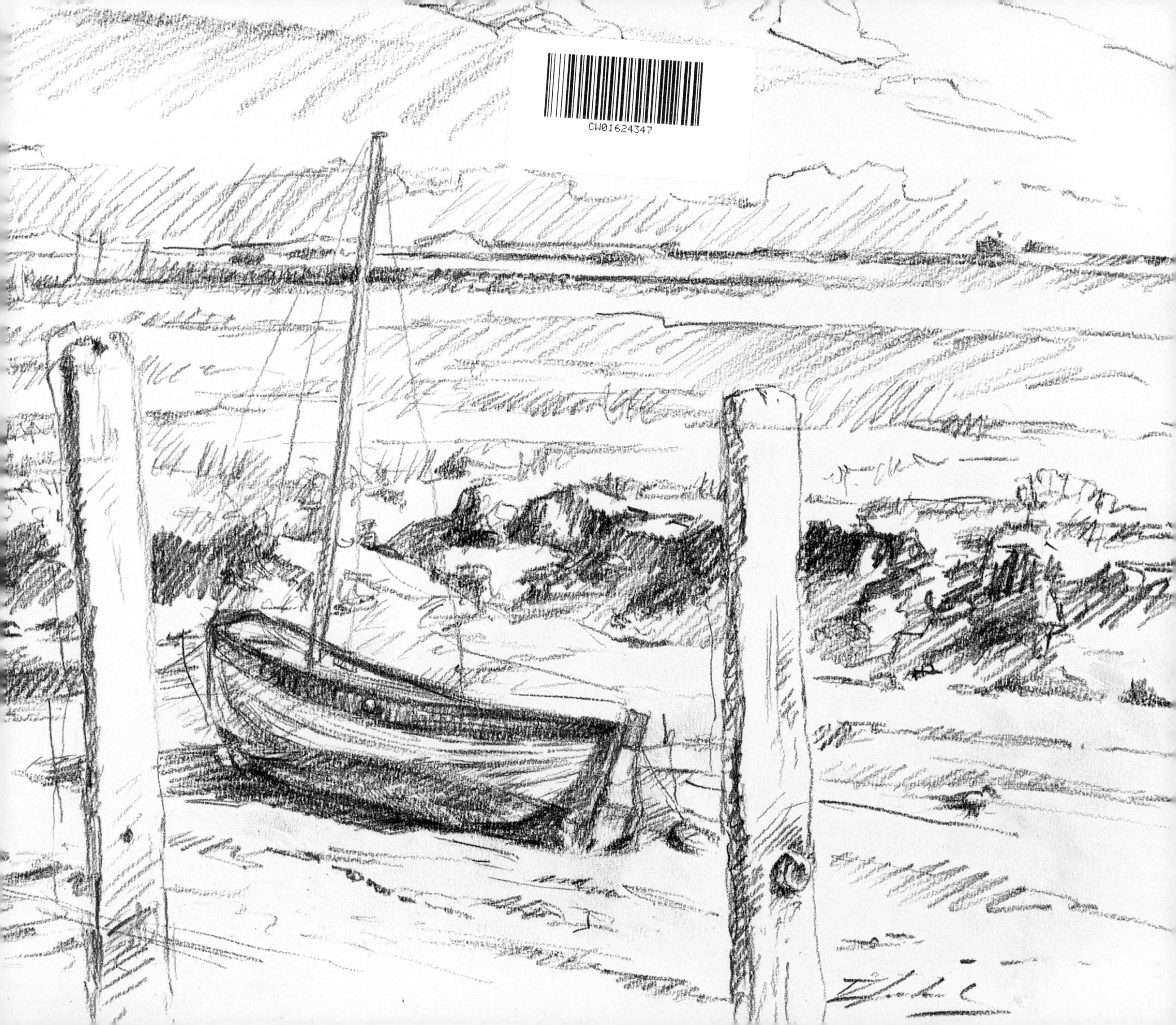

North Norfolk
A Painted Landscape

An Artist's Diary

Rachel Lockwood

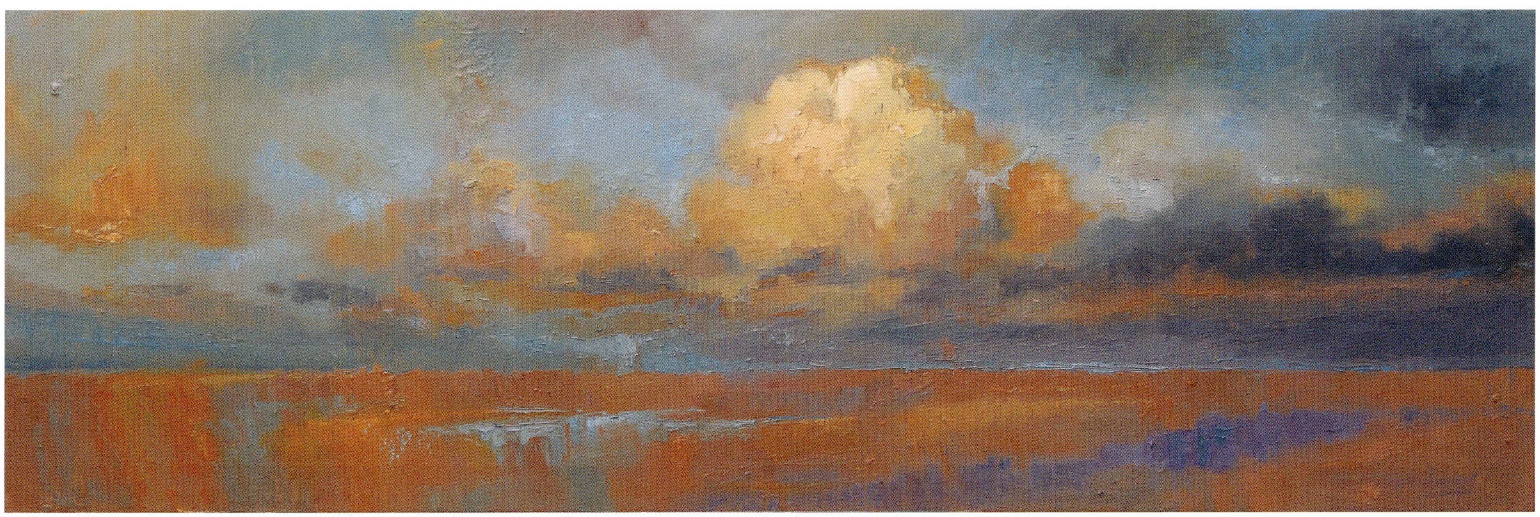

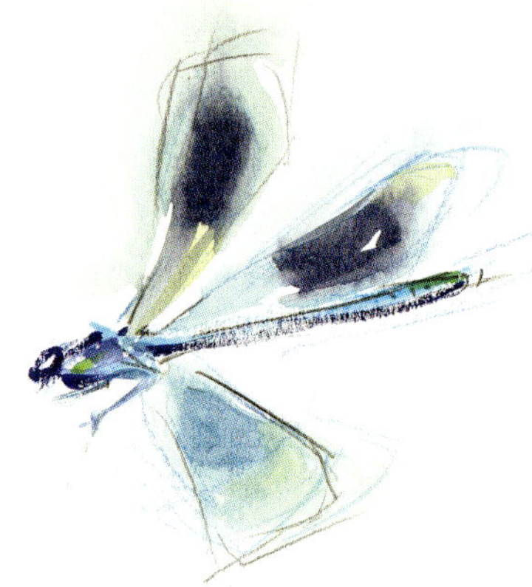

Red Hare
Publishing

First Edition
Published in Great Britain in 2011 by Red Hare Publishing Ltd

Red Hare Publishing Red Hare Studio The Field Holt Road Cley next the Sea Norfolk NR25 7TX
Tel: 01263 740947
info@redharepublishing.co.uk
www.redharepublishing.co.uk

ISBN: 978-0-9569976-0-9

Printed in Britain by Crowes Complete Print Norwich Norfolk www.crowes.co.uk

CARBON BALANCED PAPER
WORLD LAND TRUST™
www.carbonbalancedpaper.com
CBP0008851609111723

FSC www.fsc.org
MIX
From responsible sources
FSC® C007154

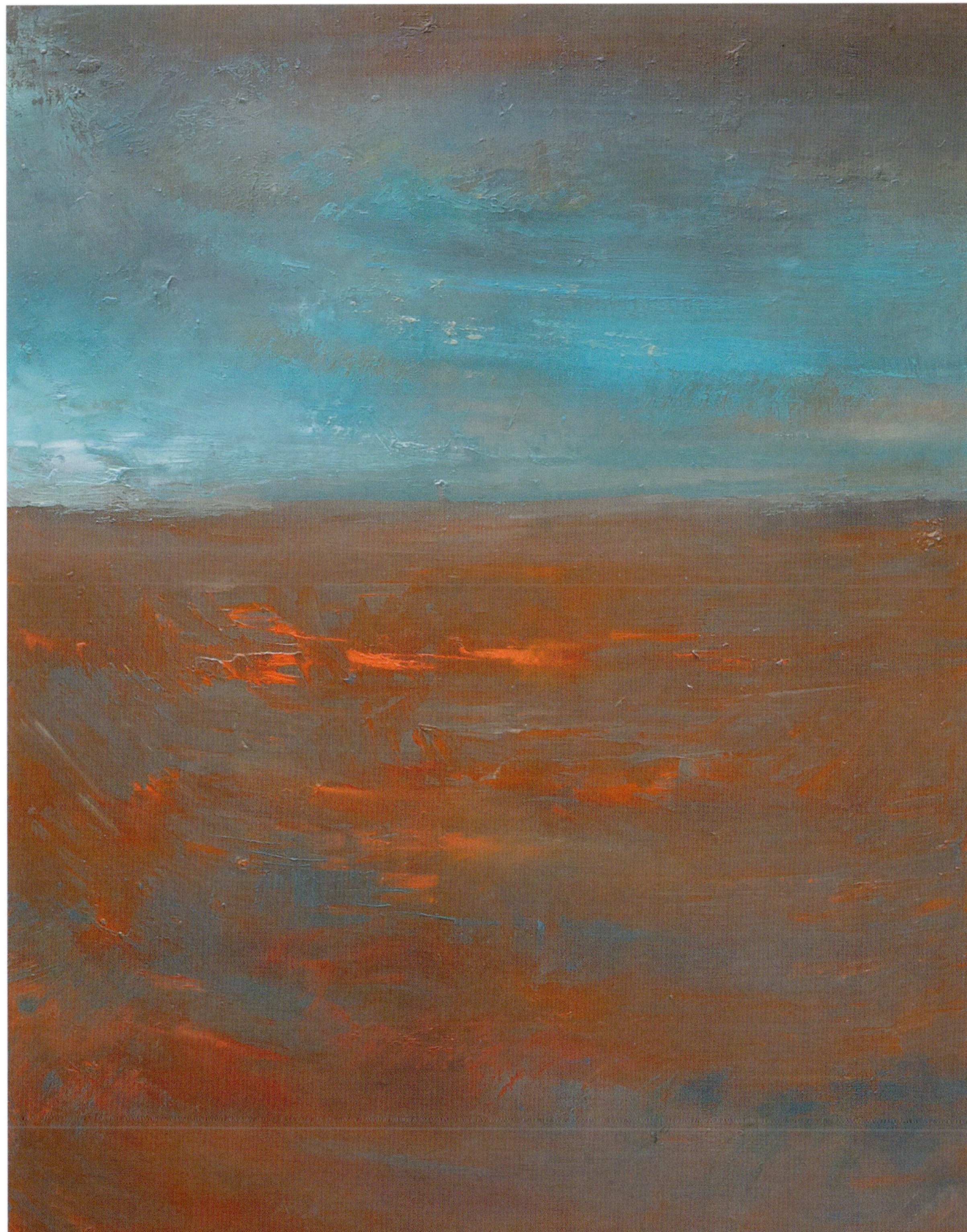

Norfolk Sea and Sky
oils on canvas 120x80 cm

Foreword

by

Virginia McKenna

It is the light isn't it? The luminous, ethereal, almost magical quality that fills the North Norfolk sky. Hardly surprising that painters try and capture this illusive colouring and how beautifully and sensitively Rachel Lockwood has achieved this. Clouds, water, reflections, open landscapes and, although we cannot hear them, we know these fields and dunes and pools are the home of calling birds, and deer and butterflies, and crickets, and we are only passing visitors to their mysterious and fascinating world.

I have, all too briefly, been one of those visitors. But I find in Rachel's delicate paintings welcome and happy reminders of the unspoilt loveliness of this corner of England. Long may it remain that way and long may Rachel continue to delight us with the subtlety of her art.

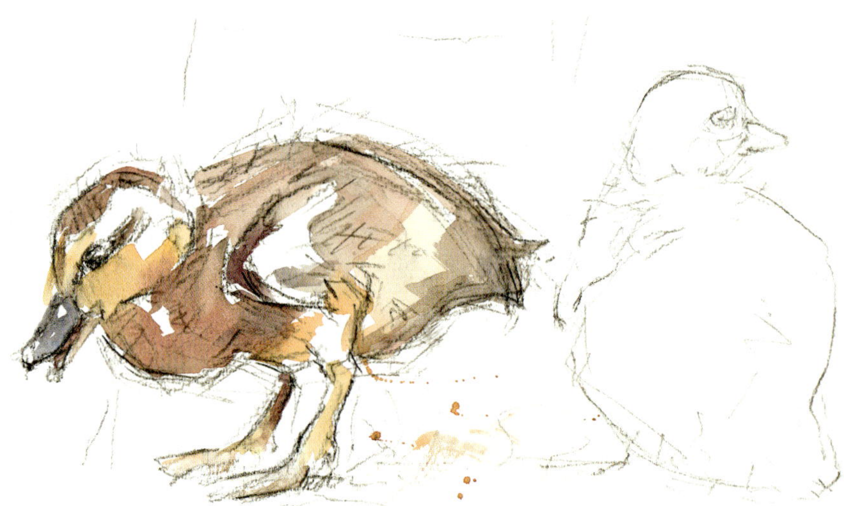

Introduction

I grew up in the north side of Sheffield, an industrial landscape of coalmines and steaming factory chimneys. Fortunately for me, my parents bought a house opposite a small area of woodland, which is where I spent most of my spare time, running wild. It was our own wilderness, a great festering jungle for our imaginations. This small woodland is where I painted my first outdoor pictures, perhaps this is where it all began.

Eventually my art education took me to London to study scientific illustration; a disciplined art course that literally delved into the bowels of creatures, dead humans and all. But my desire to run wild remained, and after years of illustrating wildlife, I decided to head for Australia – the biggest wilderness I could find that would allow me the freedom to wander. After a year of travelling around this amazing country, I spent a year in the flatlands of Holland, but I craved yet again for a natural landscape. After a visit to Norfolk, I fell in love. I had found a landscape where I could again run wild, but this time on a much larger scale than my childhood woodland patch. Now I have beach, marsh, woodland, heath, wildlife and to top it all, huge skies. Here are a selection of my paintings from the last few years that I hope shows you a glimpse of my North Norfolk through the seasons.

Rachel Lockwood

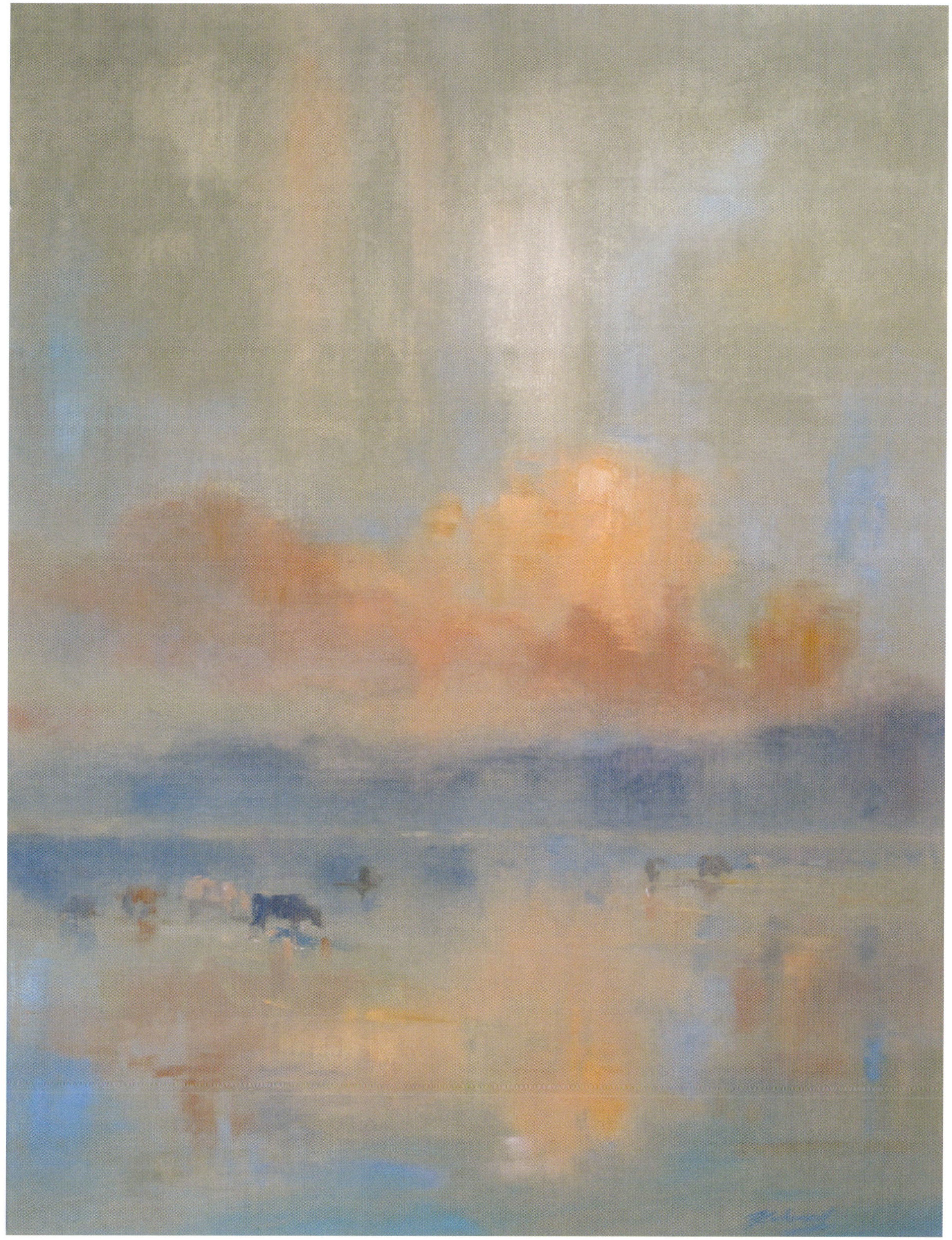

Cows On Wet Summer Marsh
oils on linen 100x80 cm

16 March

Today my favourite day of the year has arrived, that first warm day of spring; the birds are chattering incessantly about it as I walk through Cley to my studio. Heat is rising from the road and I feel my muscles start to relax at the thought of summer hopefully on its way. The air is warming up and a distant cockerel calls out over the village. I reach the field where my studio is and a cold blast of air washes over the damp grass, which reminds me that the weather could change its mind at any time. I love these days full of hope without the expectations of summer. It also sets my mind to thinking that I can again paint outside; I feel overwhelmed as to where to start.

However, first I have to finish a painting that is still wet in my studio. I can't leave it at this stage as the timing is crucial; I need to paint wet into wet to allow the colours to mingle. Another day left and it will be past that magic point. This was a view from my bedroom window in Cley, which overlooks Blakeney Freshes. The early morning mist had crept over the land and was lit by an eerie turquoise light that I'd never seen before. The mist rolled in and out within minutes, but this magical image remained with me.

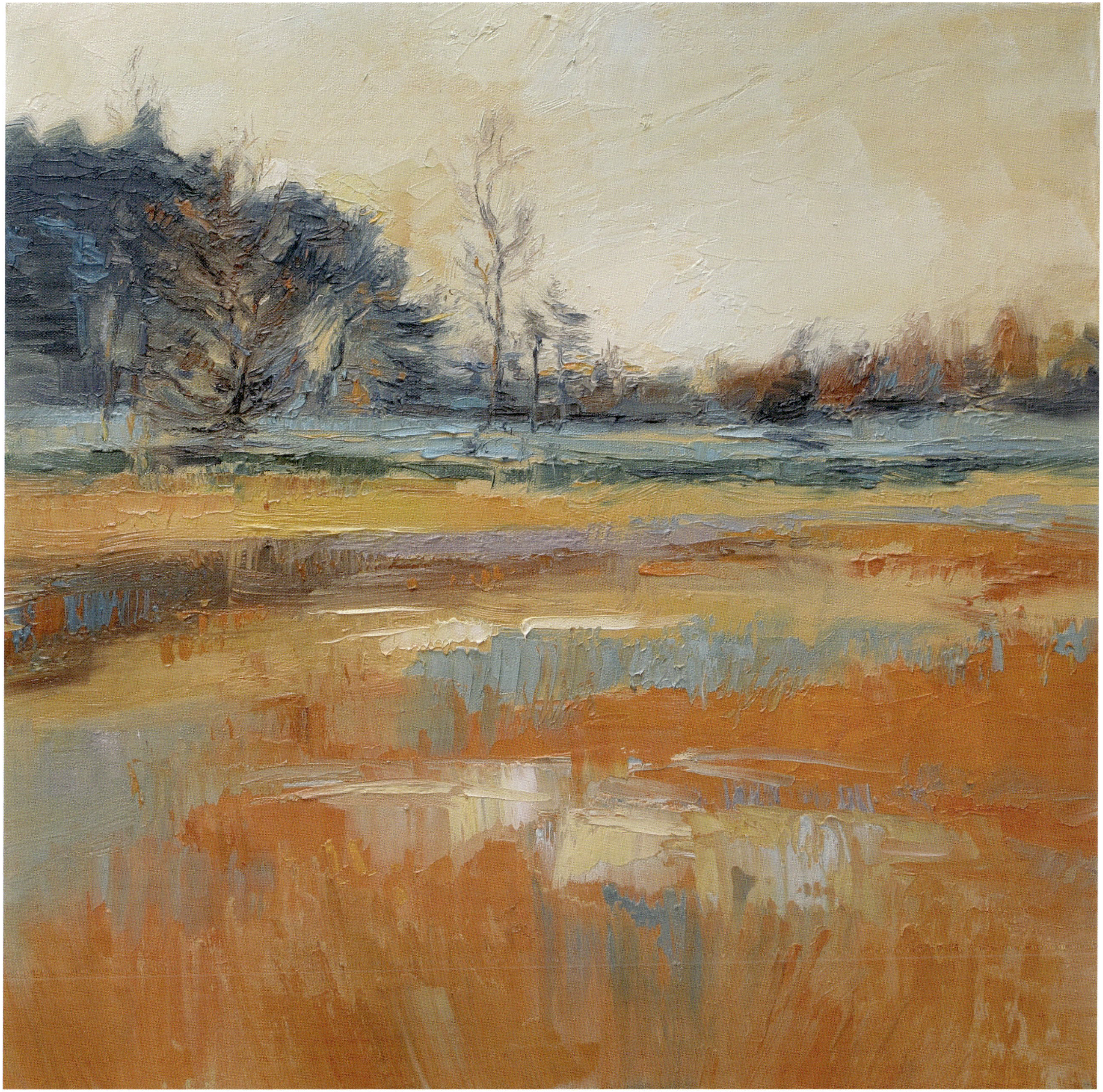

Turquoise Mist, Cley
oils on canvas 50x50 cm

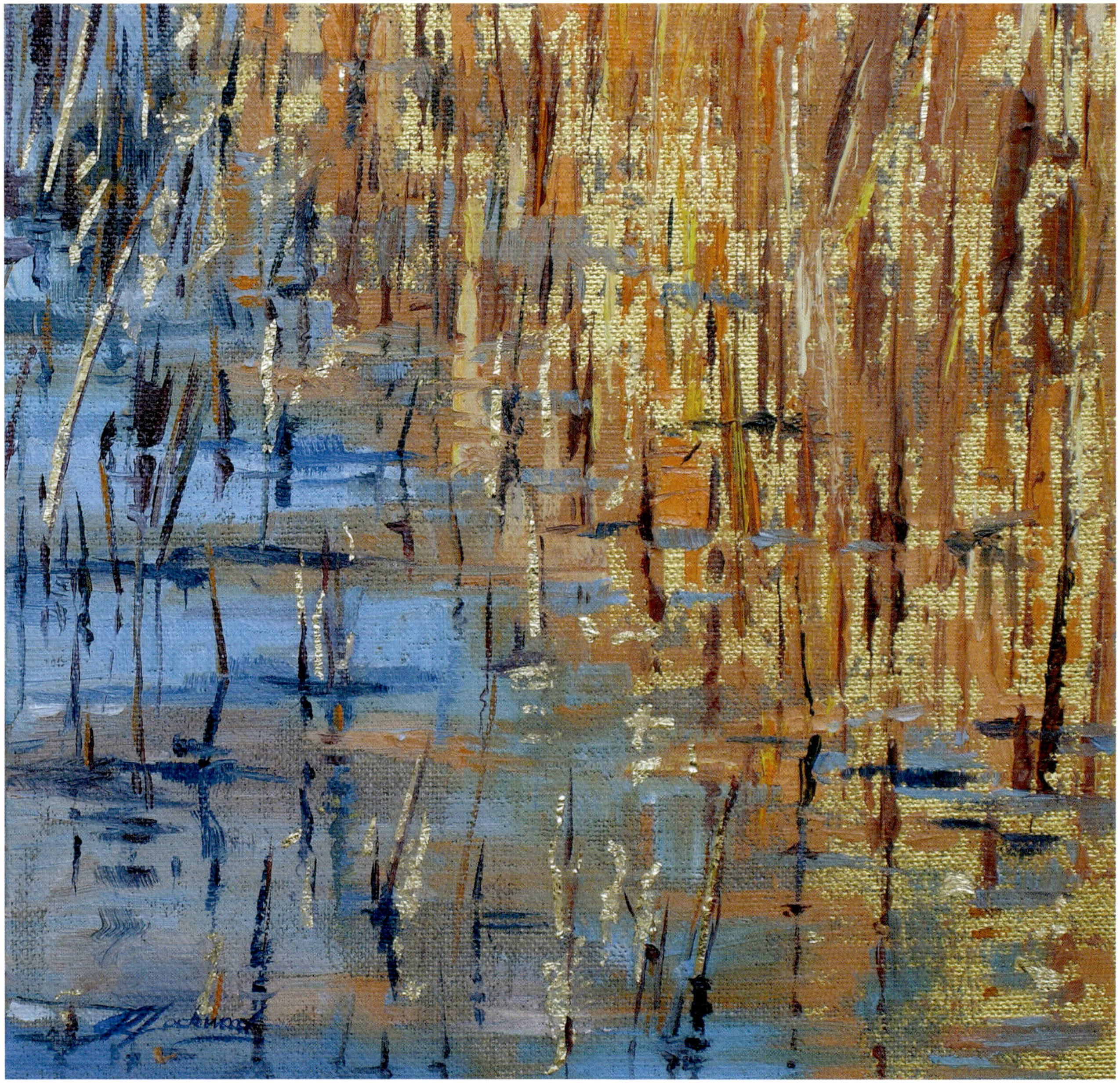

Golden Reeds
oils on canvas board
20x20 cm

17 March

The frost quickly thawed as the spring sun rose over the village this morning. Within ten minutes Sarah and I were out on the marsh, first stop Bramble Flap, a regular fishing spot for the Kingfisher. Bearded Tits called from the reeds, their metallic 'tink' giving away their position, but so hard to see. We followed the waterways for signs of wildlife, hoping to see a Water Vole. In the distance the reed cutter hacked at his bundle of reeds and I made a mental note to paint him at a later date.

The early morning light was sharp, crisp and clear, sparkling along the watery edge of the reeds. To try to capture this I used gold leaf in this painting; the glint of the gold leaf changes as you view the picture from different angles, just as I saw it.

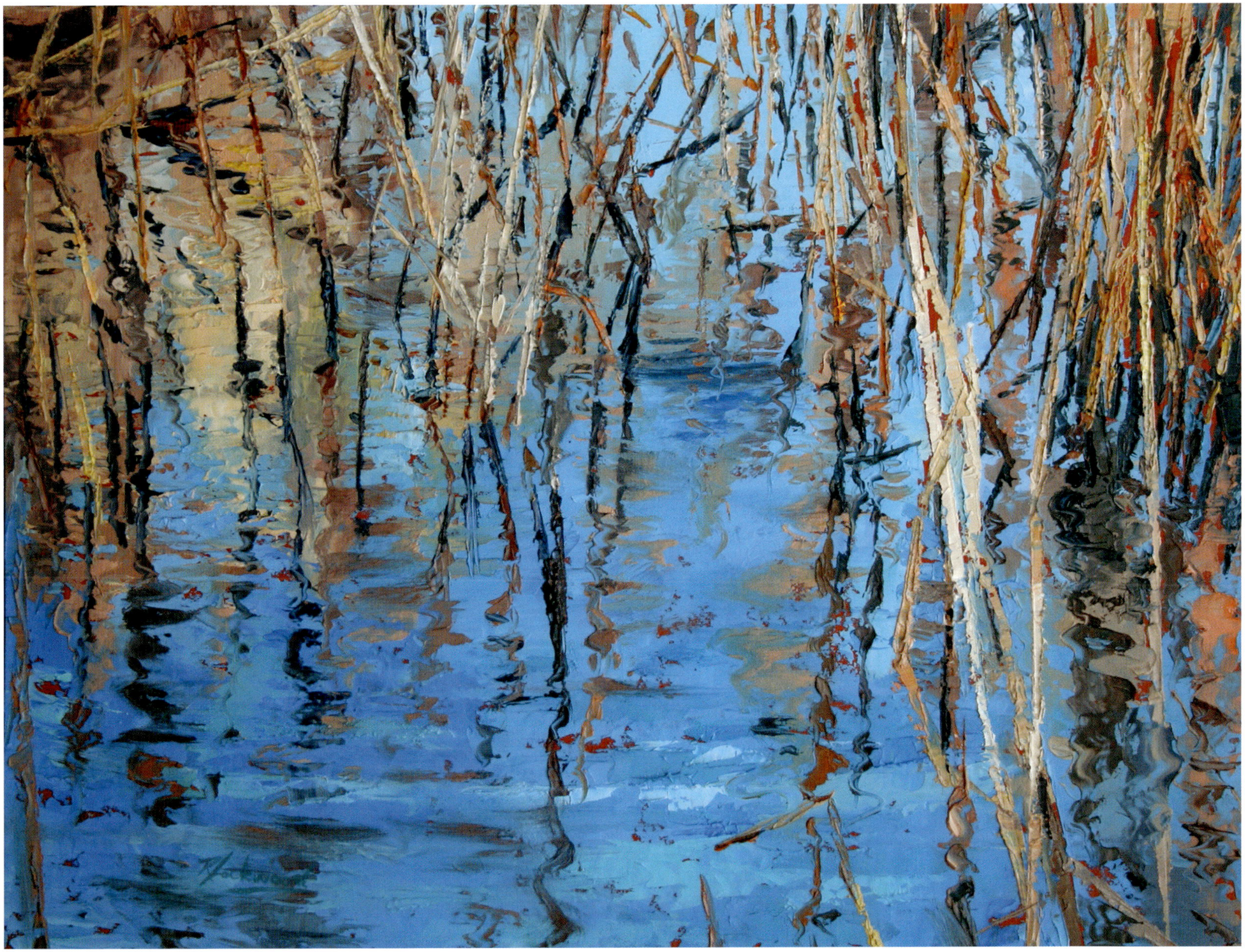

Bramble Flap
oils on canvas board
30x40 cm

Within minutes a breeze picked up, the wind rattled the reeds and the light changed. I worked quickly with my palette knife on a new small board to capture the jaggared reflections and movement of the water. The clouds stacked up and closed in and the birds quietened around me; they must have sensed the imminent bad weather that quickly took grip. It was too windy to carry on, I finished the painting in my studio, most of the time was spent picking out bits of grass.

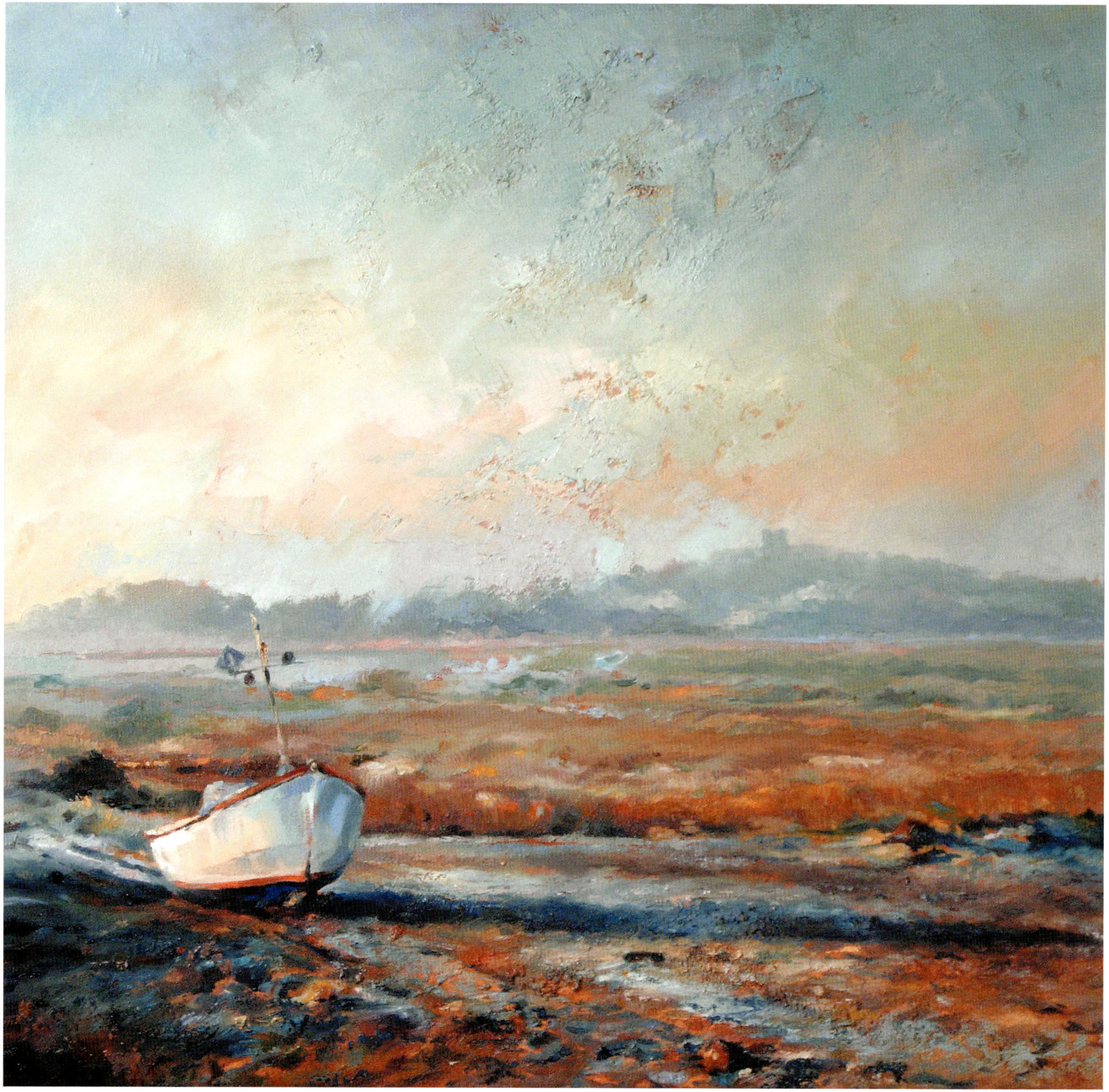

Cley After The Surge
oils on canvas 60x60 cm

18 March

Cley After the Surge (left)

The remnants of a surge tide were scattered along many beaches and marshes up and down the coast. In Cley stray boats were lifted from the creeks and left scattered across the marsh. This unusual sight gave a new perspective to the landscape. This was a view one frosty morning, long shadows of blue stretching out along the frozen shingle.

I painted another large picture of a frosty morning in Cley (top right). I was happy with what I had captured, but the picture was just too cold. Although I was pleased with the light, it gave an icy chill and as a result probably put some people off. Sadly I was swayed by the comments of those that viewed it and as I wanted it to sell at the time, I painted over it and turned it into a warm summer's day (the painting on the right). In essence I had painted a new picture and I was really pleased with the results. It was a pouring out of feelings I felt about a summer's day in Cley. The picture then sold straight away, but I can't help the regret of having destroyed a record of that frosty morning.

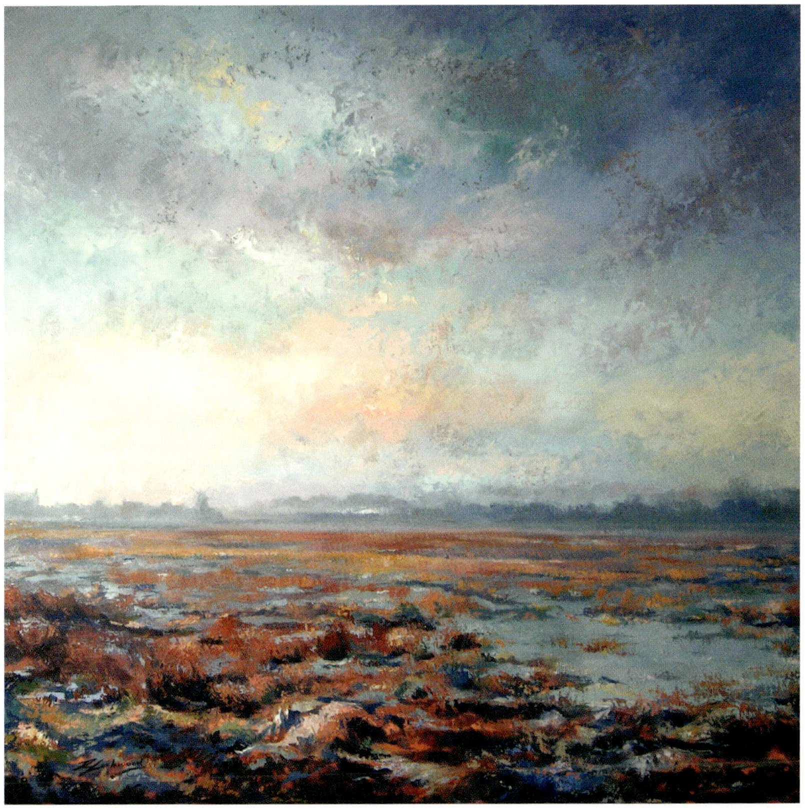

Cley Marsh Frost
oils canvas 90x90 cm

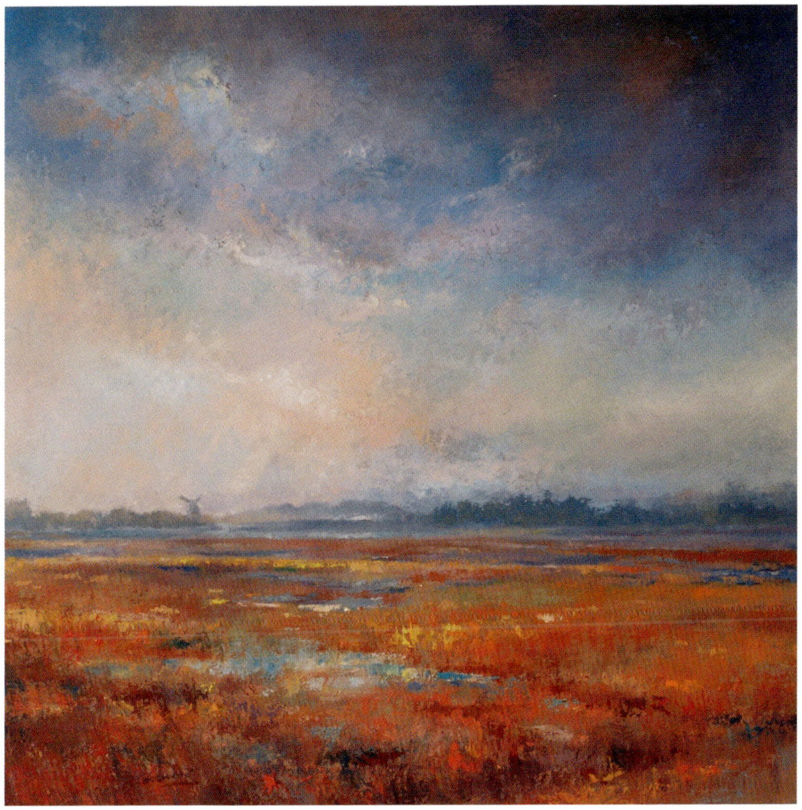

Beautiful Cley
oils on canvas 90x90 cm

19 March

One of my favourite spots in Cley is the East Bank. This path marks the eastern-most boundary of the Norfolk Wildlife Trust's Cley Reserve. On one side there is a vast sea of reedbeds and on the other, grazing fields full of geese, split by a waterway. The bank allows me a slightly elevated view of the reedbed and on this day a perfect spring cloud filled the sky. After watching the clouds for an hour, I walked back to my studio and began a painting. By the time I put paint to canvas, the image in my mind from earlier had been enriched by my imagination, but it still encapsulates the feelings I had for that moment.

21 March

Another great spring day has come again, with patches of sun breaking through the thick slab of grey that has covered everything for the last few weeks, squeezing out the light. I saw a similar thing a few days earlier, a smear of bright light slid across the land for twenty seconds and was gone.

The stray cat that has been hanging around the studio managed to make it through the winter, so we celebrate the coming of spring by sharing a slice of smoked mackerel. I leave it in a place I know it will come to later on. The rest of the day's rituals begin. I gather paper and sticks for the log burner and set it going, fill the kettle and make the tea. The smoke from the chimney swirls outside the glazed door and off across the field. I look up across the studio to the painting I worked on yesterday and wonder whether I need to do more. This painting happened very quickly, it came out in one day but it achieved exactly the effect I wanted – this is rare. I decide to walk away from it, put it on one side and come back to it later before I do something foolish. I've been preparing my first hand-stretched canvasses which has taken me days. Annoyingly they've all wrinkled and I hate the thought of having to re-stretch them all. My woodburner doesn't work well some days and when I open it, smoke billows out and fills the apex roof. The smell is wonderful but I wonder how many cigarettes this equates to. I turn on Radio 4 and set about re-stretching the sagging canvasses. I decide to leave the painting of *Rain* as it is.

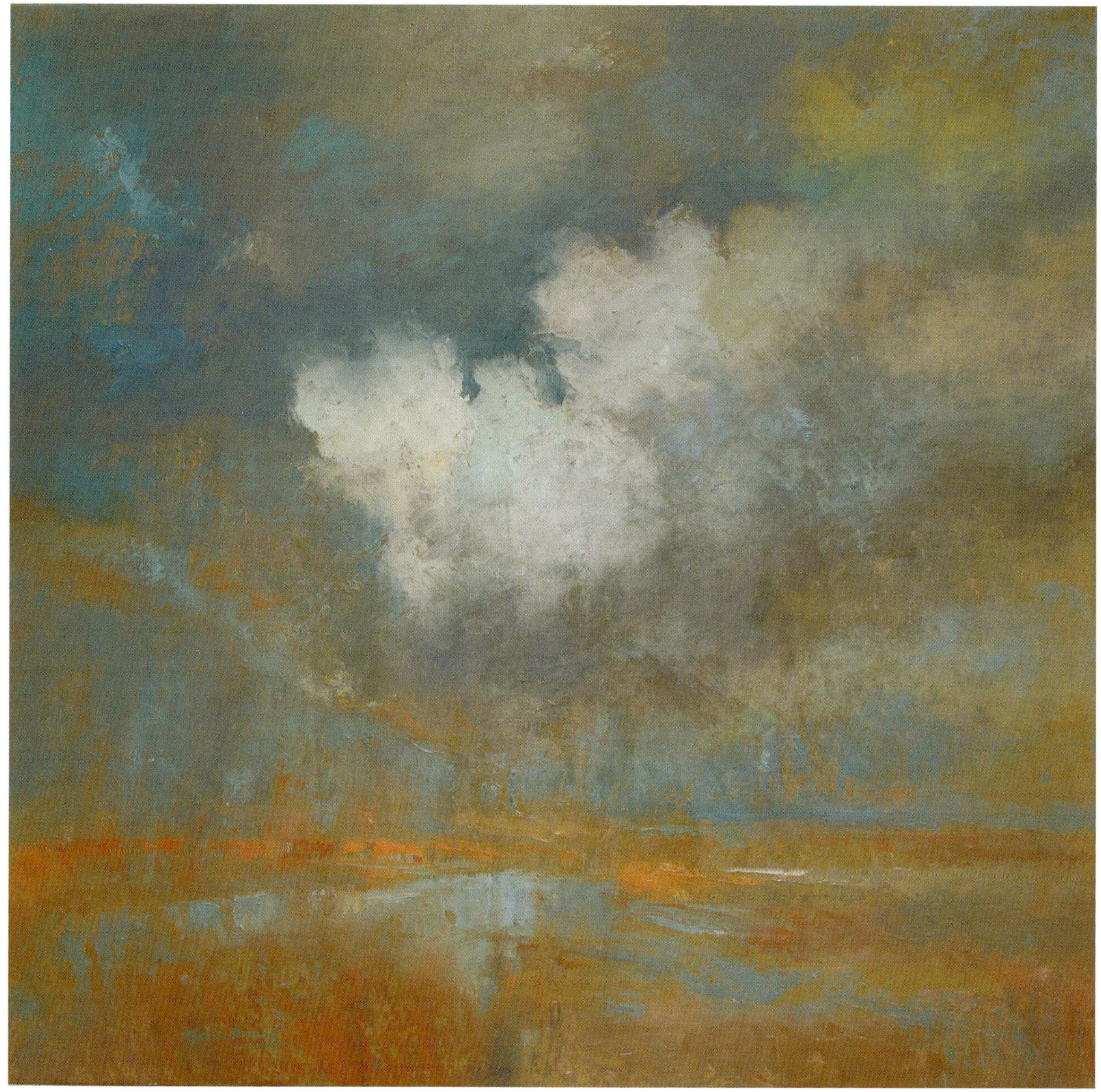

Spring Cloud, Cley oils on canvas 100x100 cm

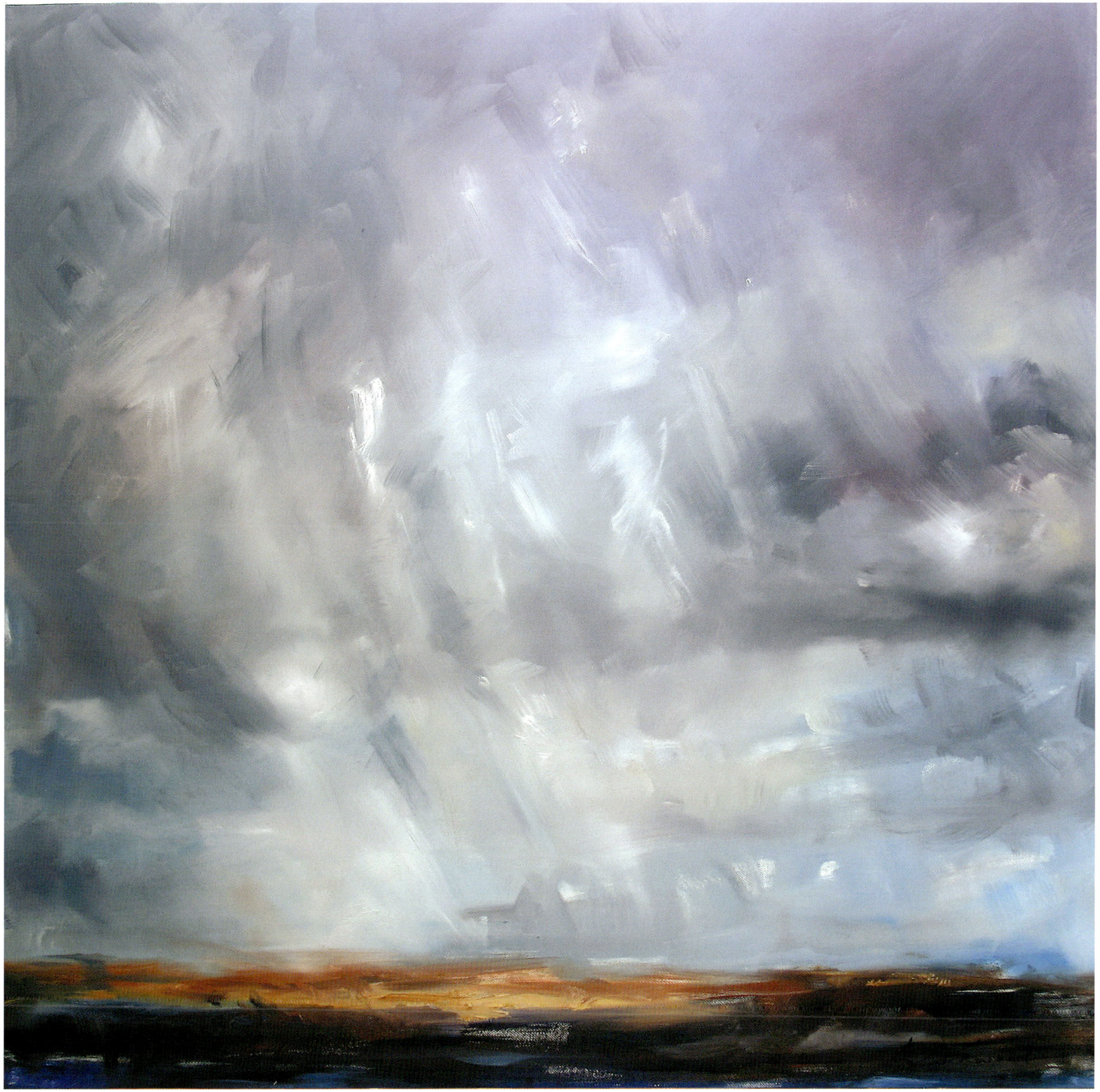

Rain oils on canvas 90x90 cm

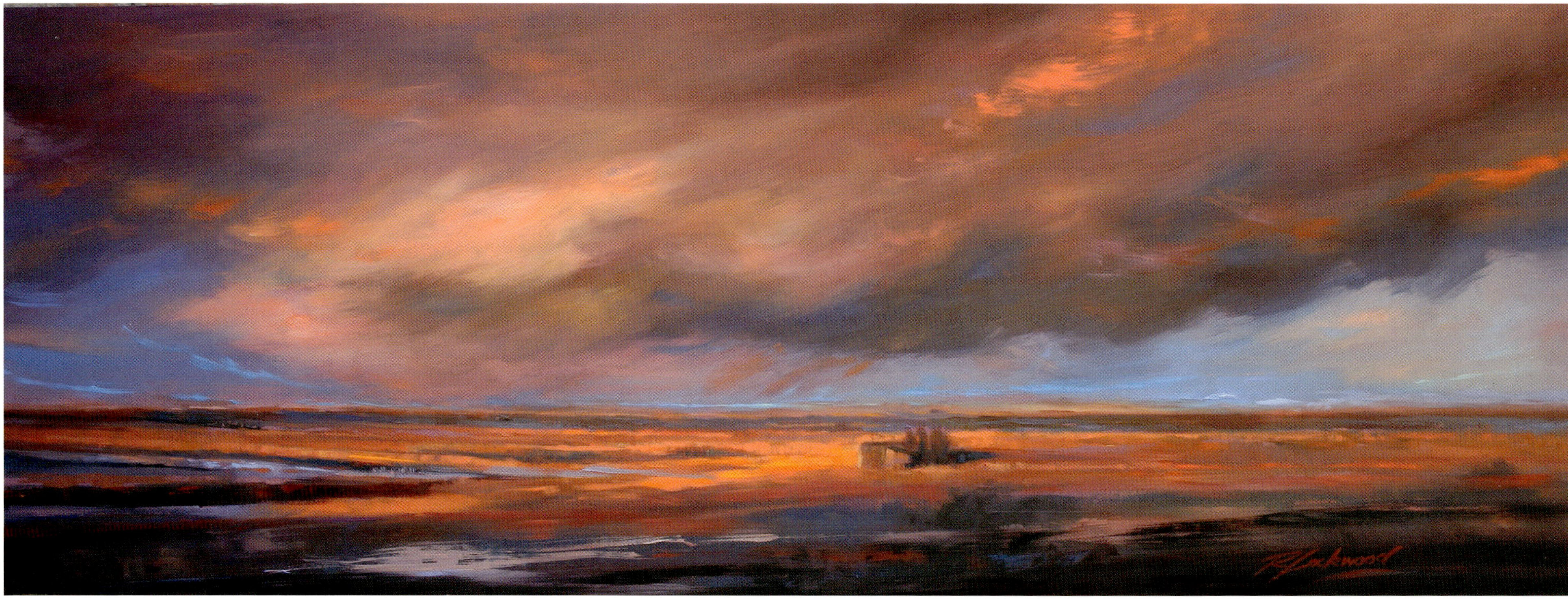

Cley Bird Pools oils on canvas 40x90cm

23 March

The cat flap clattering in the flat this morning already told me before I set out of the blustery day ahead. It was bin day and Basti from the deli opposite was chasing a half-tipped sack of rubbish around the three-way road. After helping, I set off for the studio for another day of painting indoors. The Skylarks were not deterred and lifted high on the wind, singing away. Blackthorn blossom is beginning to burst in the sheltered spots of the hedgerows, some of which is scattered along the road, caught by muddy pools. A minute later and I'm at the studio field, welcomed by the sight of a pair of hunting Marsh Harriers. After lighting my woodburner and making the tea, I watch the harriers slide away over the Hangs towards the heath.

At the end of the day I walked the long way home down Old Woman's Lane. A storm was rolling in from the sea, a crumpled front that looked like an upside down tsunami - dark and angry, travelling fast across the sky eating up the softer spring clouds. It was streaked with paler clouds filled with rain and sleet, making contact with the ground as though about to turn into a tornado. I phoned Sarah who brought the car and we chased the storm. The wind blew off the sea and whipped up sharp rain and sleet. It grew darker and darker, then the setting sun caught the softer white clouds, turning them an airbrushed orange, peach and pink. It was the most dramatic storm we'd ever seen.

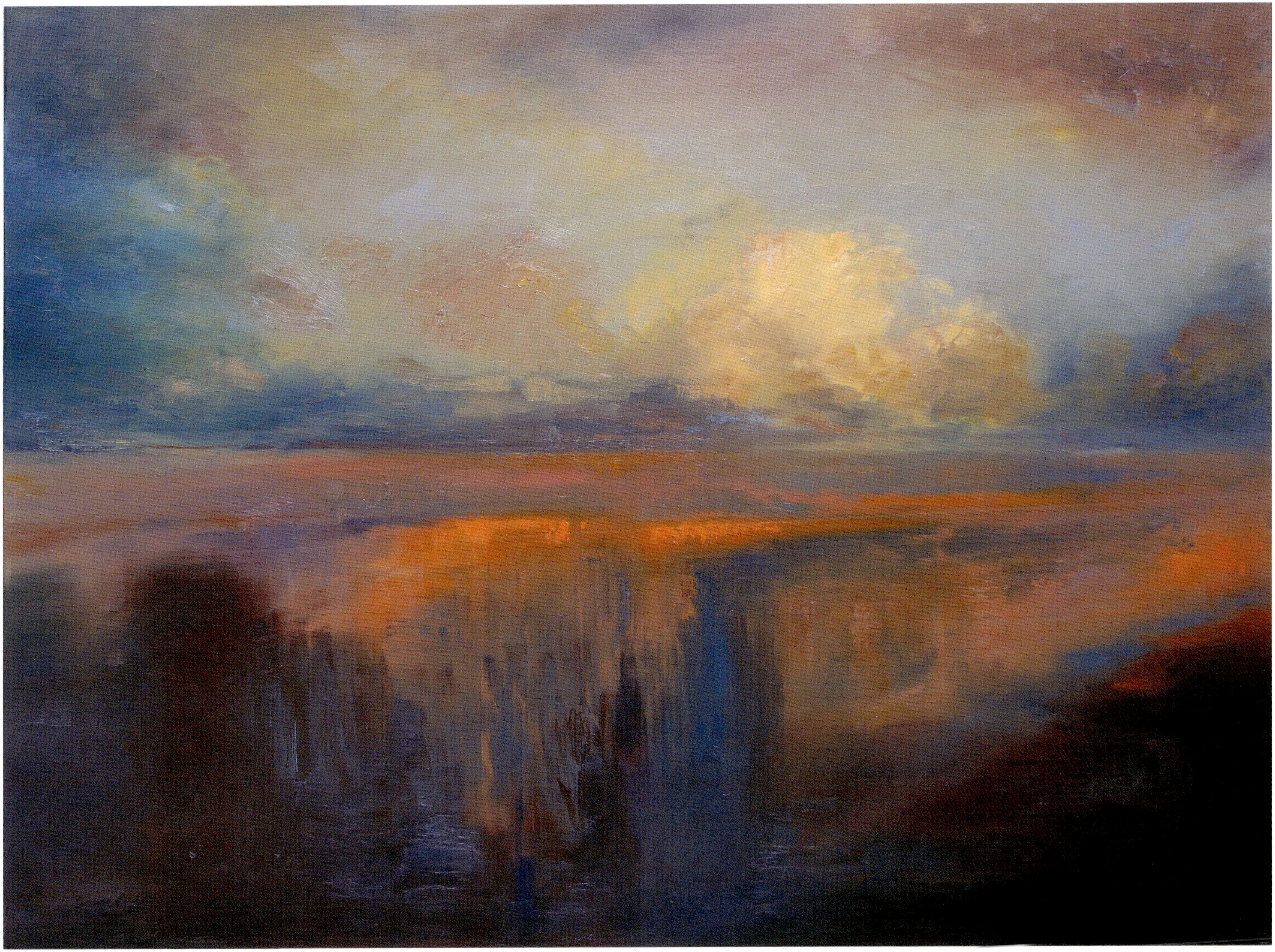

Walking On To The Marsh oils on canvas 80x100 cm

27 March

Winter has returned with icy air. I opened my curtains this morning to see a hazy mist of smoke rising from the marsh, then a leap of fire in one place, then another. The reed cutters were busy burning stubble after collecting the reeds.
I'd been awake since 4.30 feeling restless, so I quickly got ready and went to stand over the sluice gate, giving me a clear view of the cutter and the flames. He continued to make pile after pile of reed stubble, then carried the burning embers from one pile to the next. The bright gold of the flames reflected in the river, warming up the surrounding light. The flames were fast and almost manic as they leapt from one pile to the next, they then died down so quickly, it felt like an anticlimax. The hypnotic scene made my adrenaline race, and after tearing myself away I busily planned the picture in my head on the way to the studio. I knew it was something I'd have to work on straight away, not think or fuss about – just paint. I didn't even stop to light my woodburner, instead I think my adrenaline kept me warm.

It's good to know that a thriving cottage industry survives on my doorstep. Norfolk thatch is still used today, and some say it's the best quality thatch in the world, well it has to be – it's from Norfolk!

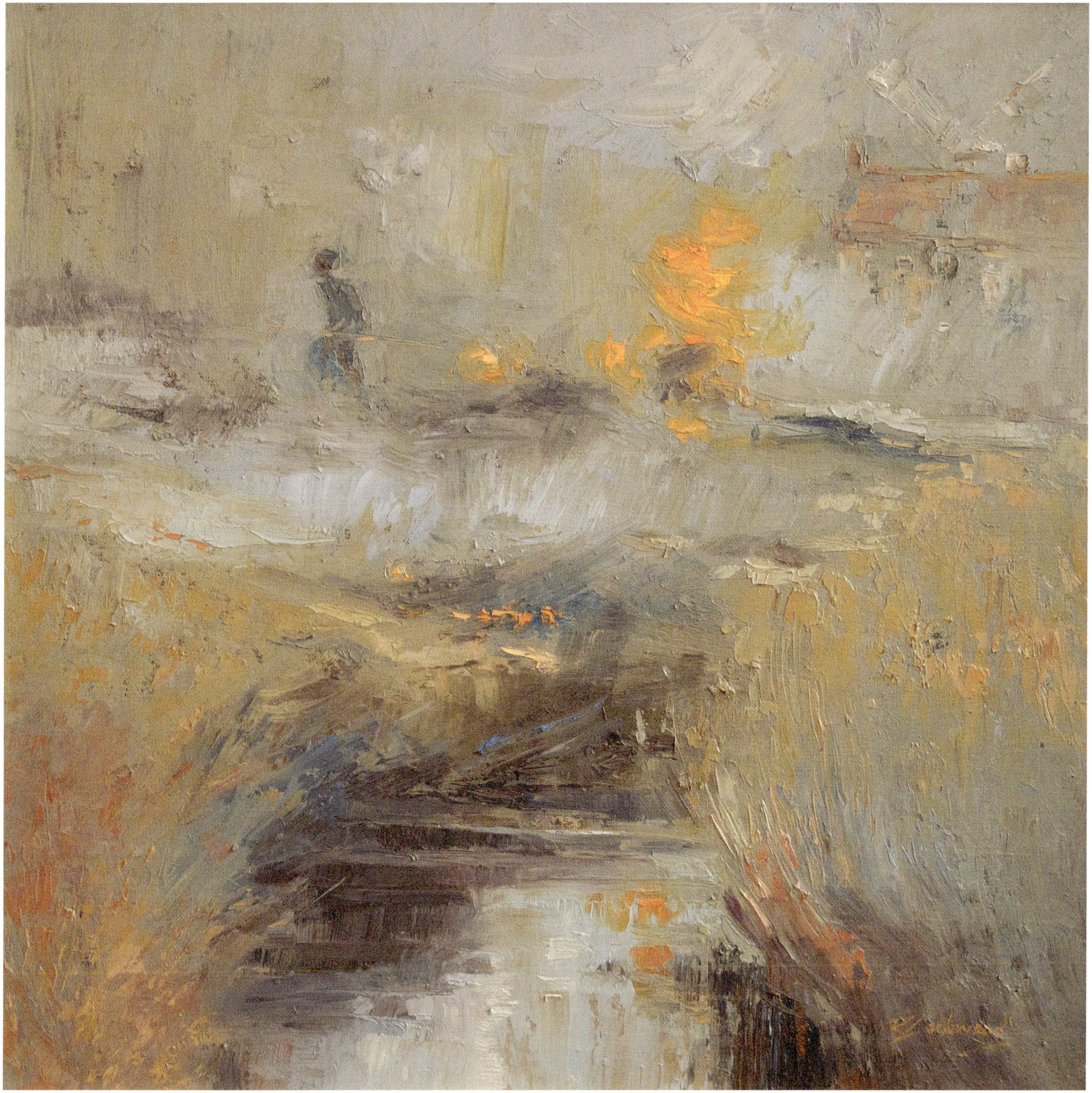

Reedcutter, Cley
oils on linen 50x50 cm

29 March

The light and colour pulled me out of my bed this morning. Constant spring showers have flooded the marsh, creating pools that reflect the sky. These pools set amongst last year's grasses, still warm and soft in colour, inspire so many of my paintings. Once the light is right, the marsh glows.

I decided to walk out onto the marsh towards the beach. A splashing sound in one of the pools made me stop, a closer look revealed a Mallard having a wash. In the distance, a Curlew called, its bubbling notes echoed over the marsh. The air already had a hint of warmth and a turquoise sky was growing over the sea, pushing out the morning chill.

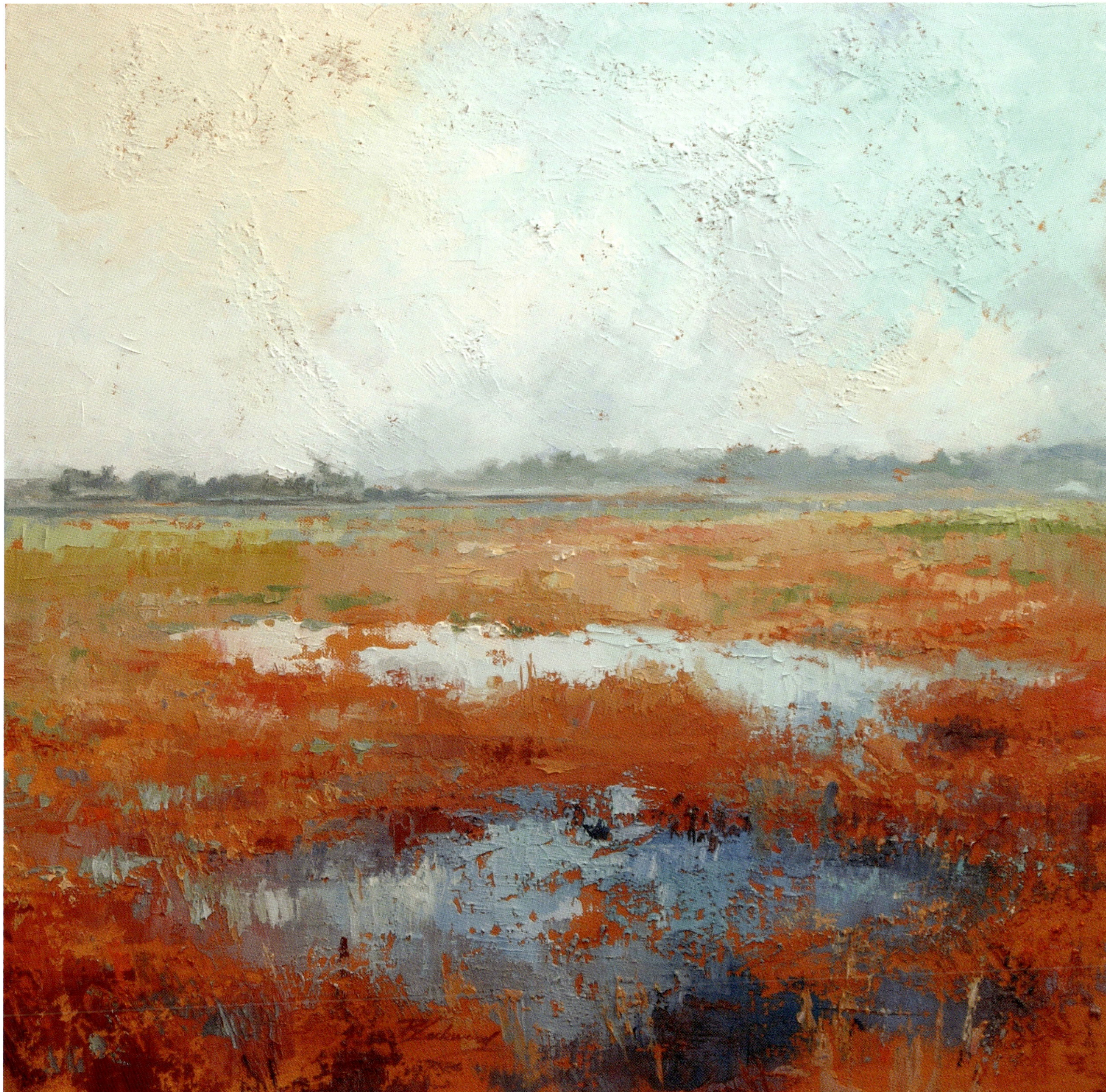

Cley Marsh Pools
oils on canvas 60x60 cm

31 March

Grey dank weather has returned this morning. It's another challenging day with no break of light to cast a shadow. But one of the positives is the woodland walks to be had. In all weather conditions, no matter what the time of day or time of year, there is always so much to see in the forest. From the colours of autumn leaves that still lie on the ground, with new growth coming through, to the wildlife that lives within.

The sky has become a more sulphurous grey, no hint of where the sun might be, so I go to one of my secret forest locations. The trees here crazily wriggle their branches upwards, as if searching for the light also. It's one of those closed-in days, low cloud and silence in the forest. I've seen very little wildlife so far, only the cracking noise of twigs from wary Pheasants amongst the muffled trees and the odd crow that suits this eerie landscape.

It begins to rain heavily, so I return to the car and wait with a flask of tea and big bar of chocolate. Determined to stay out all day, I nestled down in another part of the forest with huge candelabra oak trees breaking up the lines of straighter trees. Another pheasant tiptoed by and a wet pigeon flapped and rebalanced. A Woodcock then broke cover, twisting and turning and is gone. This is a favourite spot of mine for seeing deer, but still no sign.

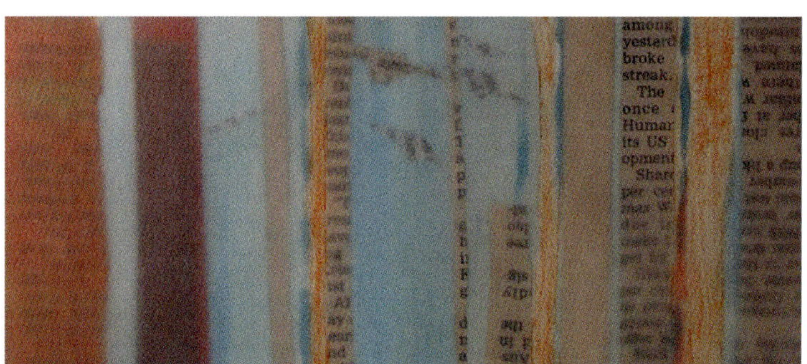

Tranquille colour swatch mixed media on paper

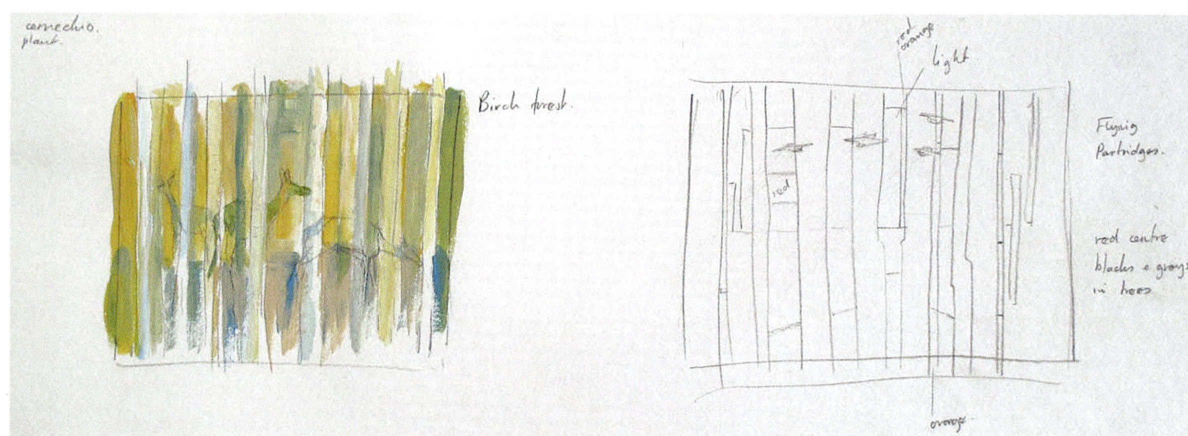

Tranquille working sketches pencil and watercolours on paper

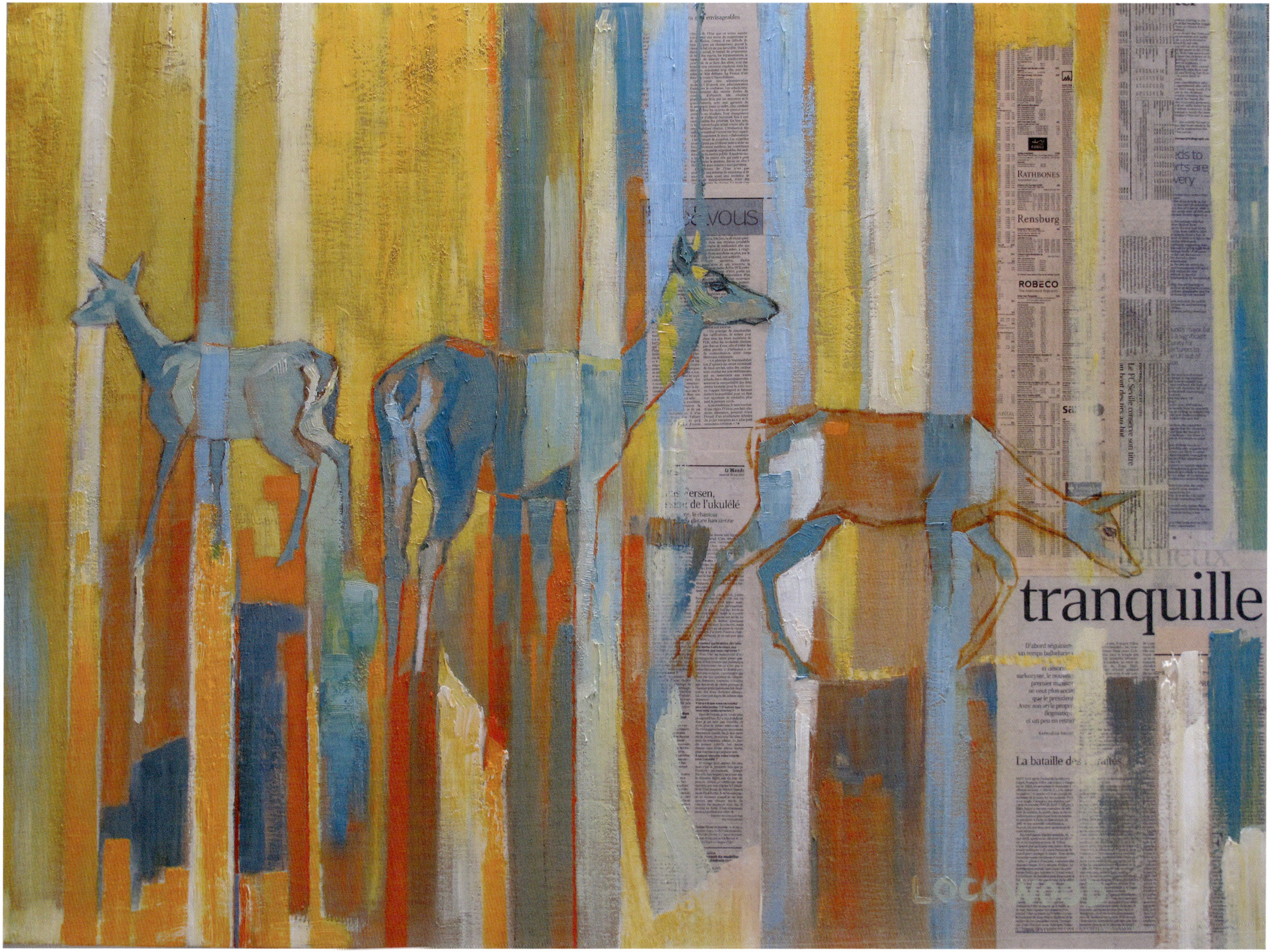

Tranquille mixed media on linen 90x120 cm

31 March *continued*

The rain has finally stopped but I have to wait for the Archers to finish...it's just a habit. I sketch the trees around me as I wait, then finally set off again in another direction. Here the area is a newer plantation set back from the public path. The ground is well trampled and used by resting deer, I see fresh droppings and chewed saplings, but still no sign of them. A cracking noise draws my attention as I walk further up the hill and there ahead, camouflaged against the foliage and tree trunks are about ten Red Deer. Three are already standing, staring at me, not moving. One looks away, one eye still on me, the others rise and another puts its head down to casually eat; but my presence is too much of a threat, it's too late to hide myself and off they go, gradually breaking up and disappearing amongst the trees. I hear the sound of them crashing through and then they are gone.

Being able to get so close to a wild animal as large as this is invigorating, and for me it always seems quite magical. Usually they're so silent and serene, you could almost be forgiven for thinking you hadn't seen them at all.

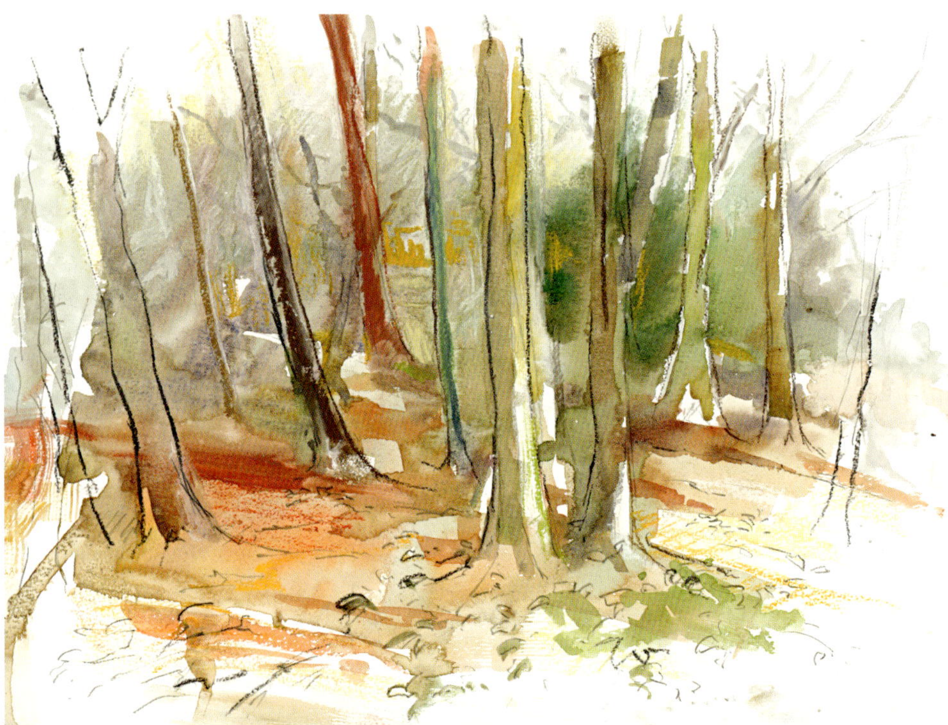

Woodland Sketch
watercolours and
charcoal on paper

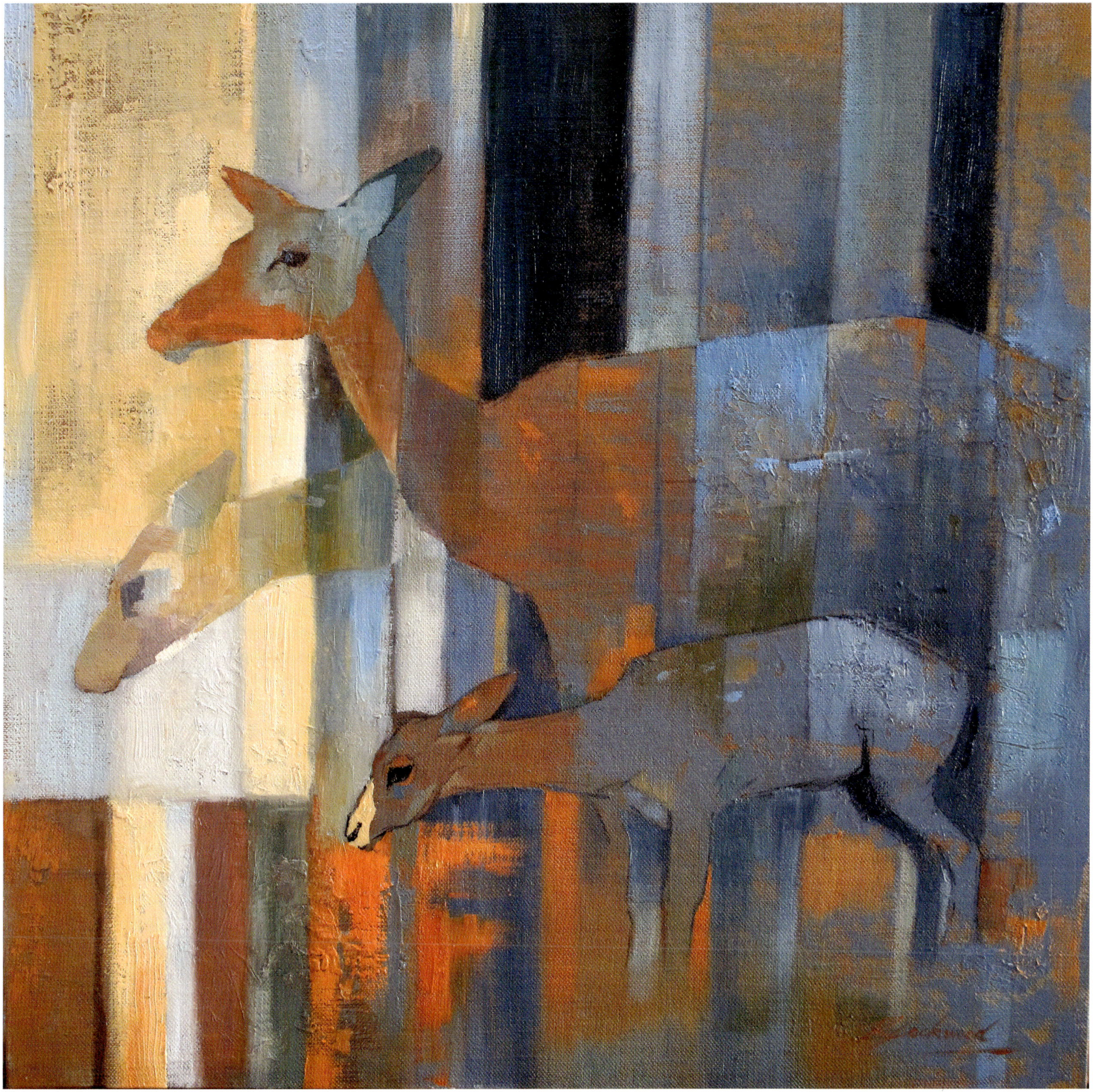

Out Of The Woods
oils on linen 40x40 cm

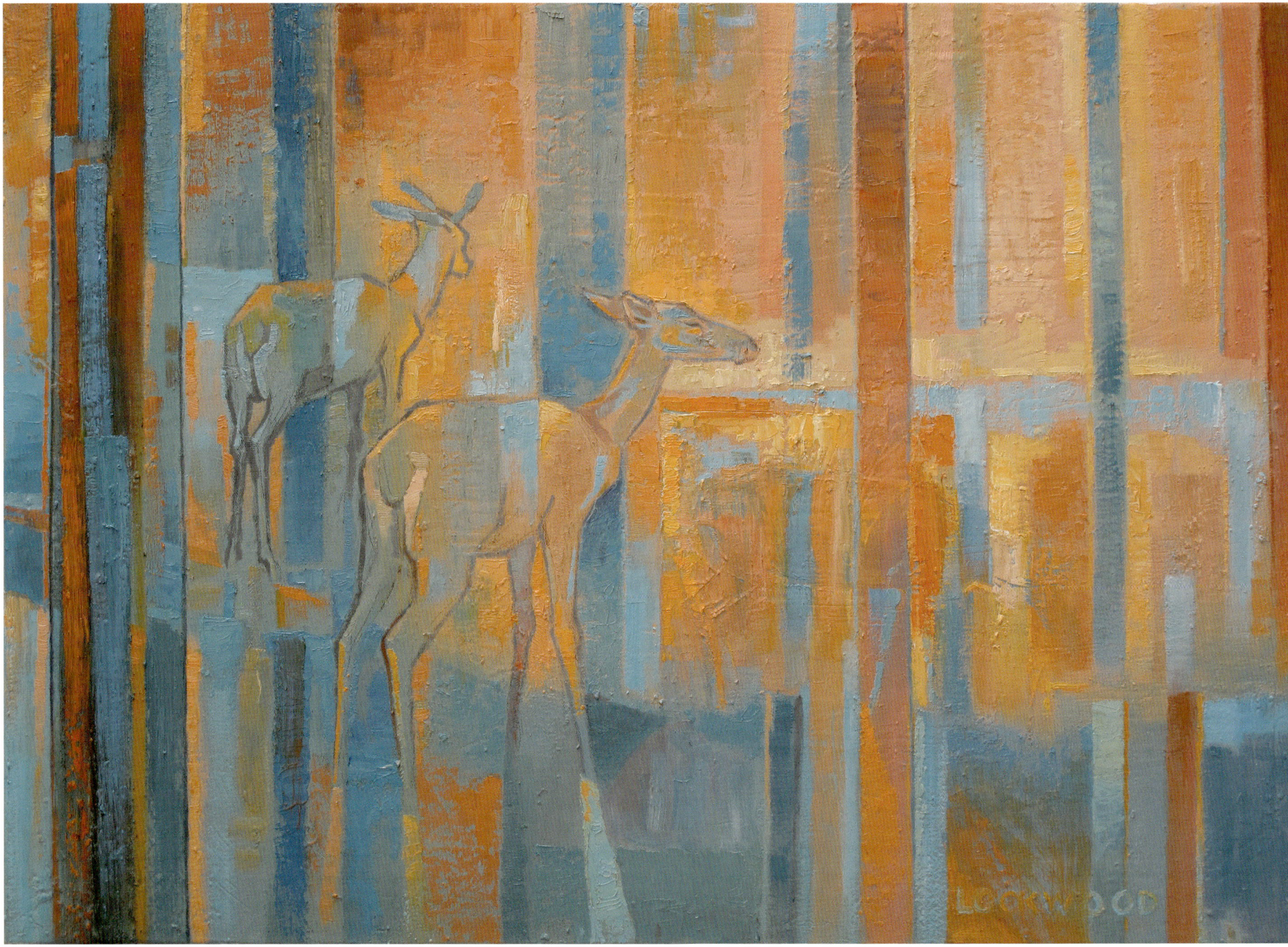

Forest Edge Deer oils on linen 50x70 cm

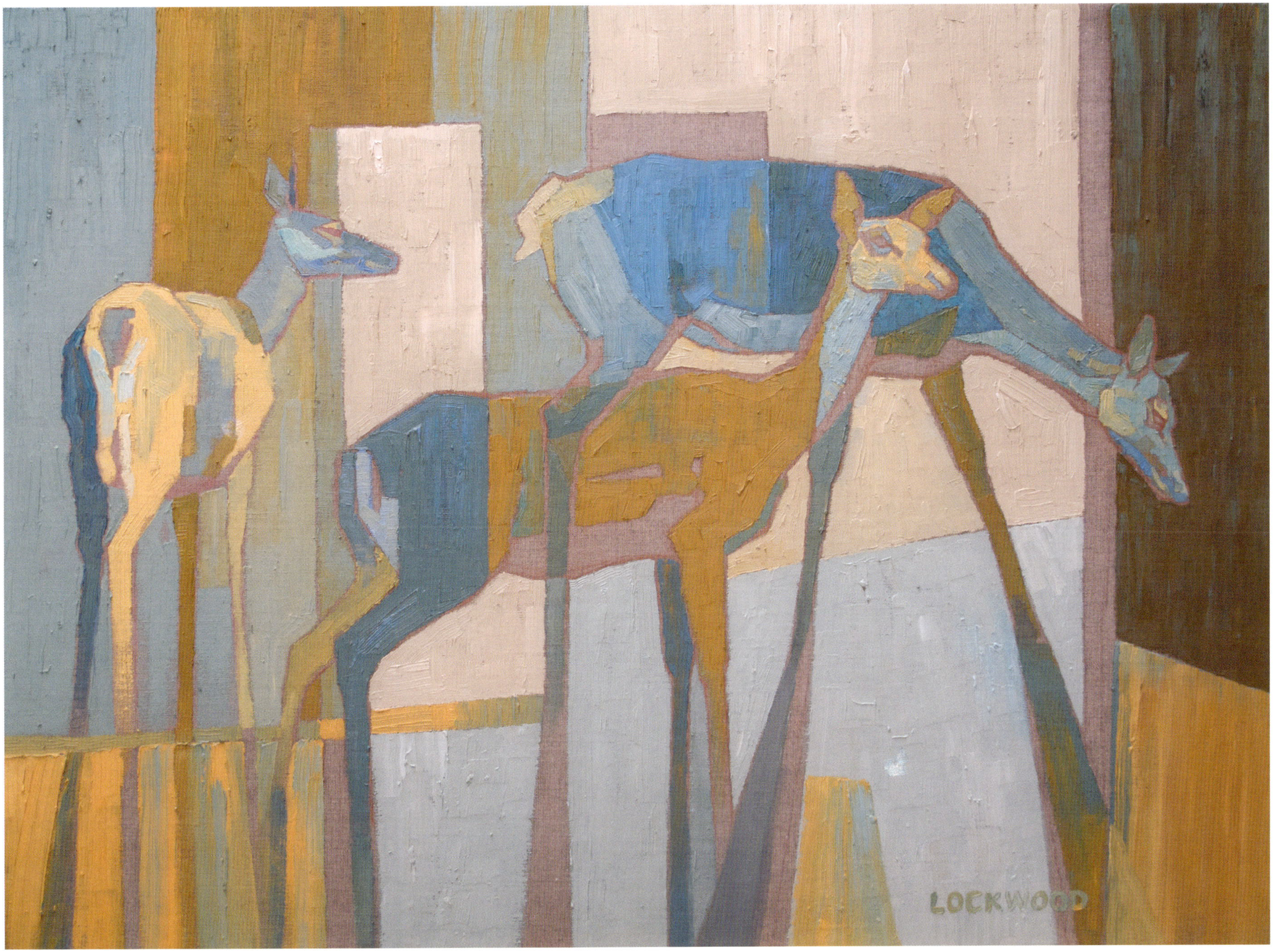

In the Shadows oils on linen 90x120 cm

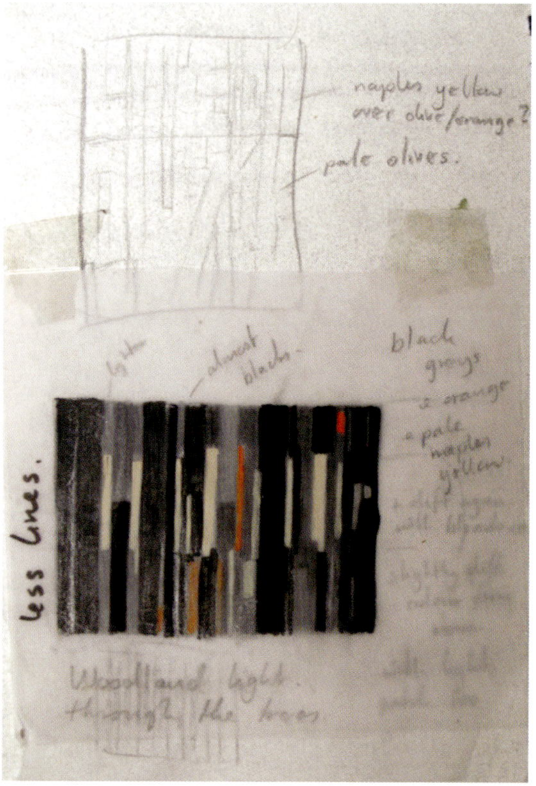

Light Through Forest sketch and swatch
crayon on paper

3 April

I have to go back to the garden centre this morning, but as I drive I can't stop the patterns of different patches of woodland imprinting on my memory. The silver lines of birch and greenish-blues and mauves of old cash-crop pines zip by, flicking and flashing in the light – they're mesmerising. I've never really looked at them so much before, but now the colours and patterns are really leaping out at me. How they change during the light of the day. A beam of sunlight striking one tree, then bouncing off another. Every day a new set of patterns and colours emphasised all the more from passing them by at high speed in a car; light glittering through like a strobe light. It's as if each woodland is calling out, like individual beings standing by the road, waiting, calling you into this quiet world of theirs, wanting you to walk amongst them.

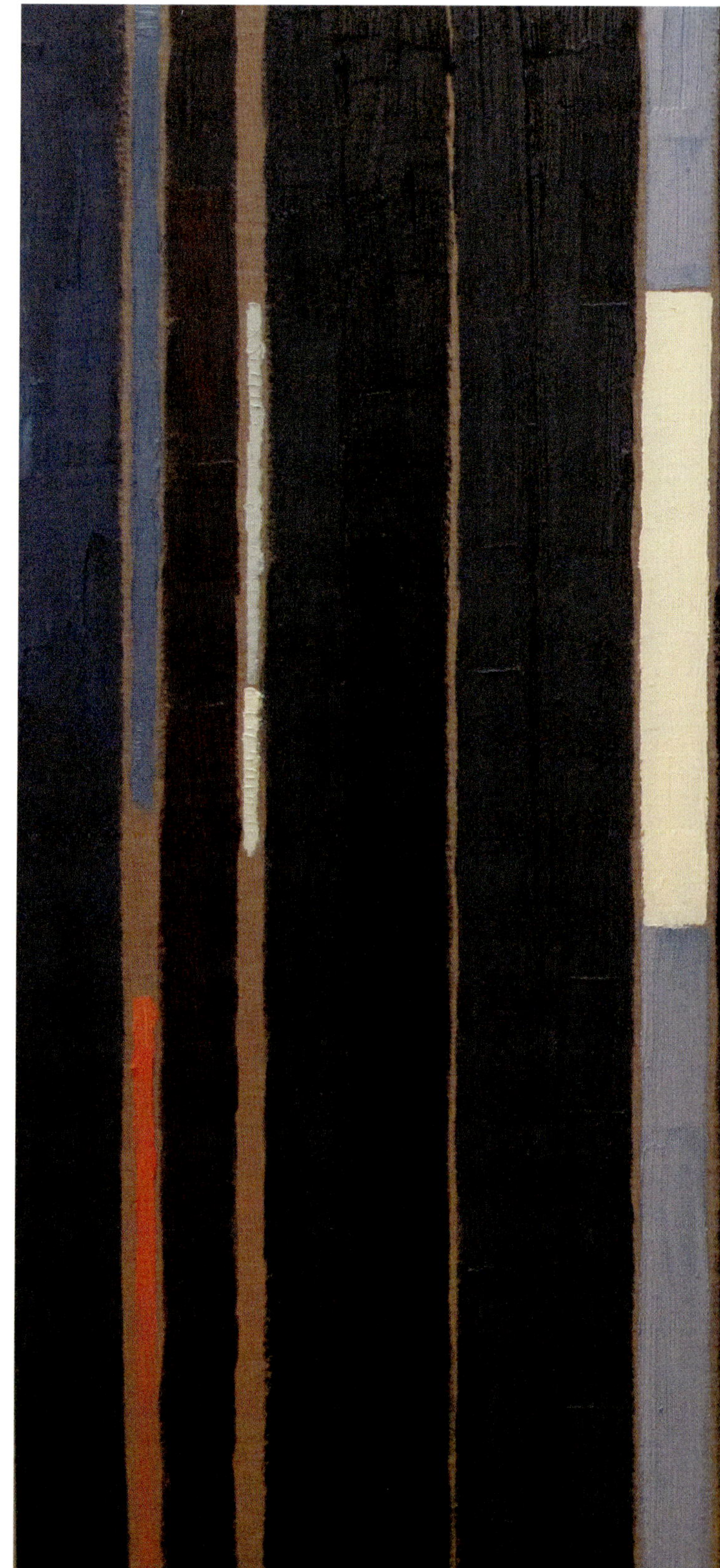

Light Through Forest
oils on linen 70x120 cm

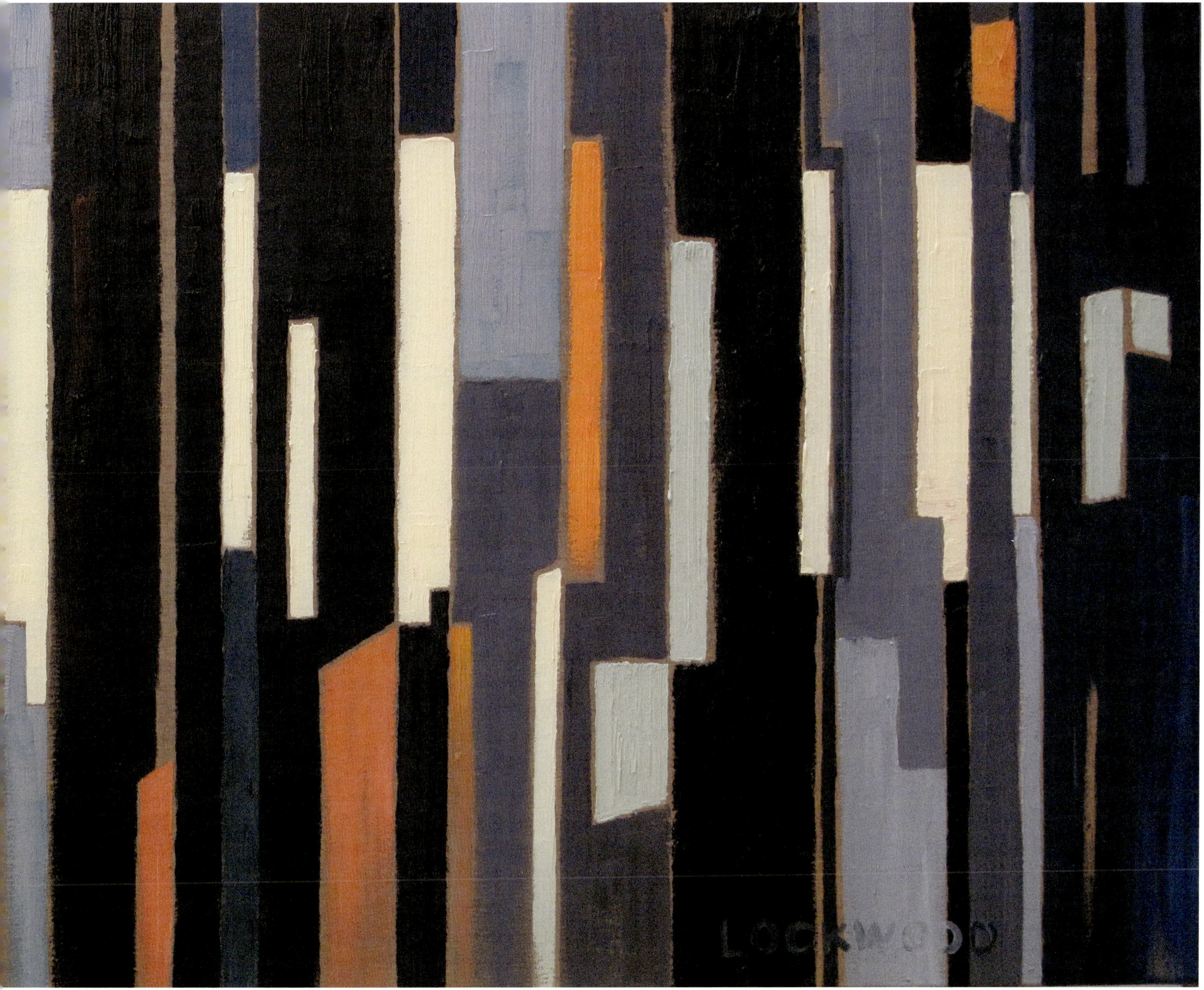
LOCKWOOD

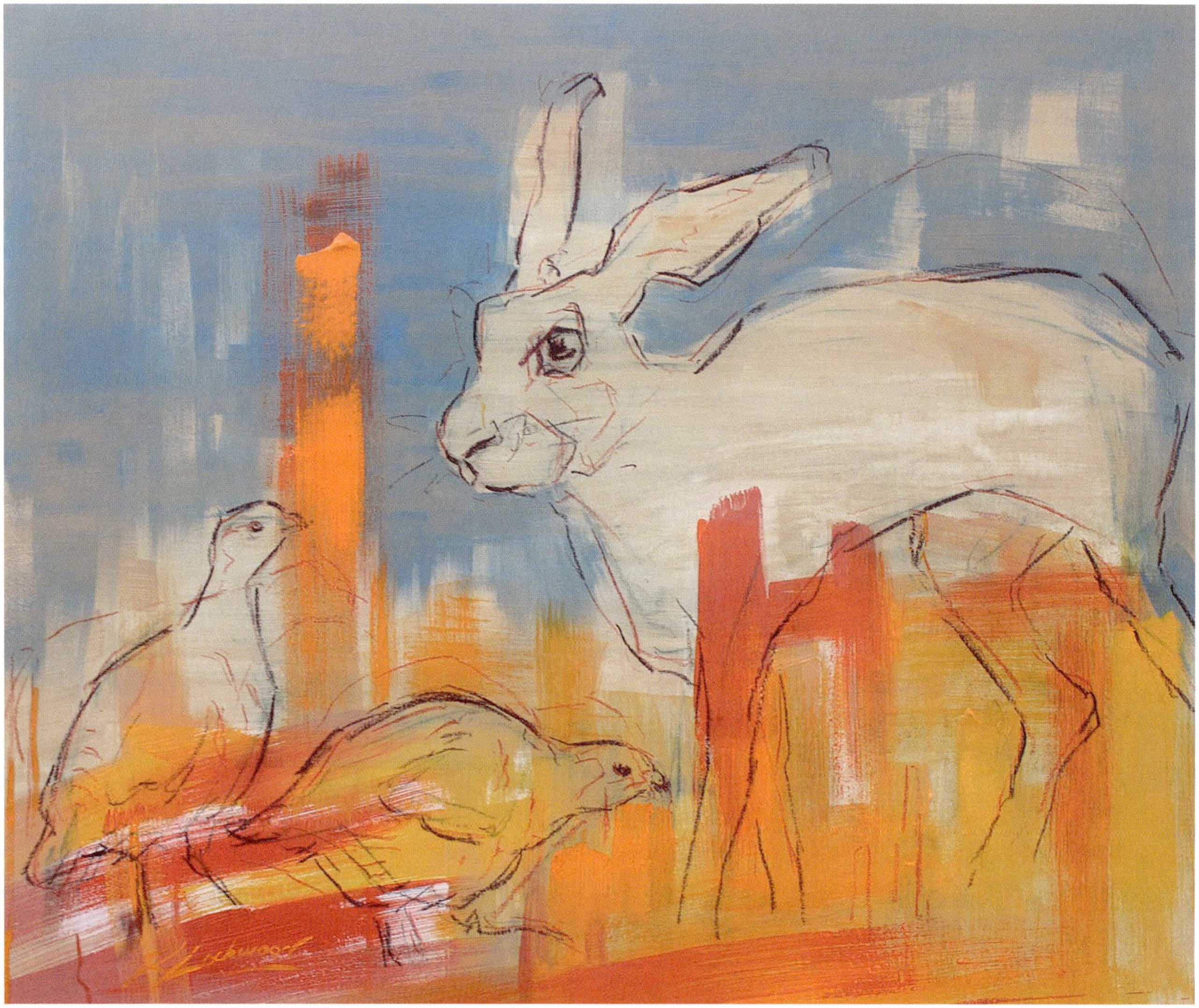

Hare and Partridges Study VI
mixed media on board
90x70 cm

6 April

After many years of searching we have finally found male adders fighting on Salthouse heath – a rare and wonderful sight. After a couple of hours of being engrossed by this I looked up to see hares racing across the flinty fields in the distance. As soon as the snakes had finished, we drove to the edge of the hare field, using the car as a hide. It gave me a chance to watch and sketch their behaviour, and as we were watching, two adolescent Roe Deer stepped through a gap in the hedge and into the field, stunning beautiful creatures with nerves on tenterhooks. They looked back at us and were unsure, so took flight spooking each other as they ran. Then two Red-legged Partridges entered the scene and approached the Hares, looking at them as if to say 'what's all that about?' And after looking around, they all went their separate ways.

Sometimes trying to capture what I see means changing my materials. I really like the immediate effect of sketching as it allows me to capture more of the movement. Sometimes the sketches themselves develop and find their way to becoming final pieces.

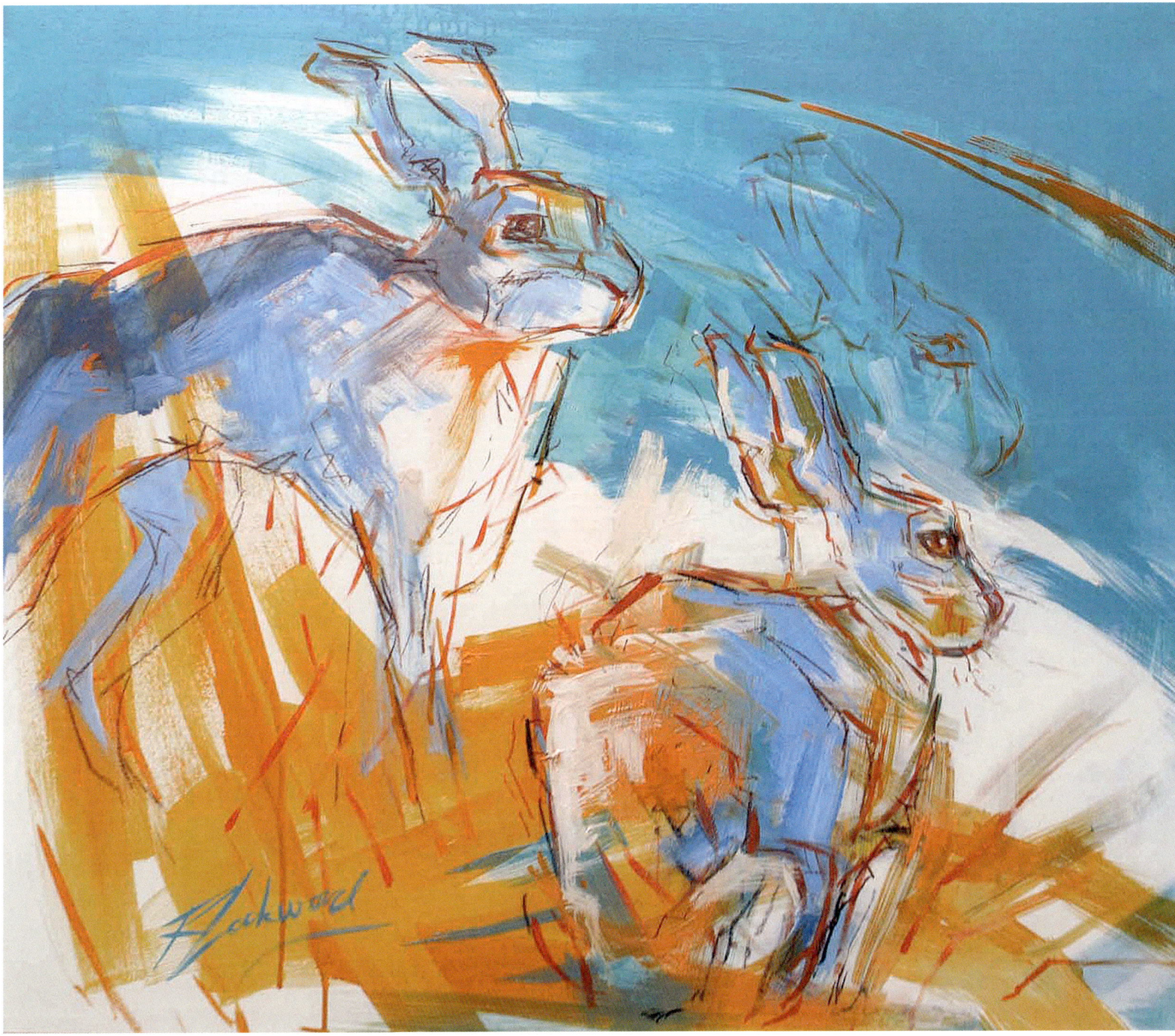

Hare Study V
mixed media on board 90x70 cm

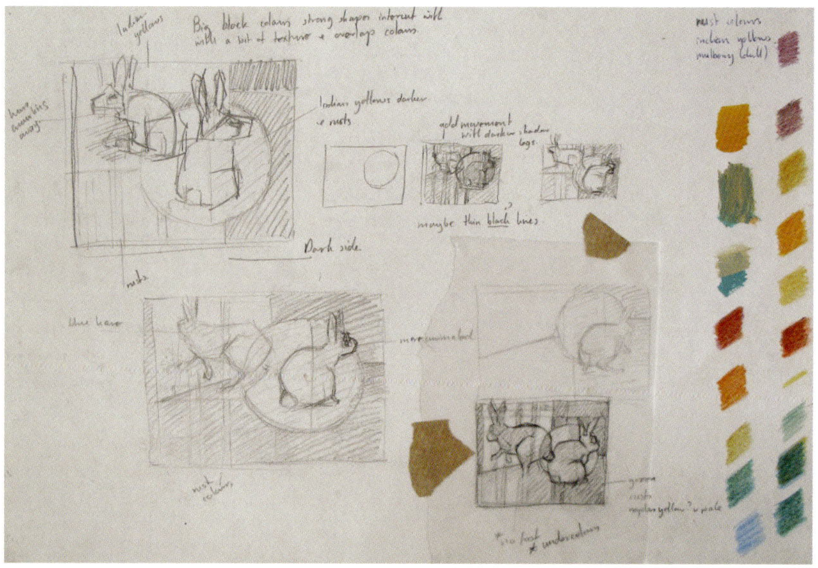

Hare in Spring Stubble Sketches
pencils on paper

8 April

Golden stubble fields of old winter crops are one of my favourite places for searching for wildlife. The colour and texture of the stubble and movement of the wildlife led to a change in the style of my work here. I wanted to capture the fleeting moments of watching wildlife and the impression that the landscape left on me. The repeated structures of the land in my memory are beginning to permeate through in the strangest places, and gradually becoming more prominent in my work.

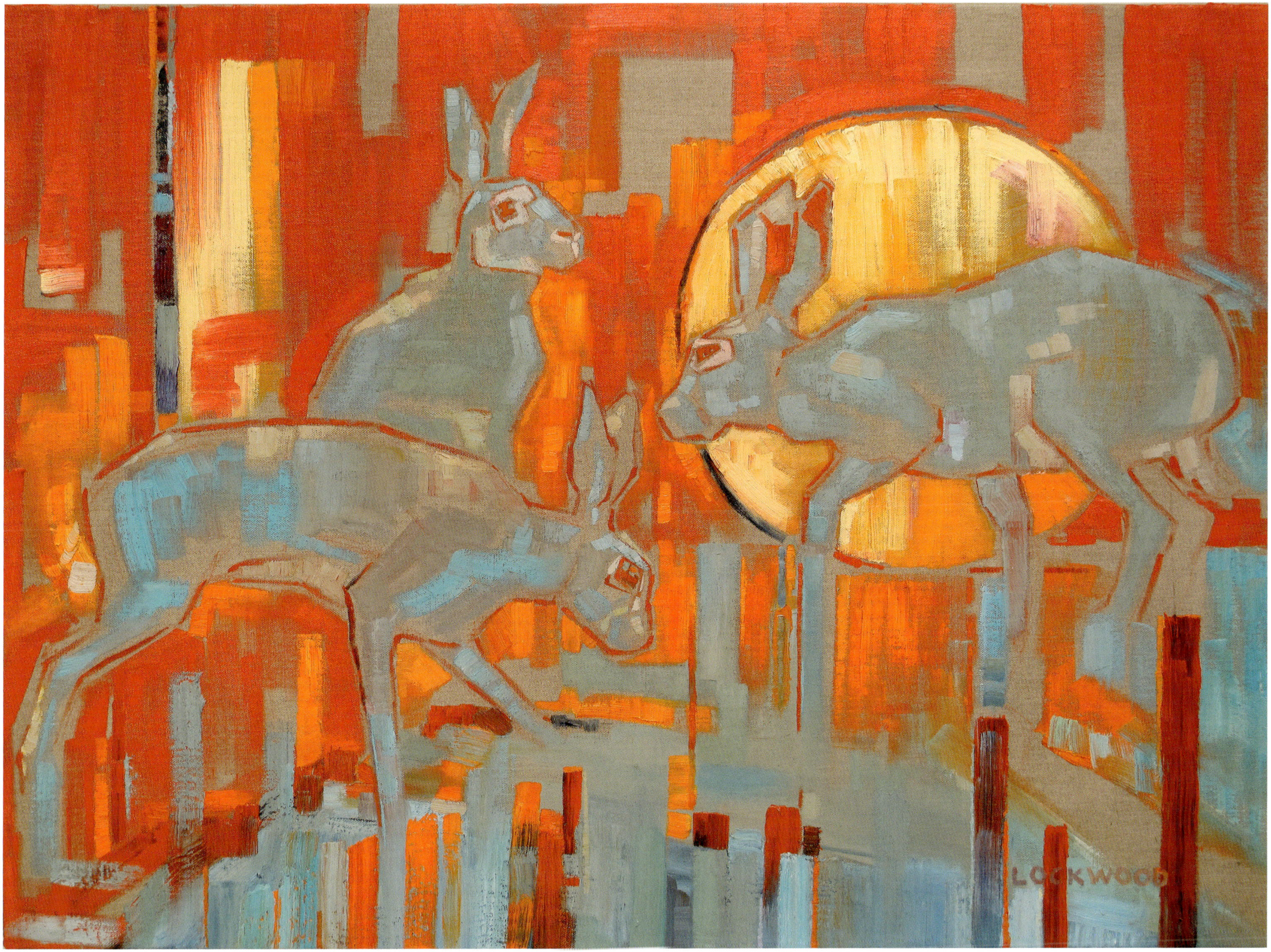

Hares In Spring Stubble oils on linen 90x120 cm

14 April

It rained this morning when it was meant to be dry - no surprise there. I went out with Martin and a couple of friends today on a hare safari. Sadly, the hares had gone to ground, lying flat in their forms against the flinty soil. The crops were already beginning to grow and so was the set-aside. All hopes of seeing a hare seemed to be withering away. But Martin didn't falter in his quest, and with full land owner's permission, we entered the set-aside. The dry grasses brushing the underside of the car and the heave-ho of the fully laden suspension of the VW hatchback made us feel as though we were on a boat set out on a rolling sea. We scraped and bounced along the furrows, checking each one for slight variations that could have been Hares. It took a while before we saw our first, a pair belting towards the edge of the field, disappearing into a dip. This broke the spell and a minute later we came across others, rising like blocks of flinty earth themselves. Quick as a flash, off they went again and were gone. We scoured the fields one by one, the sunlight teasing, warming patches of game cover. Every now and then, a Pheasant or a Partridge would emerge, notice the car and quickly turn back, and in a rather comic way, would duck back into the foliage. In the end we saw quite a few but they were all incredibly nervous.

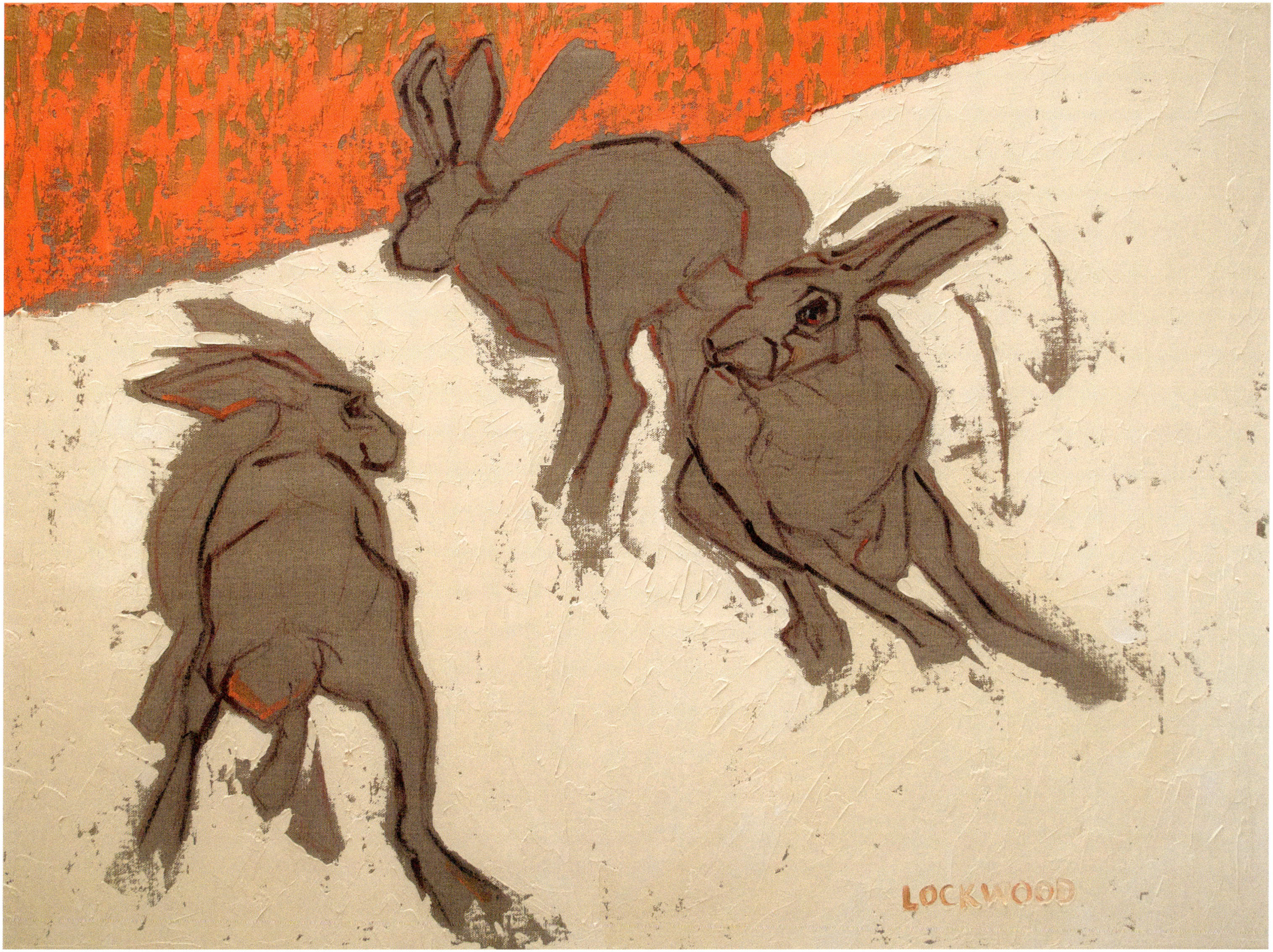

Winter Hares mixed media on linen 90x120 cm

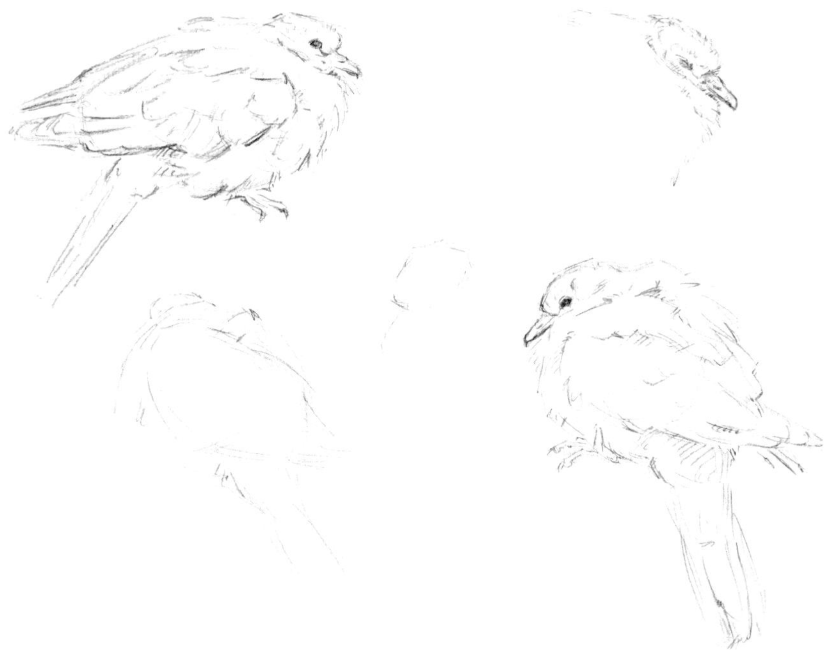

28 April

On my way to the studio this morning I found a juvenile Collared Dove. I couldn't help do a few sketches while I gave it some food and let it recover while it warmed by my stove.

It is a spectacular year for blossom. White Blackthorn blossom is curving over the roads, like frothing waves about to crash. Bright perfect pink cherry blossom lights up Cley's shadowy alleyways and picks out gardens I've never noticed before. They are singing and humming with insects; big, fat, heavy bees strain to lift their bodies, just managing to get from one flower to another. I feel like I've been placed in a fantasy world where the temperature is just perfect and the wind is barely a breath of perfumed air. The blossom is still flowering with freshness not yet fallen, shoots of fresh green foliage, backlit and vibrant. I don't want anyone to pinch me, I don't want to wake up from this. It is that magic moment in the British year and it's absorbing all of this that feeds my work.

I couldn't resist taking some of this perfect blossom home to my studio, and as soon as I put it in a vase I knew I had to paint it. Although it was a very quick painting, it felt good doing it, and it helped me get into the mood for working on my large exhibition pieces.

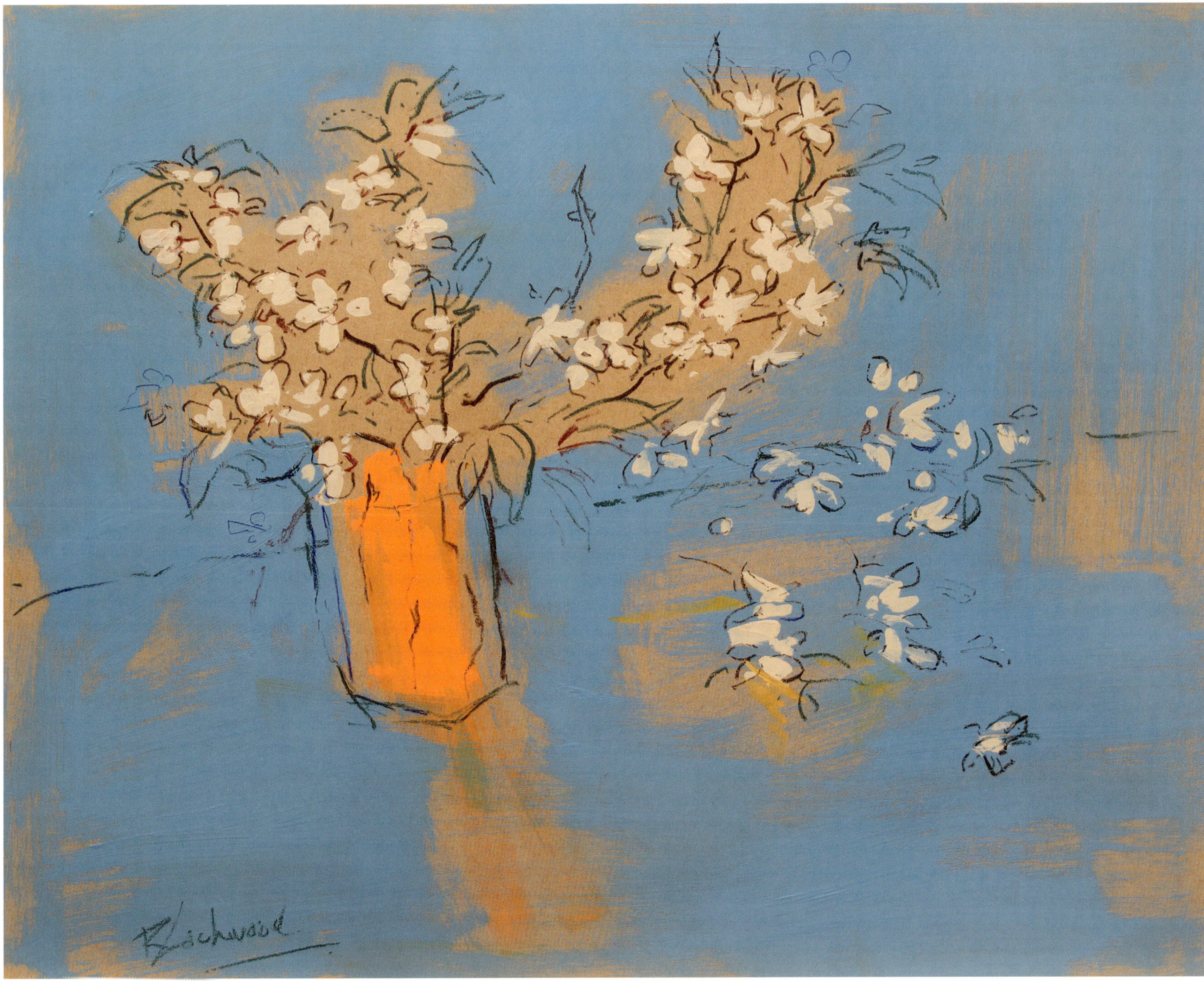

Blossom Study mixed media on panel 60x90 cm

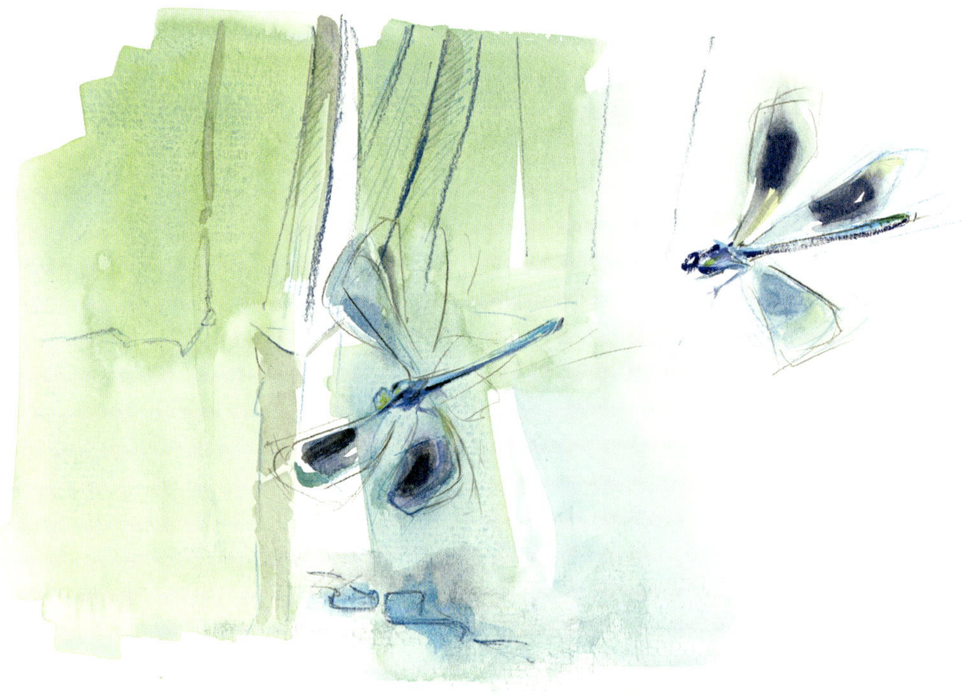

Demoiselle Sketch
watercolours on paper

10 May

Setting our canoe up on Glandford Ford, Sarah and I headed upstream not really knowing where we were going. We wanted to explore this idyllic stretch of river hidden by its tall sides, so made our way slowly, trying to identify the water plants on the way. The first of this year's Demoiselle Dragonflies flounced around Flag Iris and nettles, always just out of reach. Every now and then, they skimmed the surface of the water, creating subtle ripples with a flick of their bodies.

We moved up further through dark tunnels of arched trees and old brambles that dangled down, snagging at our clothes and hair. Feeling like ever the adventurers, we broke through in to more clear patches of river. The sunlight was fresh and warm, enough to bring out this years newly hatched insects. After reaching so far we decided to turn back as we were worried about entering private property. We turned around and slowly and silently drifted back again. It was good to find more evidence of wildlife, flattened paths leading through the long grasses, away from the water's edge, and Freshwater Mussel shells glinting their broken insides in the water below, maybe the remnants of an Otter's meal. Upon entering the ford again, we surprised a group of Mallards as we broke cover and then left reluctantly to return to the studio. So many pictures were inspired by this one trip.

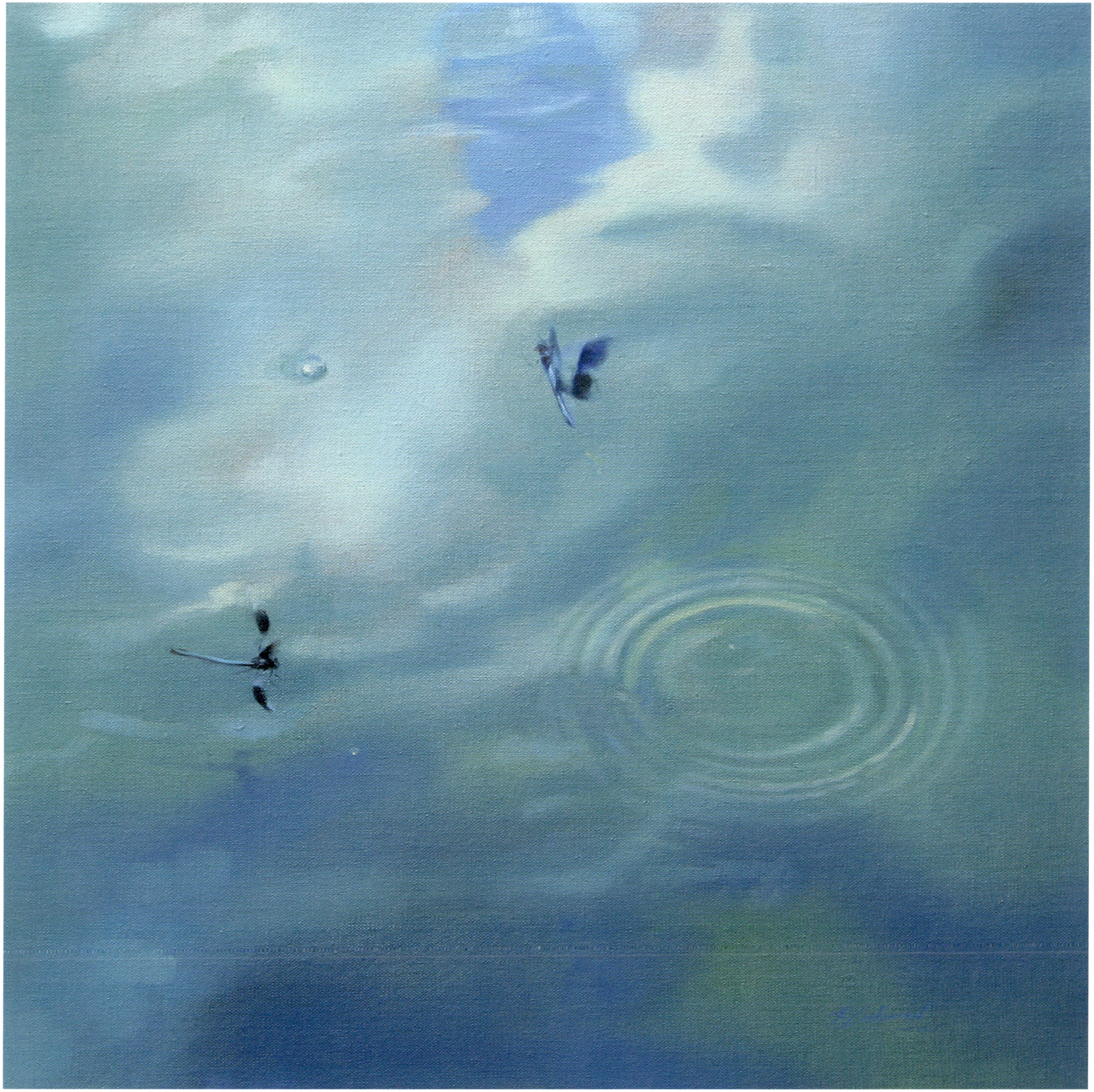

Banded Demoiselles And Ripple
oils on canvas 60x60 cm

12 May

I think of cleaning the studio floor but I am procrastinating, anything to put off the start of my next big picture. I need time to think and plan its stages, sometimes I find this the hardest part of the picture – the daunting blank canvas. I consider the layers and try to plan in my head where to begin, but it just won't come today. So after desperately rummaging through my storeroom, I find a Demoiselle painting left unfinished from last year. It never really worked for me, it seemed too empty; it needed something else. I decided to add two goldfish. Although I know this isn't strictly speaking a natural scene, but they helped me create more depth in the painting, and the colour combination added more vibrancy. I like the challenge of painting the layers within the water, the gentle movement and depth; it's as if it holds a secret, you can see so much but there is always the unknown. I add more logs into the woodburner and it's time for a cup of Redbush tea, as Mma Ramotswe would say.

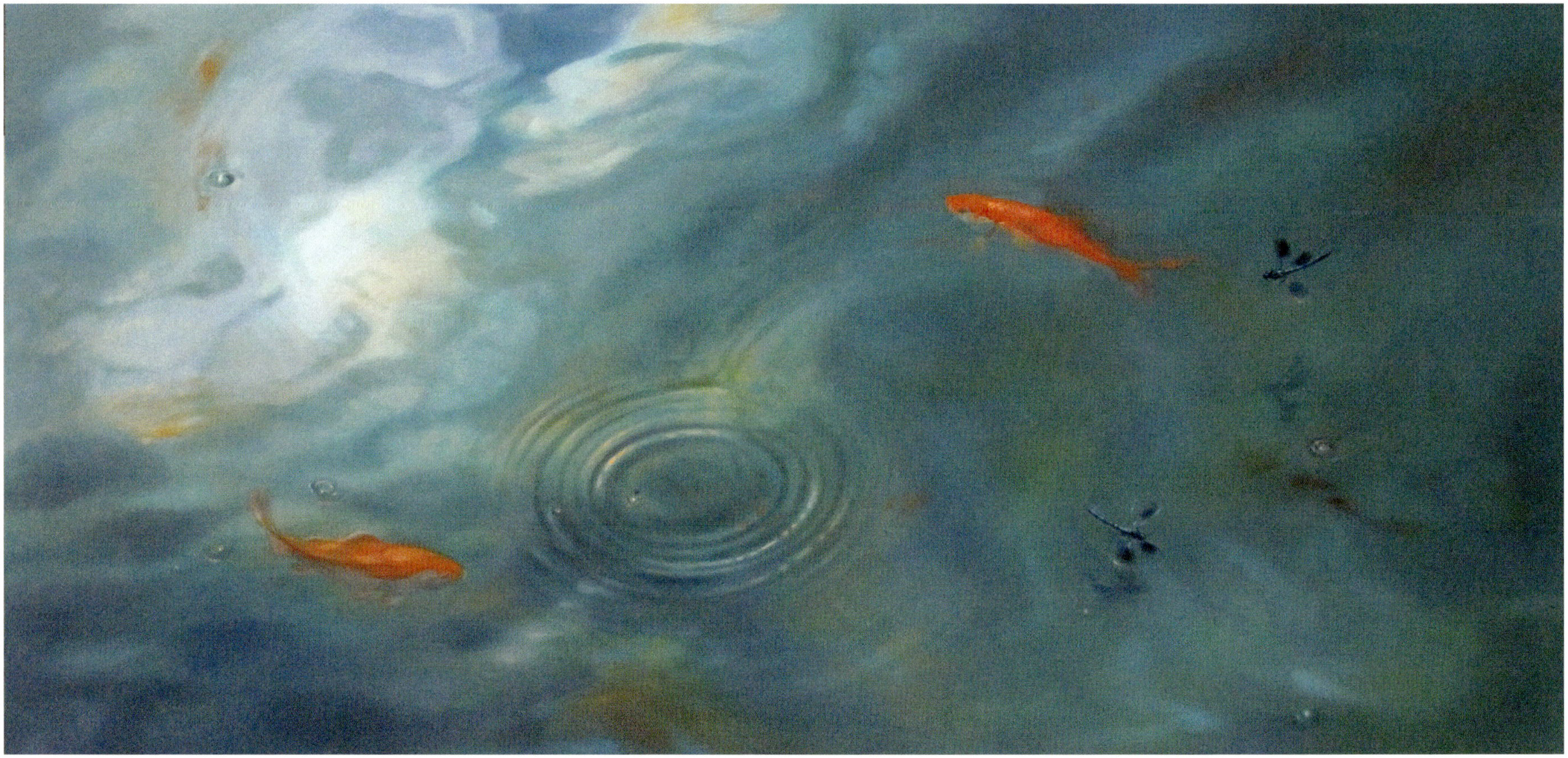

Turquoise Pool With Goldfish oils on canvas 80x100 cm

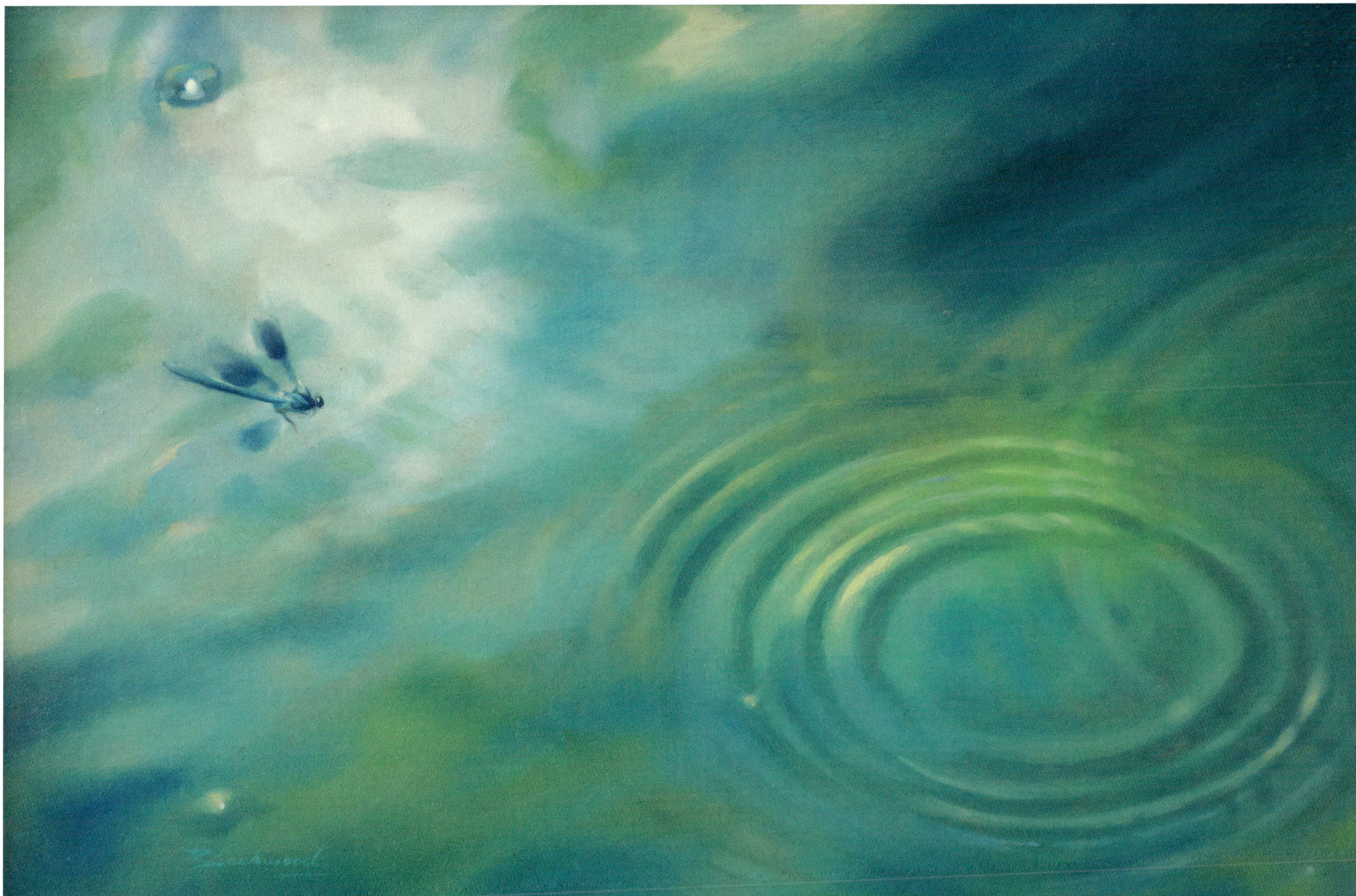

Demoiselle oils on panel 28x40 cm

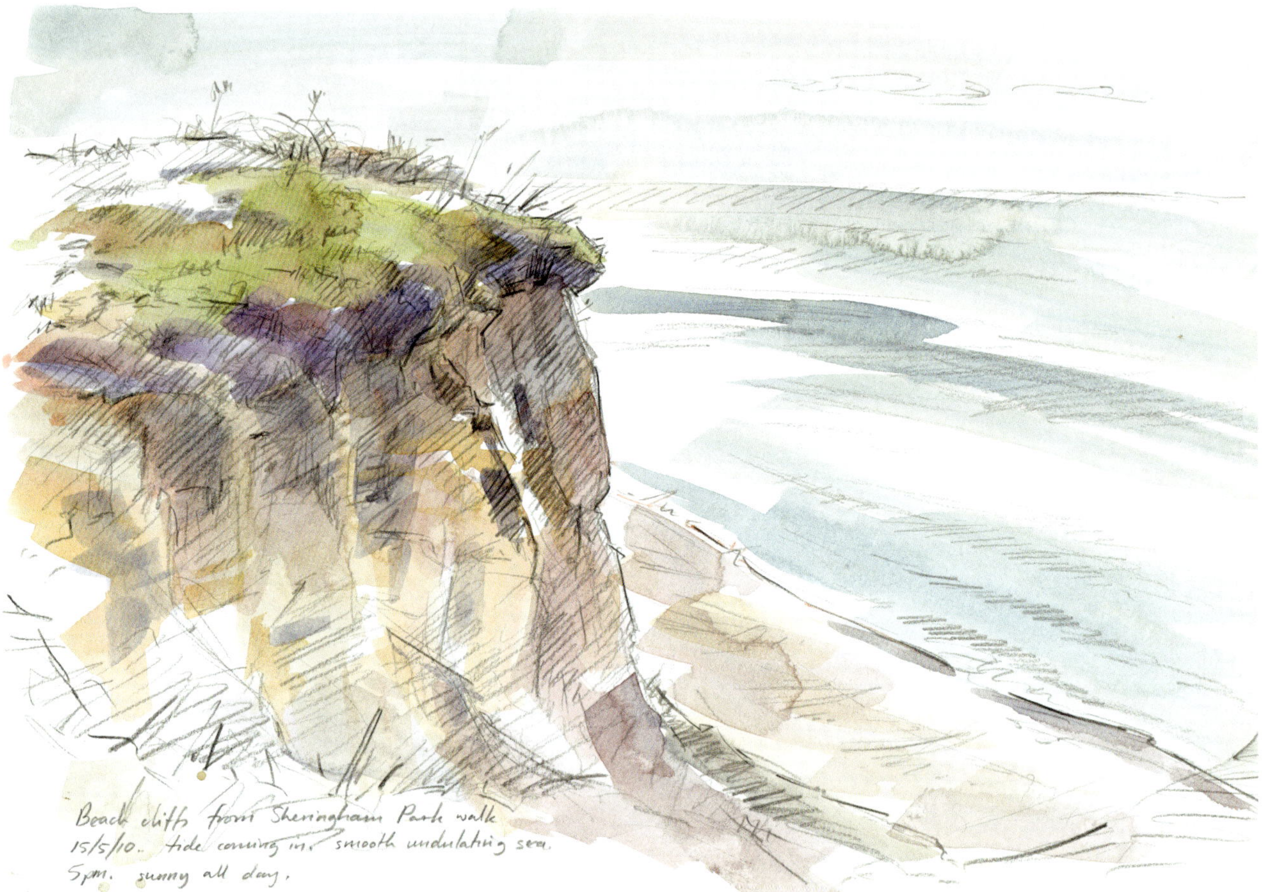

Sheringham Cliffs Sketch
watercolours and pencil on paper

15 May

It was promising to be a glorious spring day, a day for exploring the landscape and enjoying the warmth. I packed up a picnic and tore Sarah away from her desk. It was probably the last chance to see the flowering rhodedendrons at Sheringham Park; another year was slipping by and still I hadn't seen them. We took an unusual entrance into the park through woodland, hoping to see our favourite area, but the Forestry Commission had cut their crop and we were greeted by open space and fresh cut stumps and the smell of sap hanging in the air.

From one of the watchtowers we saw a view that could have almost been from the Himalayas. Azeleas and rhodedendrons spreading out far into the distance towards the coast. We took the track heading for the sea; Whitethroats were out in abundance, singing from the hedgerows. Finally we came to the cliff edge and looked down to the sparkling sea. Skylarks rose from the tufted grassy tops and another Whitethroat sang its heart out from a nearby bush. I set out my sketchbook to capture a memory of the day. The sea rolled gently mid-tide and we threw our scraps to the passing gulls.

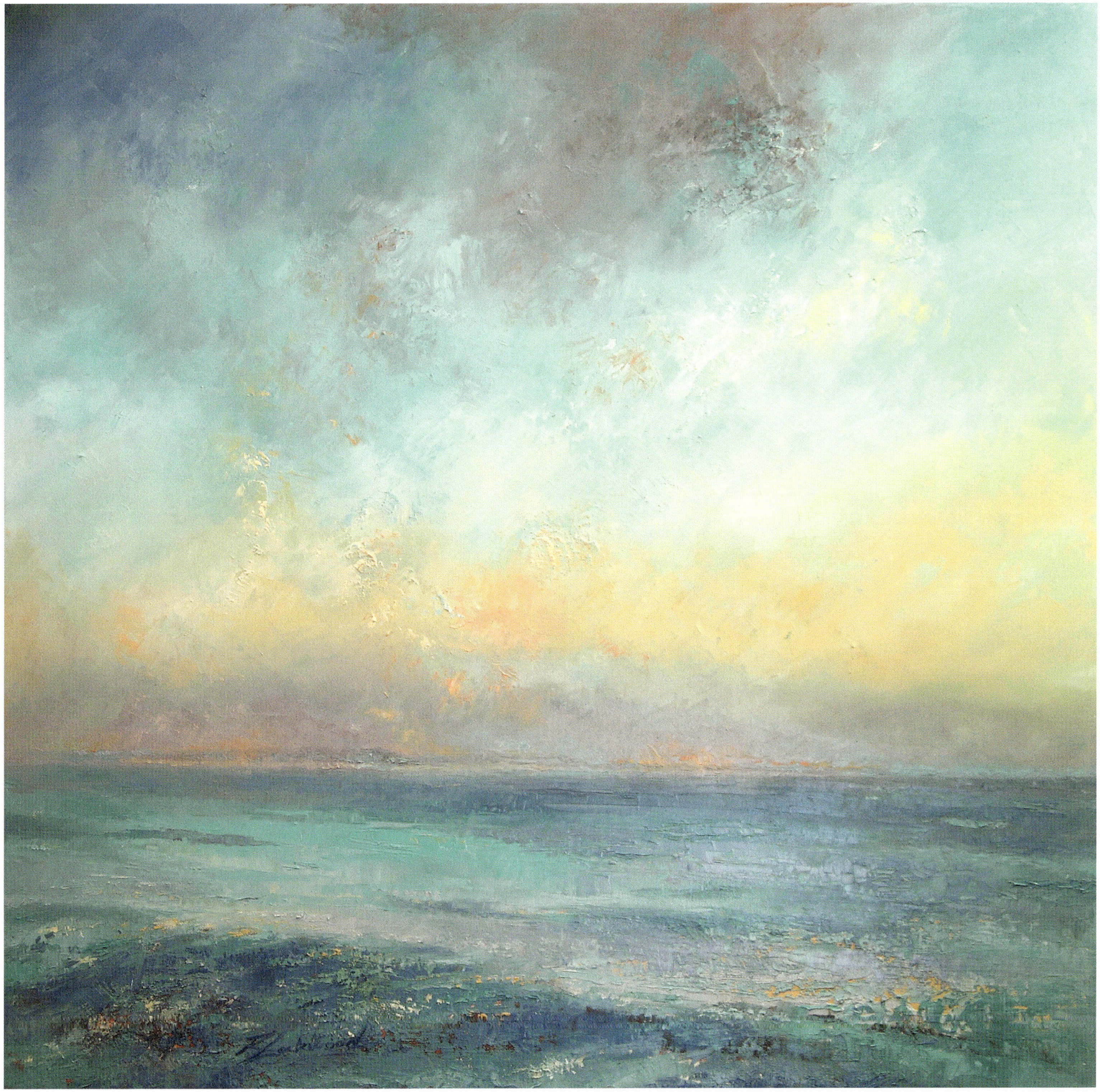

Sea And Sky, Sheringham oils on canvas 100x100 cm

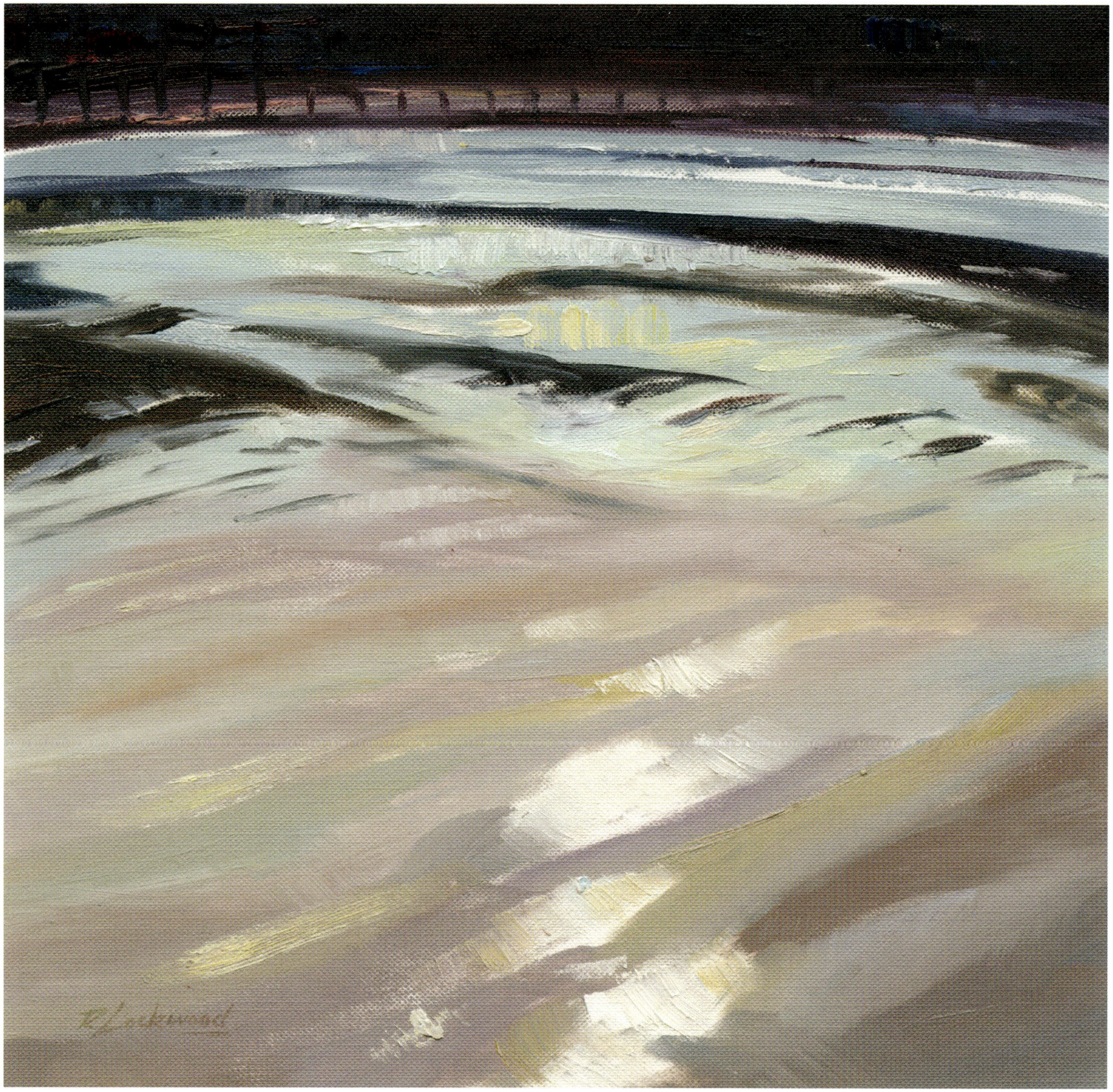

Wet Sand, Sheringham oils on canvas paper 24x24 cm

17 May

When I had my studio in Sheringham, I spent a lot of time looking out to sea and I was always amazed at the changes of colour and light across the shore. It seemed that no two days were ever the same; a wet beach would be transformed by whatever sky was reflected on it. It was necessary to work quickly on these paintings here, to gather as much information as possible, the light changed so quickly the image was gone within minutes.

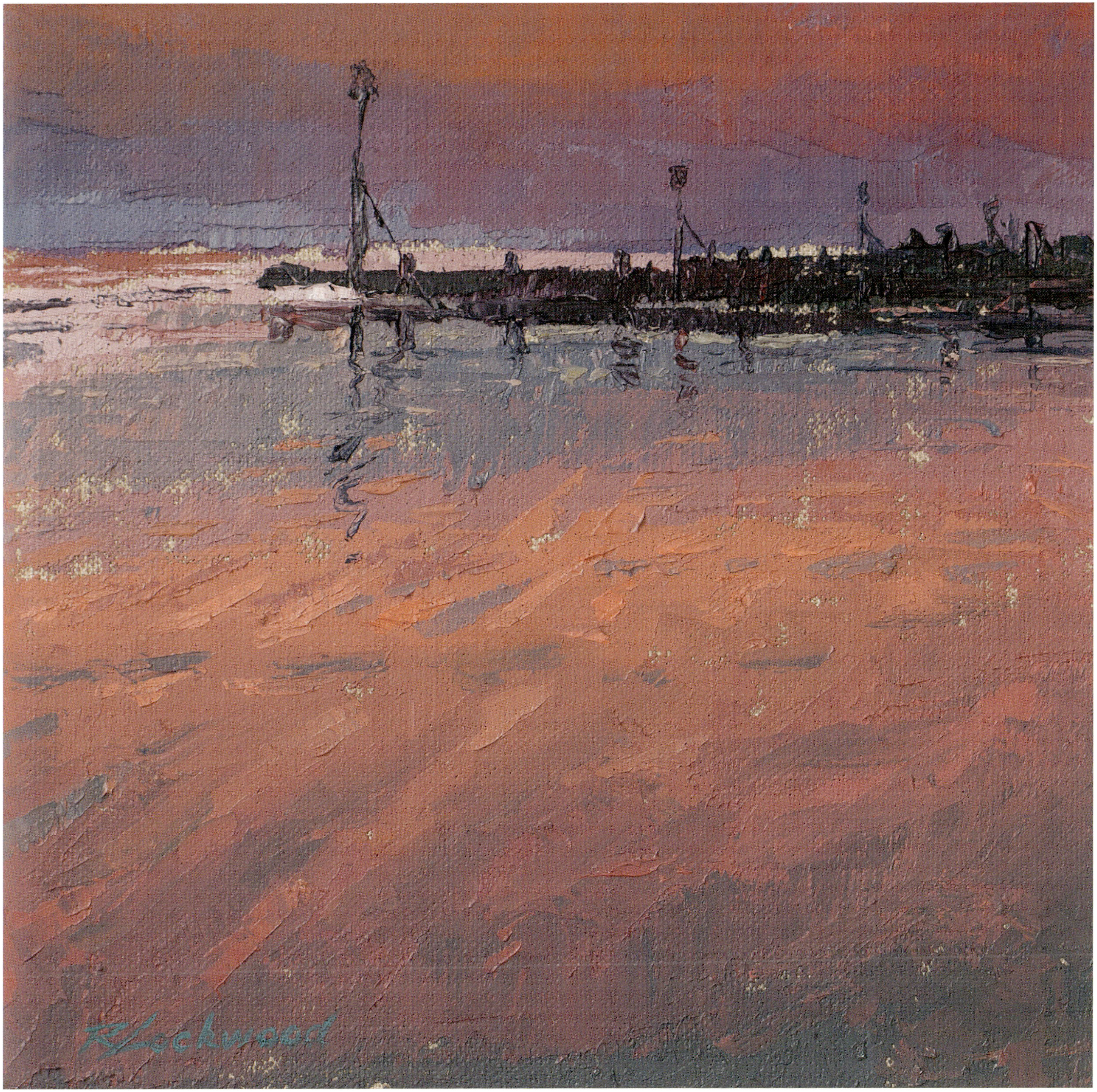

Receding Tide, Sheringham
oils on canvas board
20x20 cm

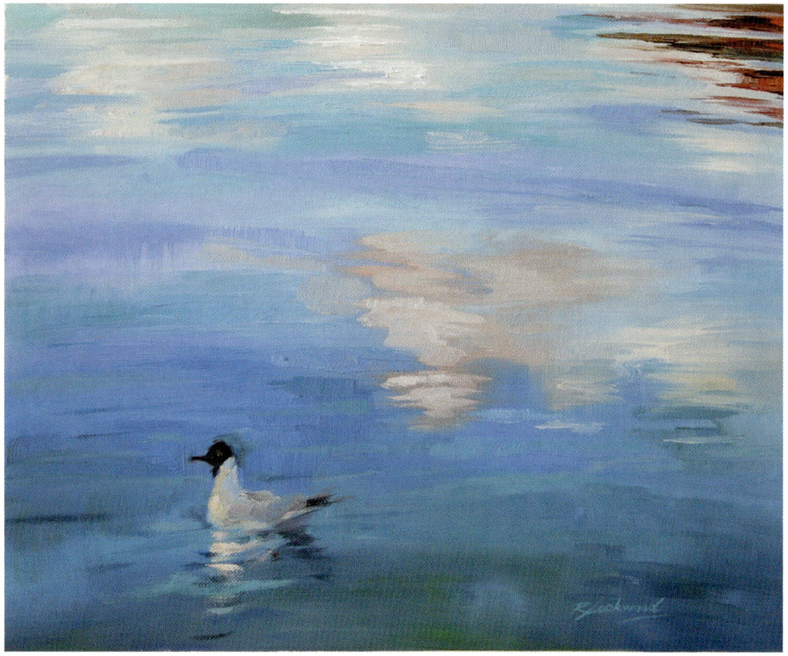

Gull and Clouds oils on canvas paper 25x20 cm

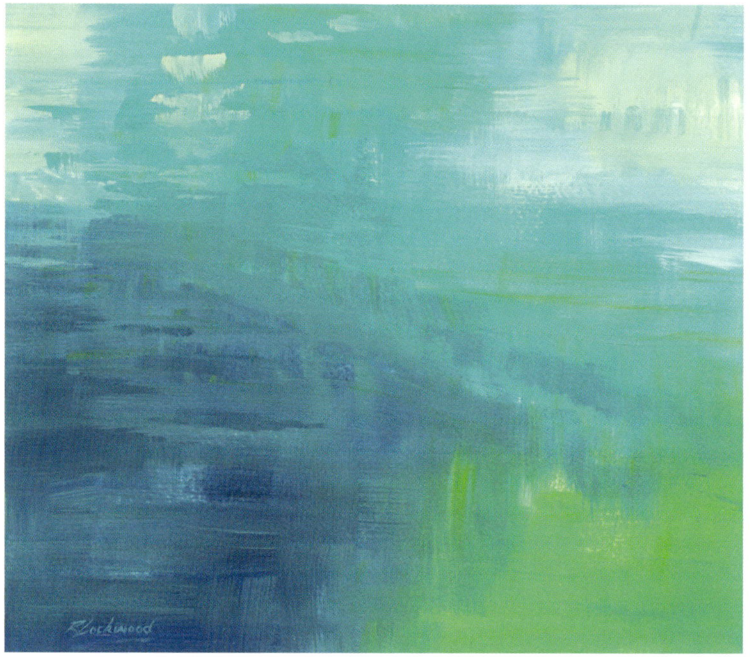

Sheringham Boating Lake oils on paper 23x20 cm

20 May

Other areas of Sheringham that caught my eye were the clifftop pools and boating lake; sparkling gems that lured me in. I studied the fish pond for about a year, visiting it regularly to see the changing colours of the lily pads. I think people thought I was a bit strange, spending so long staring at this tiny pond, simply watching the movement of the fish and the ripples they made. The boating lake was a different thing all together. I think the water here is dyed as it is an incredible turquoise blue. Here I can indulge my fantasies of tropical places - it's enough to cheer you on a cold winter day.

I sometimes start paintings outside to get the essence of the idea down, and then finish them in my studio. But the large painting here, *Red Earth* was purely a studio piece. As I said, I spent months looking at the clifftop pool, watching the light change, waiting for the cerulean blue skies to come along with a cloud to reflect on the water. I also waited for the angle of the sun to change, which would finally filter down to the bottom of the pond and light it up. The darkness of the bottom of the pond, once lit by the light, revealed a red, stained earth - probably enhanced a little by my imagination!

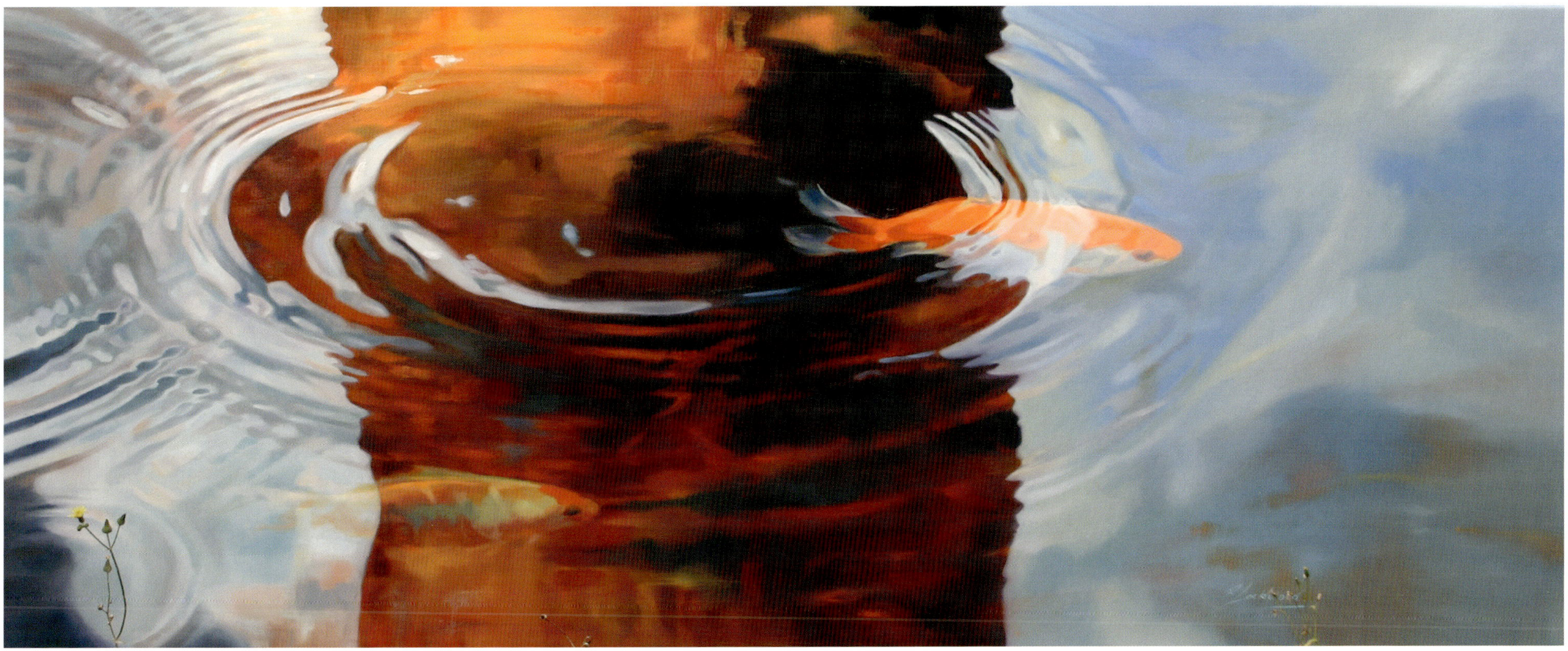

Red Earth oils on canvas 50x120 cm

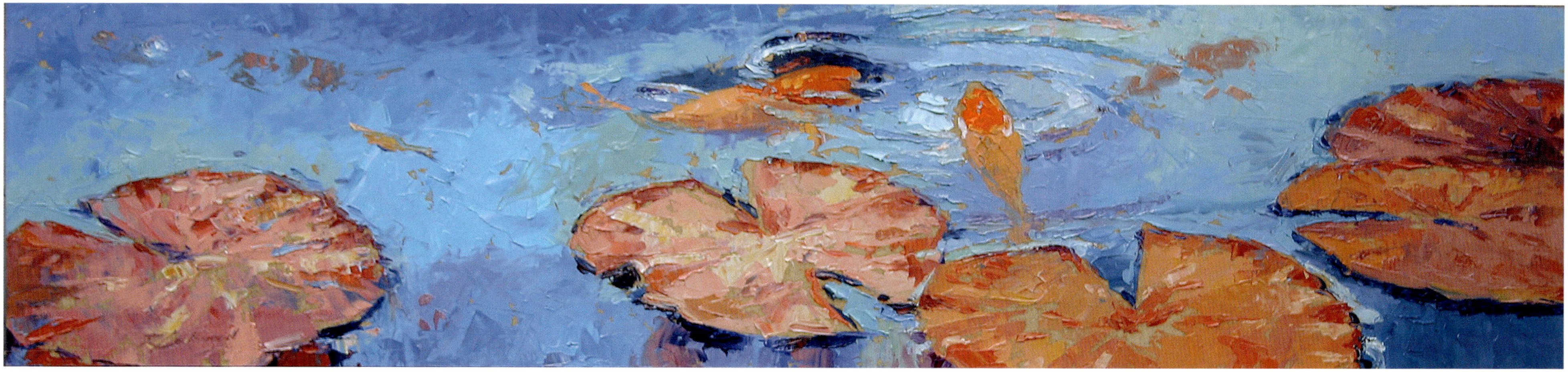

Beach Pool Lilies oils on panel 25x105 cm

24 May

This particular morning on my way to my studio I decided to take a detour down to the clifftop pool. For me, it's really important not to miss that perfect light and today was one of those days. When I arrived at the pool the council gardeners were busy tending the beds, until one of them noticed me watching the pond. I wondered if I was doing something wrong as he walked over to me, but he was simply interested in what I was watching. After a chat, he went to his van and produced a bag of fish food. He'd taken it upon himself to look after the fish and they seemed to know him. As soon as he stood over the pond they rose to the surface. I took advantage of the ripples and patterns made by the feeding fish and I took a few photos and made colour sketches. Now I had my inspiration for the day.

Sometimes while driving home to Cley from Sheringham after a day at the studio, I would slip off into adventurer mode with the aim of discovering new ponds. In fact any body of water would do. I was looking for water plants, watering holes, simple long-standing depressions in the land that had held water for years. Trickling streams, tamed and untamed, I love this combination of nature and its reflections.

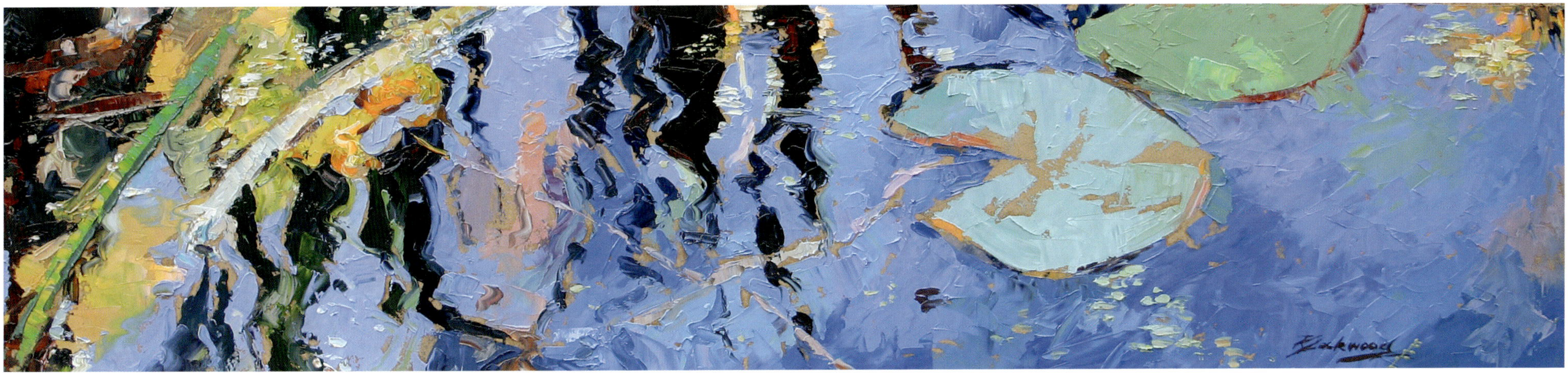

Flag Iris and Lilies oils on panel 105x25 cm

The colours were another thing that attracted me, as I am constantly drawn to blues and reds. I seem to squeeze those colours in to most of the things I paint, not always consciously. I sometimes set myself the task of painting other colours altogether but the pull is so strong that an orange or a blue finally makes its way in at some point. So ponds usually allow me free reign to use the colours I love.

This painting was inspired by a secret location along the coast. I followed a stream that ran through a village, it was heading down to the sea. Further inland the waterway became more of a babbling brook that cut properties off from the road. Makeshift plank bridges crossed the brook and on the other side I came across a hidden pool, its location given away by the sunlight reflecting off its surface, glinting through the foliage surrounding it. I couldn't help it, before I knew it I had stepped across the wooden bridge and was standing on the edge of the pool. The light streamed in, creating milky patches on the surface. A small rowing boat sat still in the shadow of a willow tree and patches of lilies, both red and green spread throughout. I held my breath to suppress my delight at finding such a gem. And with the owners' permission, visited it regularly.

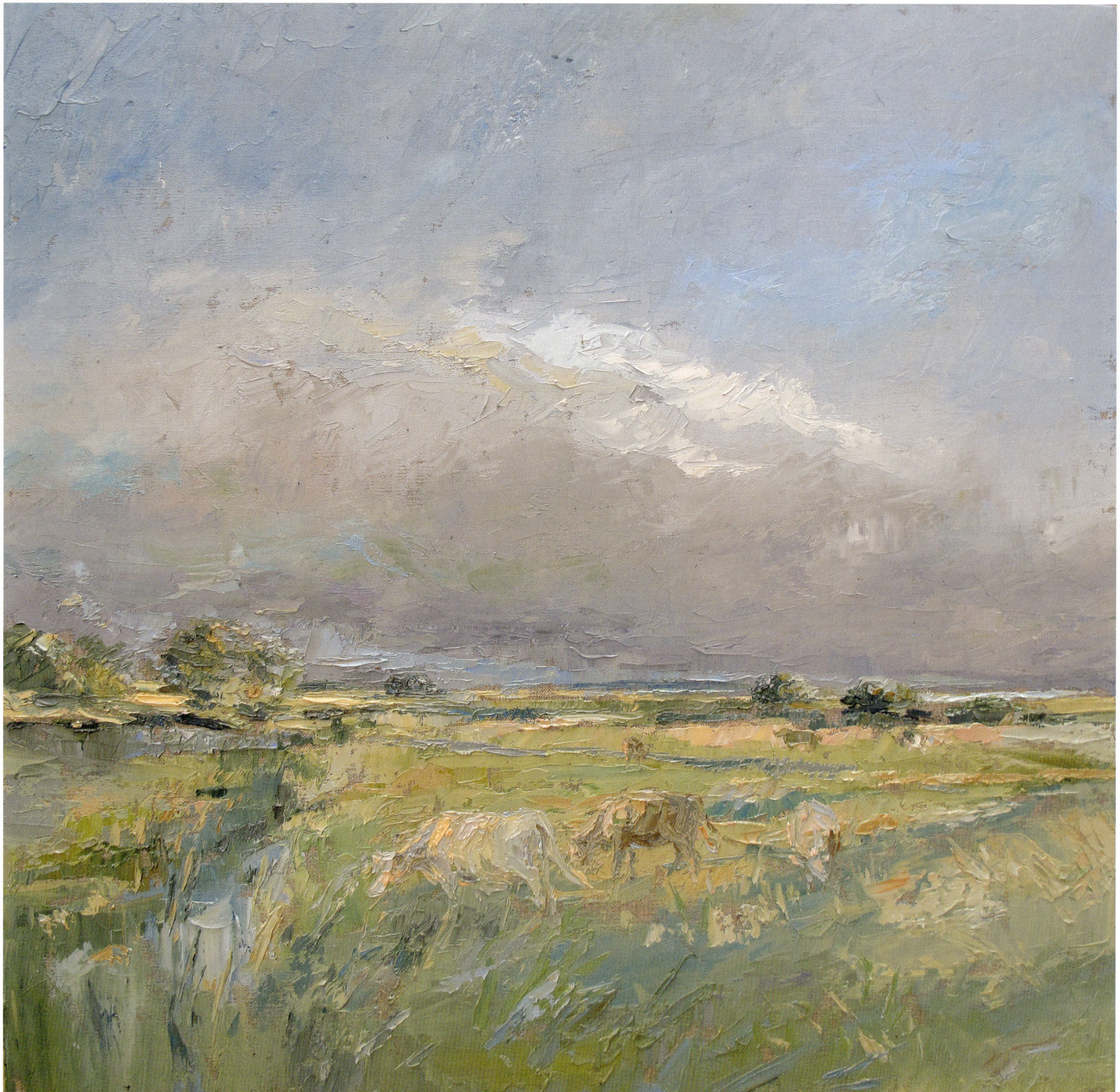

Cows On The Freshes, Cley oils on canvas 50x50 cm

30th June

It's morning and the temperature is already hot and rising. I look out of my bedroom window towards the freshes and see the cows in the distance, they're shimmering in the heat. I pick up my painting things along with a picnic Sarah has packed for me, it's almost as heavy as the easel, I wonder what she's put in there and off I go. The breeze is soft and the heat comforting, it lures me into the pleasure of painting outdoors. It takes me a while to find the right spot but finally I'm sorted. I squeeze out my oils and work quickly on the base colours, It is still early and I know that the lovely morning haze will change soon. I work in a frenzy once I've begun, laying down the layers with my knife, blending and cutting through the paint. I always lose track of the time but finally I have to call it a day. The wind has picked up and the mist has lifted, the light has finally flattened the textures and I know that I would be chasing the light if I continued. I sit beside my easel on a pile of pallets left by the reed cutters and open the box of packed lunch. Toffee aromas rise from wonderful fresh baked flapjack and homemade soda bread. It's hungry business this oil painting. I lighten the load and head back to my studio to continue with the painting whilst the scene is still fresh in my memory.

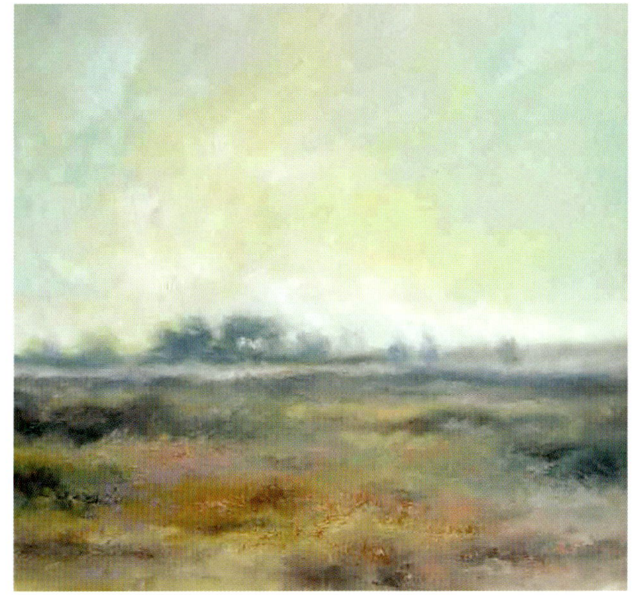

Summer Across The Marsh, Stiffkey
oils on canvas 60x60 cm

3rd July

It's another steaming day. I head for Stiffkey and park near the campsite where I can walk out across the marsh. A soft salty breeze welcomes me as I step out of the car and I stand for a while taking in the view. The summer haze and baking heat has softened the marsh grasses and the air crackles with twisting seedpods. I count these as my perfect days. I love the heat and still air.

When we put the book together, we discovered I didn't have a good enough photo of the painting top right. I went back to Stiffkey to try and recapture the moment, but I couldn't do it. I'll be taking this painting back to Stiffkey to try again!

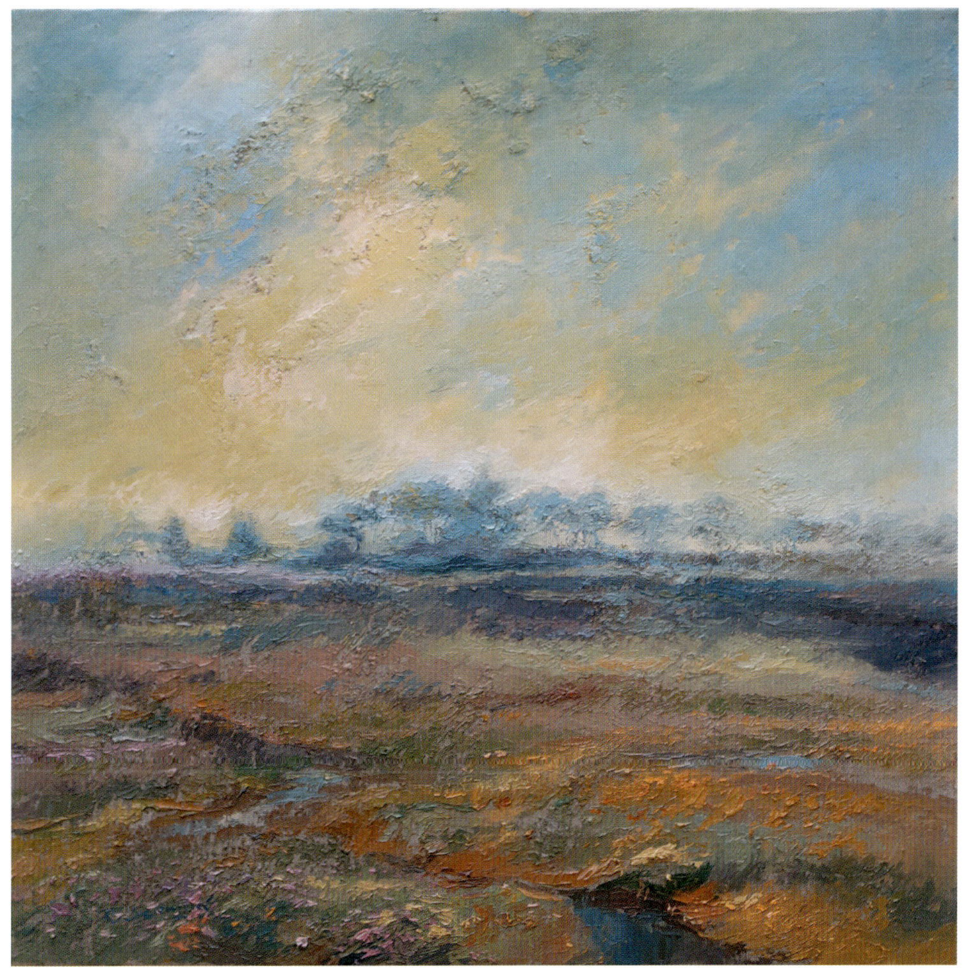

Stiffkey Marsh painting
as yet unfinished
and un-named

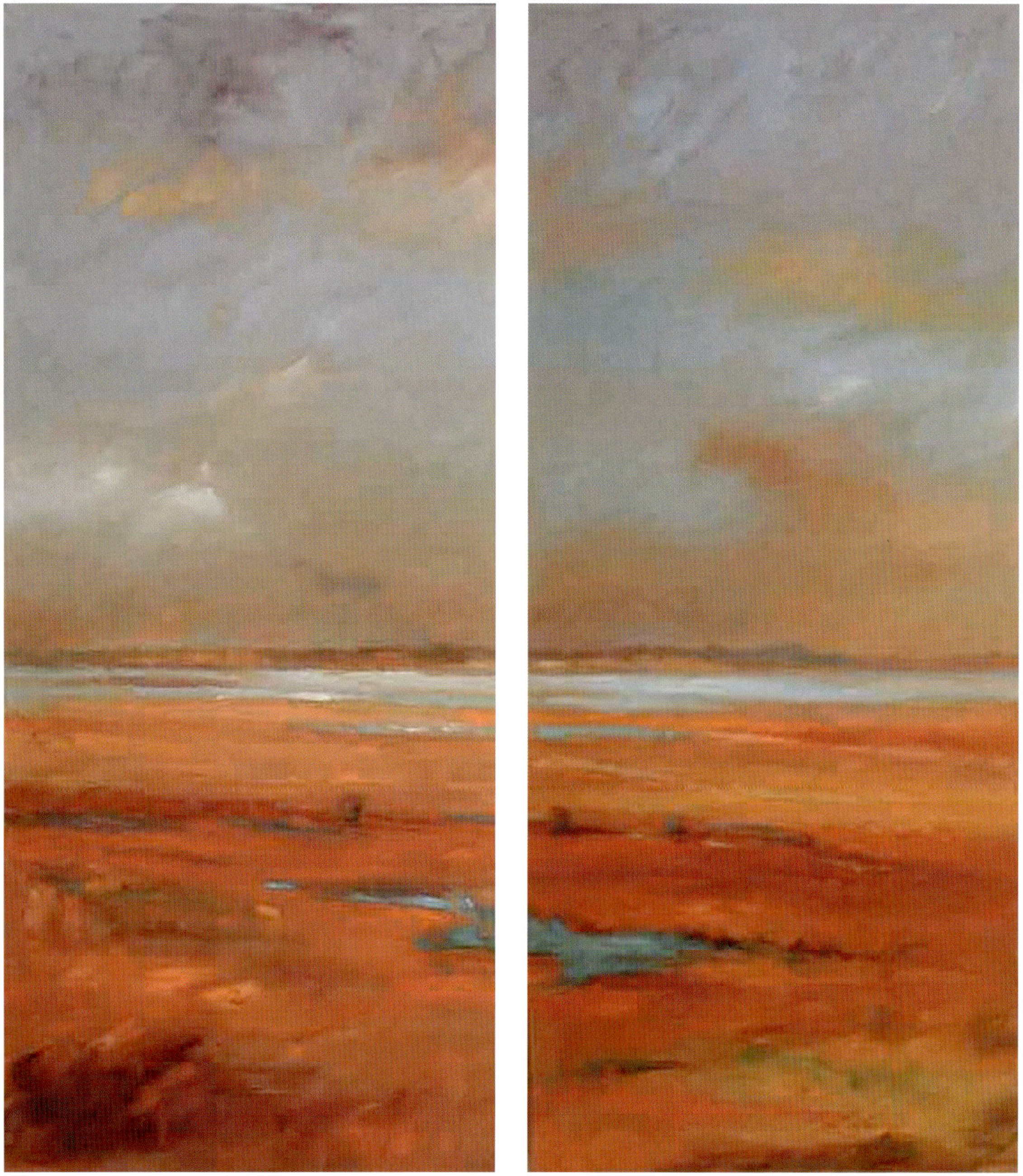

Late Light, Stiffkey Diptych
oils on board 52x123 cm x2

5 July

In *Late Light, Stiffkey* I wanted to create a window, a view to take home and place on the wall to recreate the heat of that day all year round. I wanted to capture that lovely feeling of walking out on to the marsh in the warm air, the light fading and my muscles relaxing.

I wish the viewer could listen to the sounds I experienced on that day. I remember geese, probably Brent Geese as no matter what time of the year, they always seem to be out there. And it's not too far before I upset a Redshank; their sharp, excitable cries are ever present on these marshes.

6 July

I saw this view while walking back from the sea towards the car park at Stiffkey. It had been quite wet the days before, increasing the amount of water lying on the marsh and the morning summer light had not yet bleached out the subtle colours of the marsh plants. I used a palette knife here to capture the texture and sharpness of vegetation against the cuts of water, but I had to finish the painting in my studio as the morning colours disappeared very quickly. I remember watching a Short-eared Owl on my way back; it noiselessly glided overhead, casually looking at me, undisturbed by my presence. It made me think of my packed lunch as I watched it hunt. Even though it was only eleven o'clock, I stayed a little longer to eat and enjoy the view.

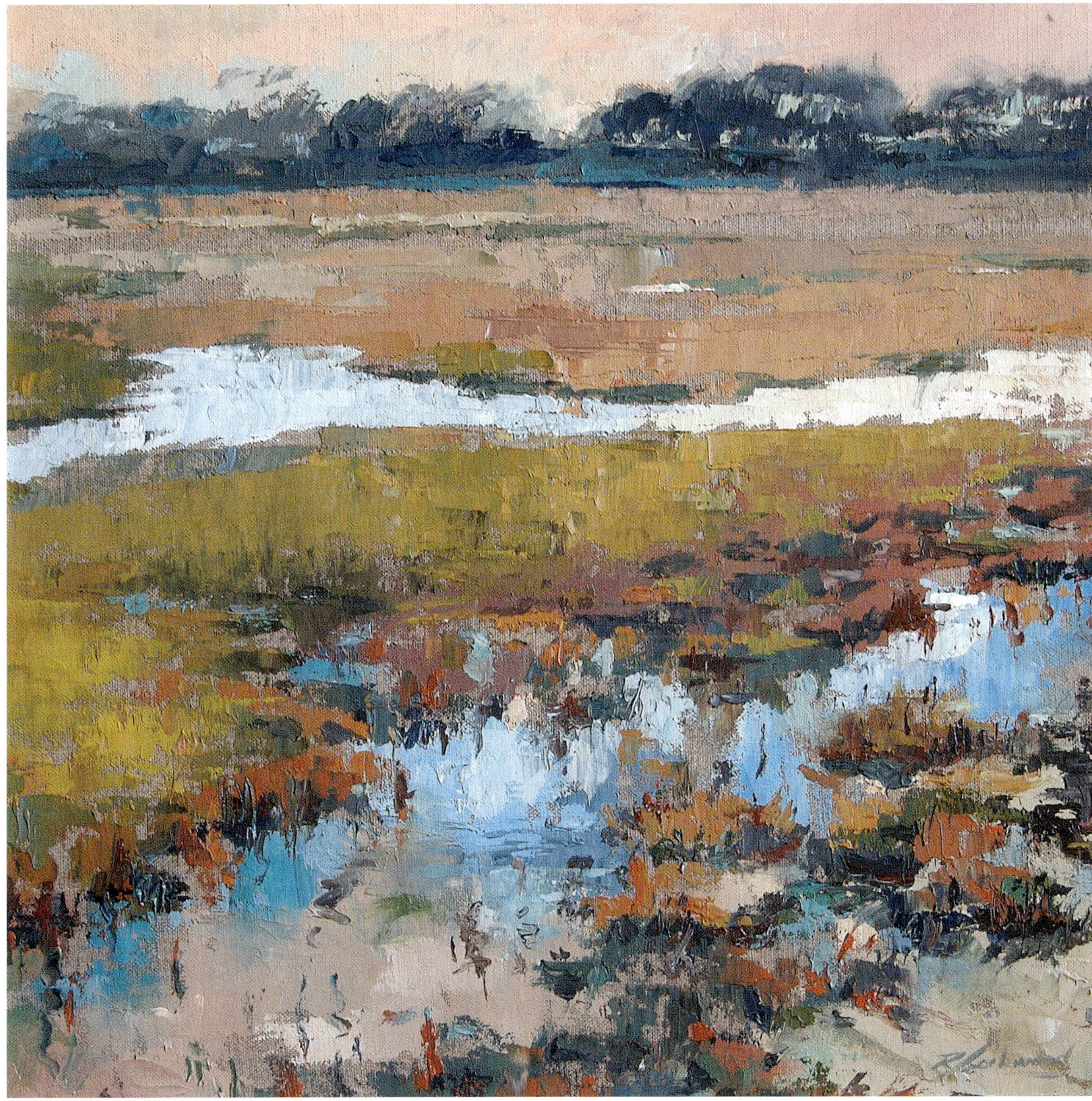

Stiffkey Marsh oils on canvas 40x40 cm

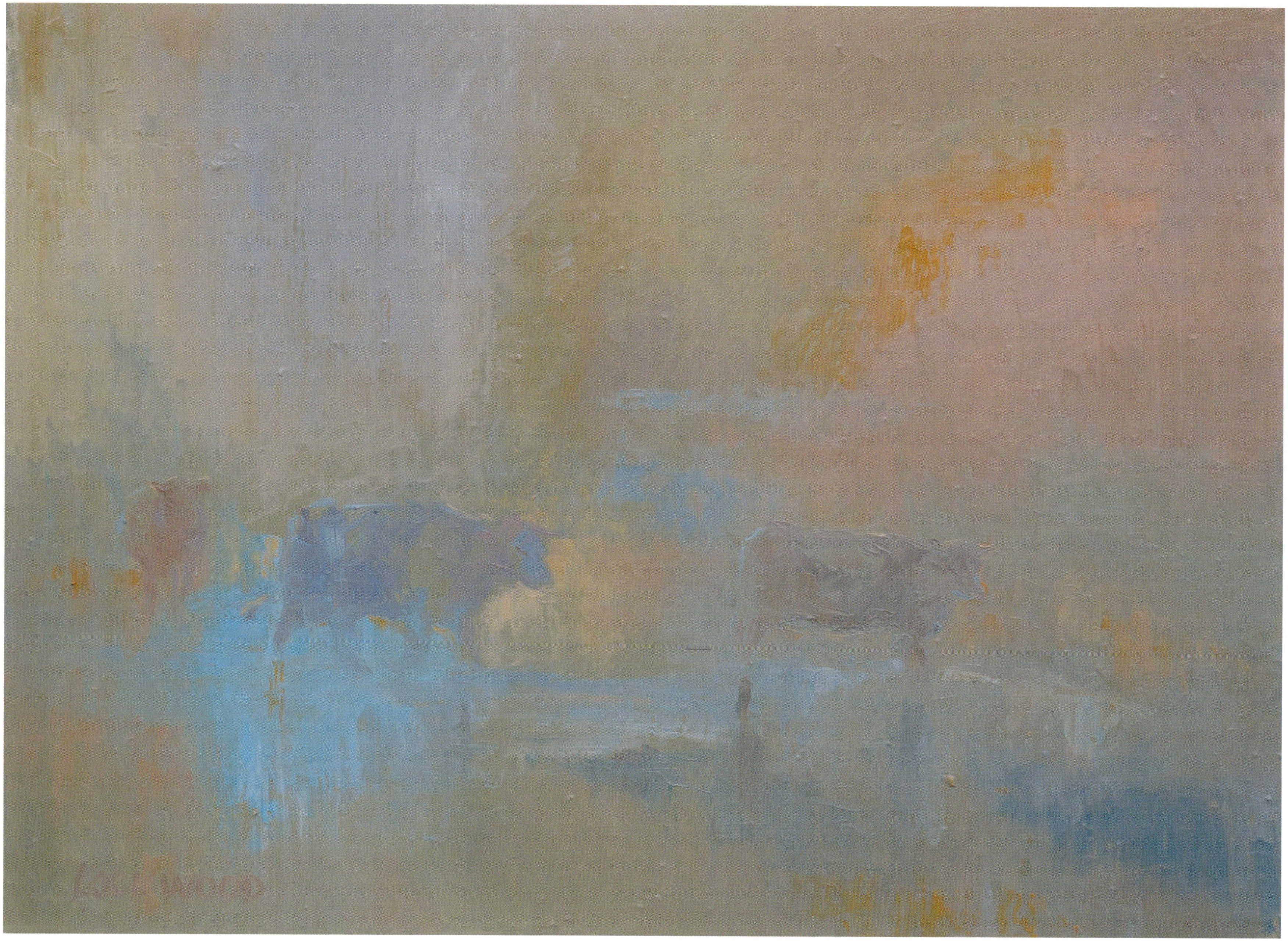

Cows in Summer Mist oils on linen 80x100 cm

8 July

Who would have thought that by the end of the day I would have set myself on fire. The day began so perfectly with the heat rising steadily, I eagerly organised a barbecue for the evening. But as I was cooking the last burger I heard a roaring noise very close by – too close. My beloved fleece had caught the flames and caramelized, but luckily I whipped it off before it could barbecue me. Eyebrows intact, I managed to finish my burger just as a thick mist began to roll in off the sea, like something out of a 1970's horror movie. It thickened further and the temperature dropped. We braved the freezing temperatures for a while but eventually had to call it a day. As it was early and still light, we headed down to Salthouse. The cows stood there just visible in the mist, the salty pools throwing out odd reflections. To make the most of this strange weather, I went out early the next morning. The air was beginning to warm up and the mist was quickly moving away, but it left me with an idea for these paintings.

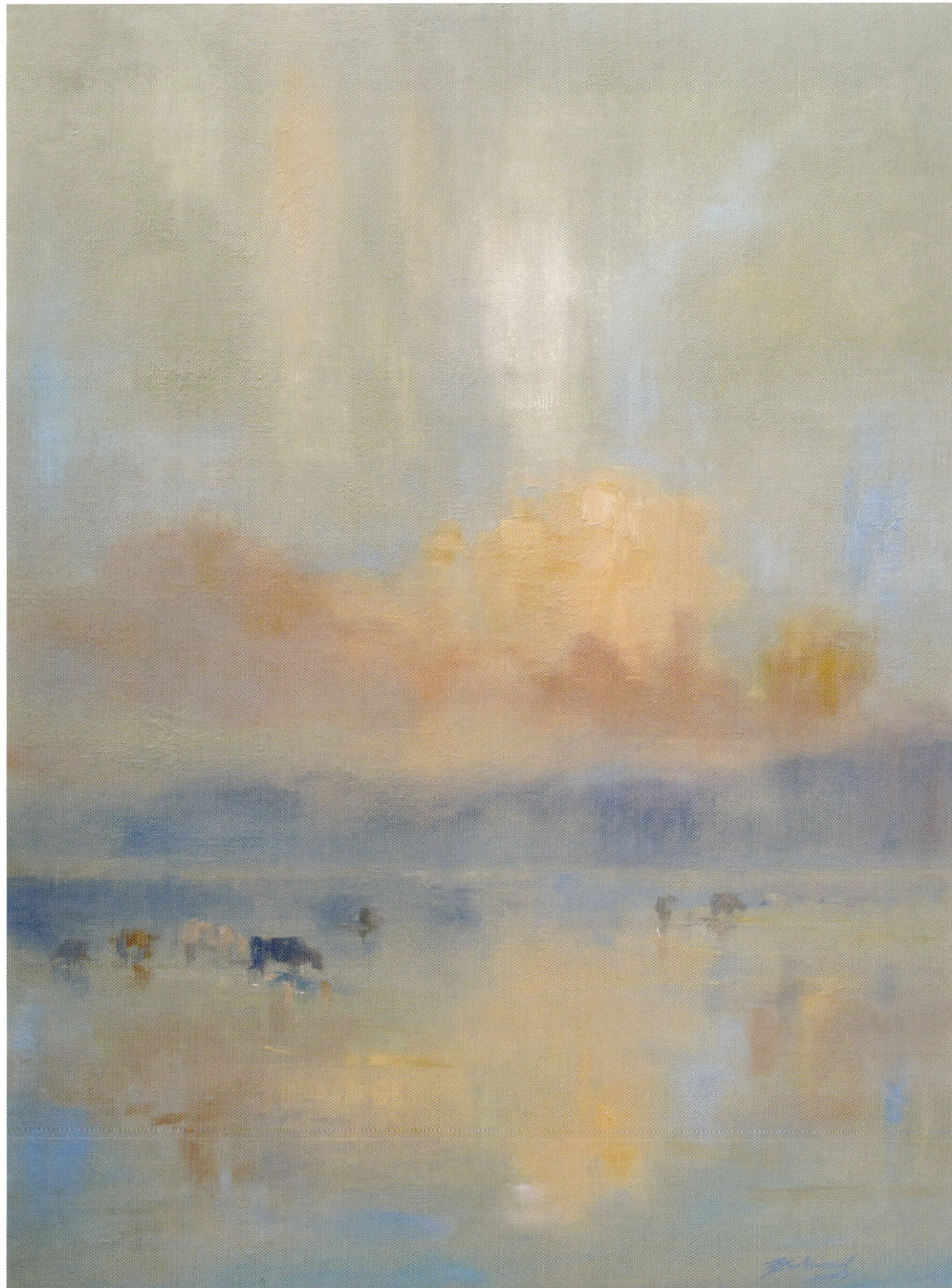

Cows On Wet Summer Marsh
oils on linen 100x80 cm

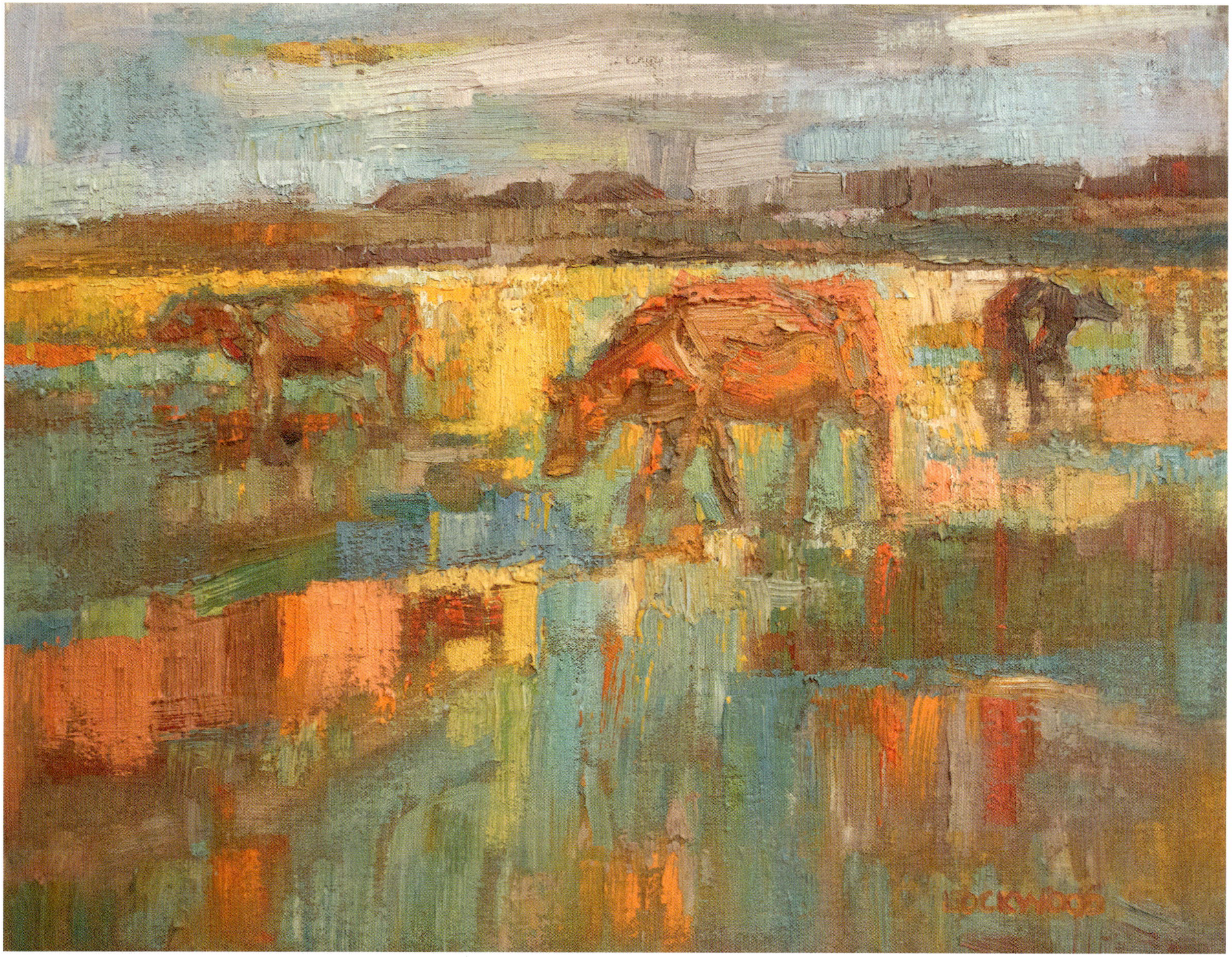

Cows, from Cley Beach Road oils on canvas board 40x30 cm

15 July

A few days later and the marsh meadows have returned to the typical sun-dried landscape of summer in Cley. I can spend hours watching the cows move lazily across the hot marsh, however, this is British weather we are talking about and after starting the painting above, thick, heavy rain clouds appeared and drenched my canvas making it impossible to continue. The water mixed with the oils making a congealed mess, interesting but it didn't really work. So I returned to my studio and left it to dry. The painting developed over the following days by adding a mark here and there, mostly subconsciously. I think it's interesting how it has depicted the striations of the marsh grasses.

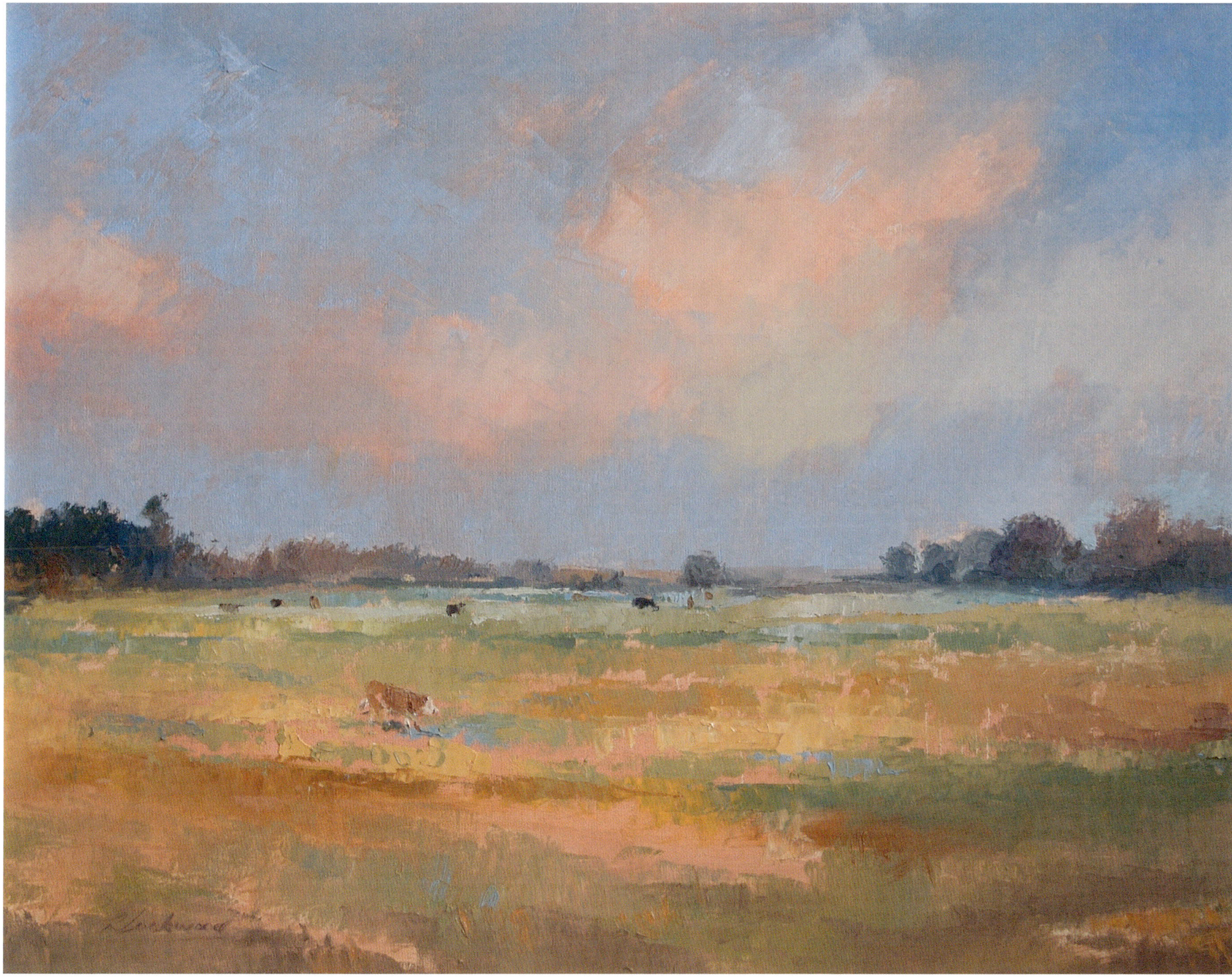

Blakeney Freshes, With Cows oils on canvas 40x30 cm

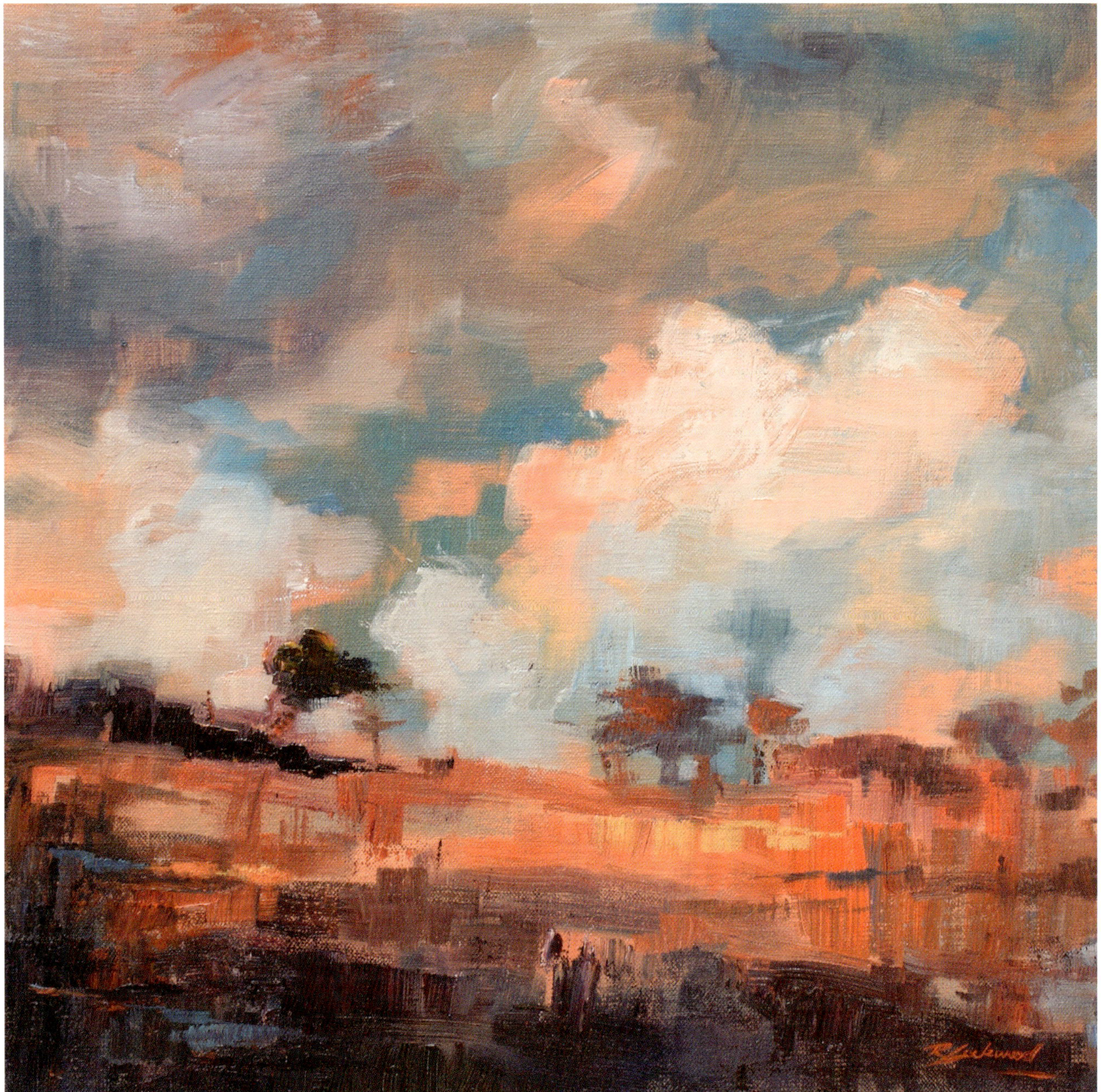

Up Cockthorpe Valley oils on canvas board 40x40 cm

I August

This morning the rain is pouring, I can hear cars outside scraping through the water, washing down the road outside the gallery. The land desperately needs a good soaking; on this particular part of the coast we've had weeks without proper rain. Pond levels are low and on the brink of drying up completely. Insects are desperately laying eggs in the shallow warm water.

In the afternoon I went inland to see some friends near Cockthorpe. The weather had cleared, leaving behind a few lazy clouds. They showed me a walk I would never have discovered, a small hidden valley that headed down to the coast. Yes that's right, a valley in Norfolk. And on the edge of the valley stood an old Crab Apple tree, the light was catching it and pink clouds were pouring over. It was such a striking image I made a mental note to paint it as soon as I got back into the studio. I wanted to remember the detail of the block textures of the cliff reflected in the angles of the clouds. This wasn't really a highly finished painting, more a collection of my ideas and memories of that moment that will hopefully develop into something else in time.

As we walked further down the valley, we came across the River Stiffkey, which gradually led us on to an estuary famed for its mussels and the men that work the waters there. The light glistened on the discarded shells and resting boats and the cerulean blue water. We all stood quietly, watching the light disappear, another painting brewed in my mind.

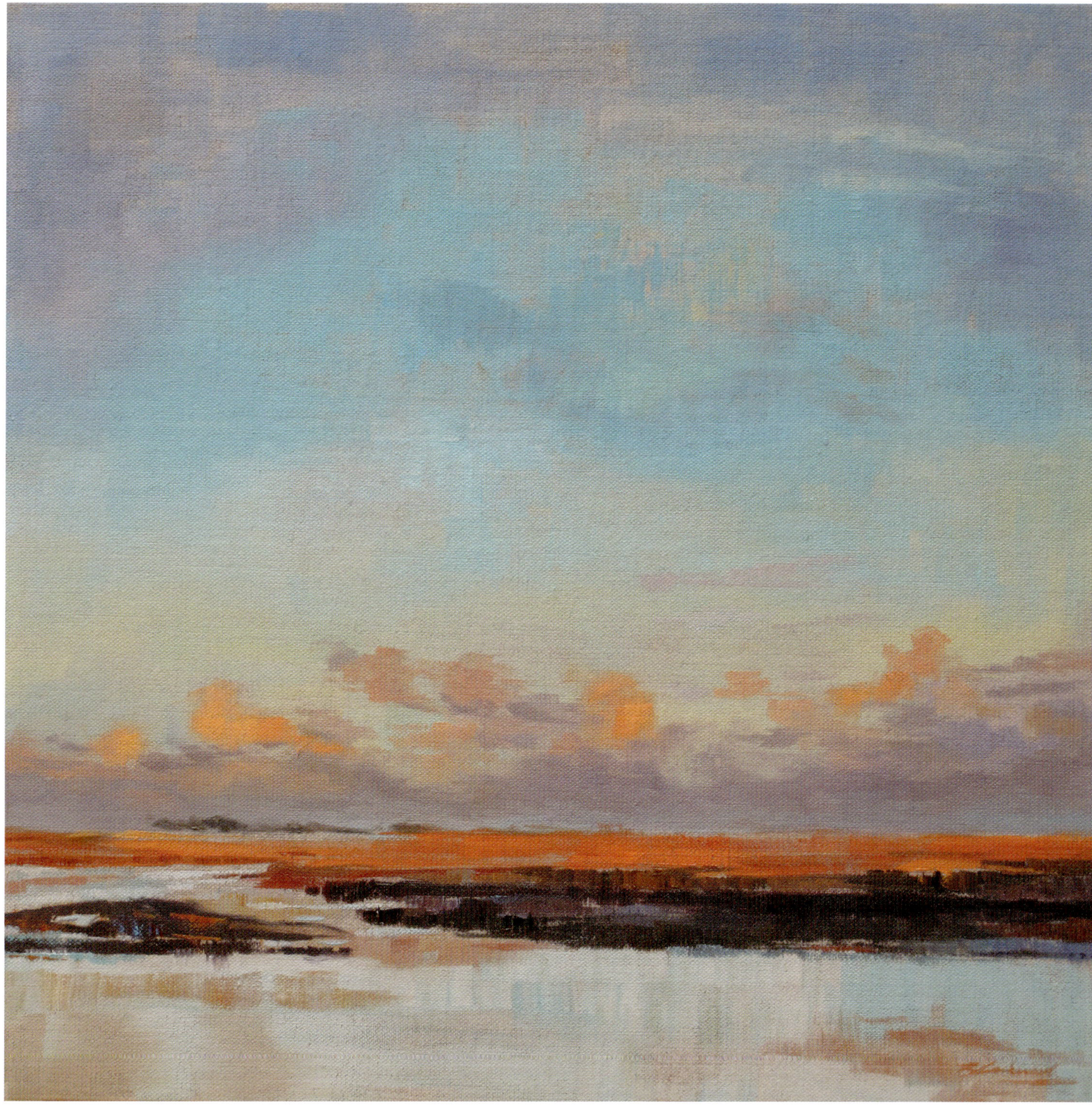

Marsh and Sky   oils on linen board   30x30 cm

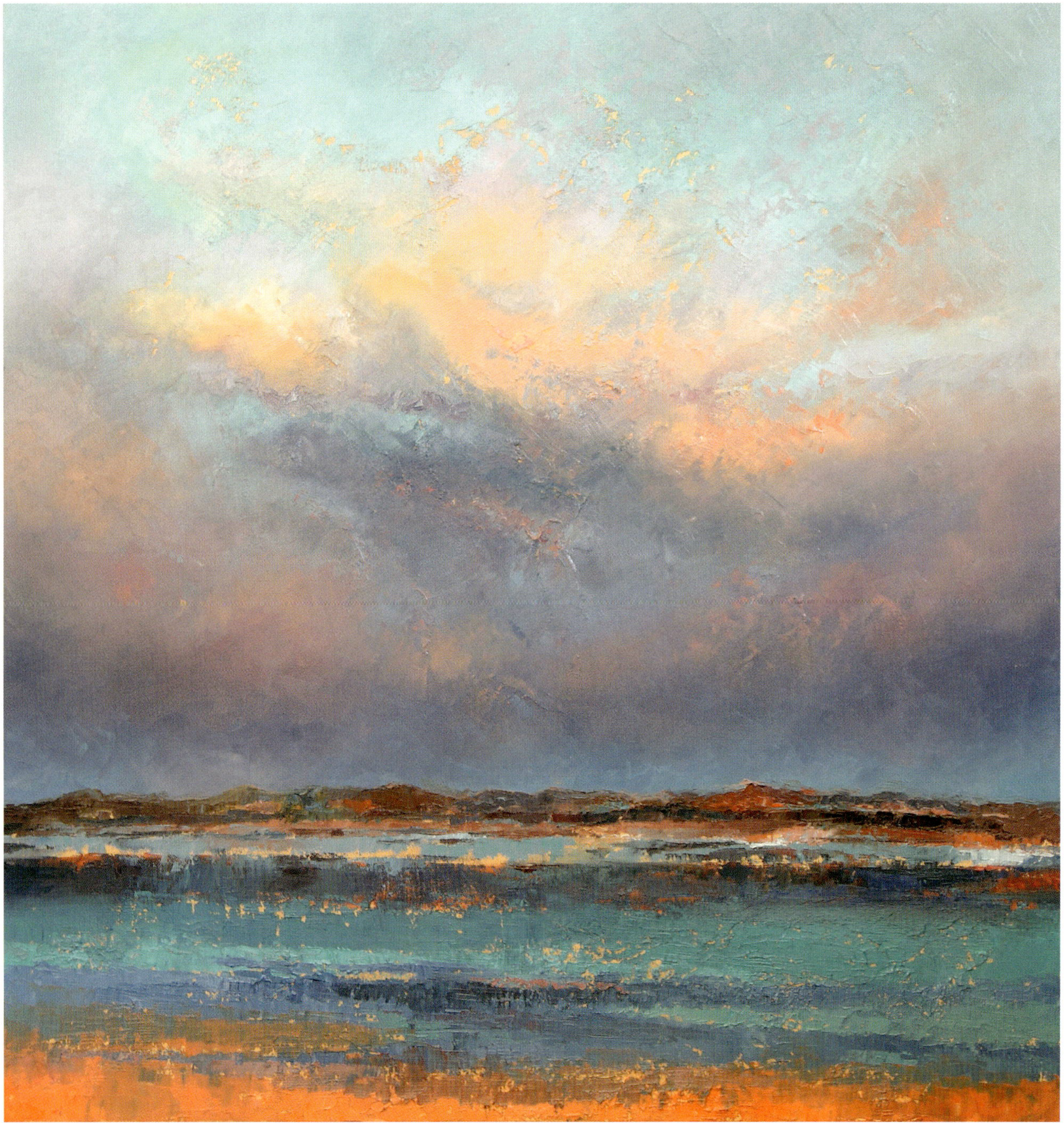

Evening Sail From Wells to Morston oils on canvas 80x80 cm

15 August

Some friends who ran our local café asked us if we wanted to go for a sail this evening as they had to bring their boat back from Wells. We had to wait for them to cook sausage and mash for a late arrival, it's so laid back here that they let the customers finish their meal and see themselves out. Nothing gets in the way of an evening sail when the weather and tide are right.

We rushed up the coast, dropping one car off at Morston Quay on the way, just managing to get to Wells in time to make it back on the tide. Although it was a beautiful evening, the swell of the open sea started to make me feel sick. Luckily I managed to keep calm, despite our captain's fight with his sails. I concentrated hard on the land and horizon, busily planning a picture as we sailed by. I made mental notes of the colours of the coastline; I remember the sea being especially opalescent that evening.

While our hosts were busy preparing their boat for sail, I took advantage of the water reflections in the harbour at Wells. Although it would have been an obvious choice to paint the many boats in the water, I found the reflections they were making far more interesting. I saw one particular reflection that I thought would sum up all the essential elements of the harbour. I used the buoy to give a final clue to the scene, and to add perspective.

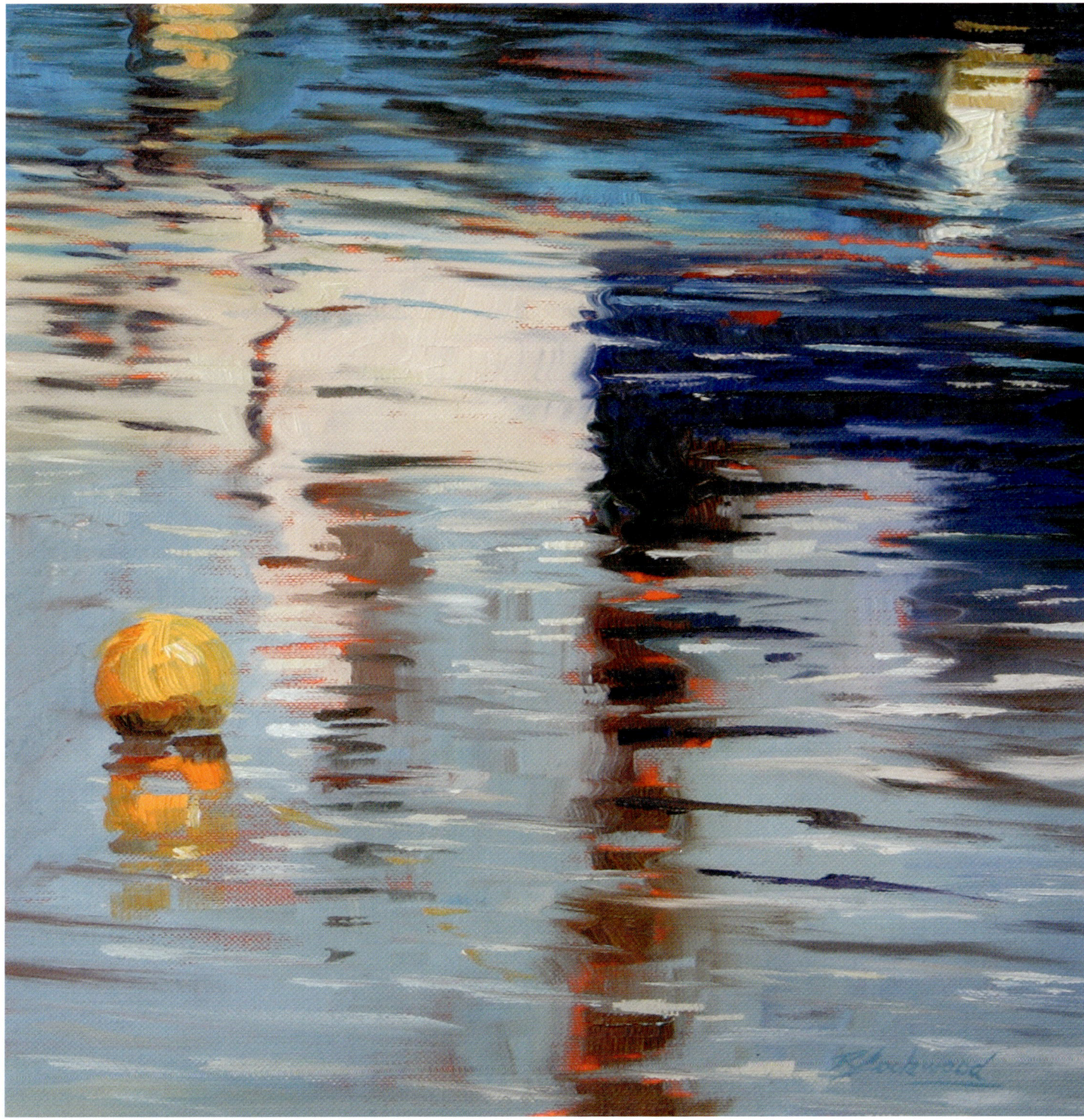

Buoy And Boats, Wells oils on canvas paper 25x25 cm

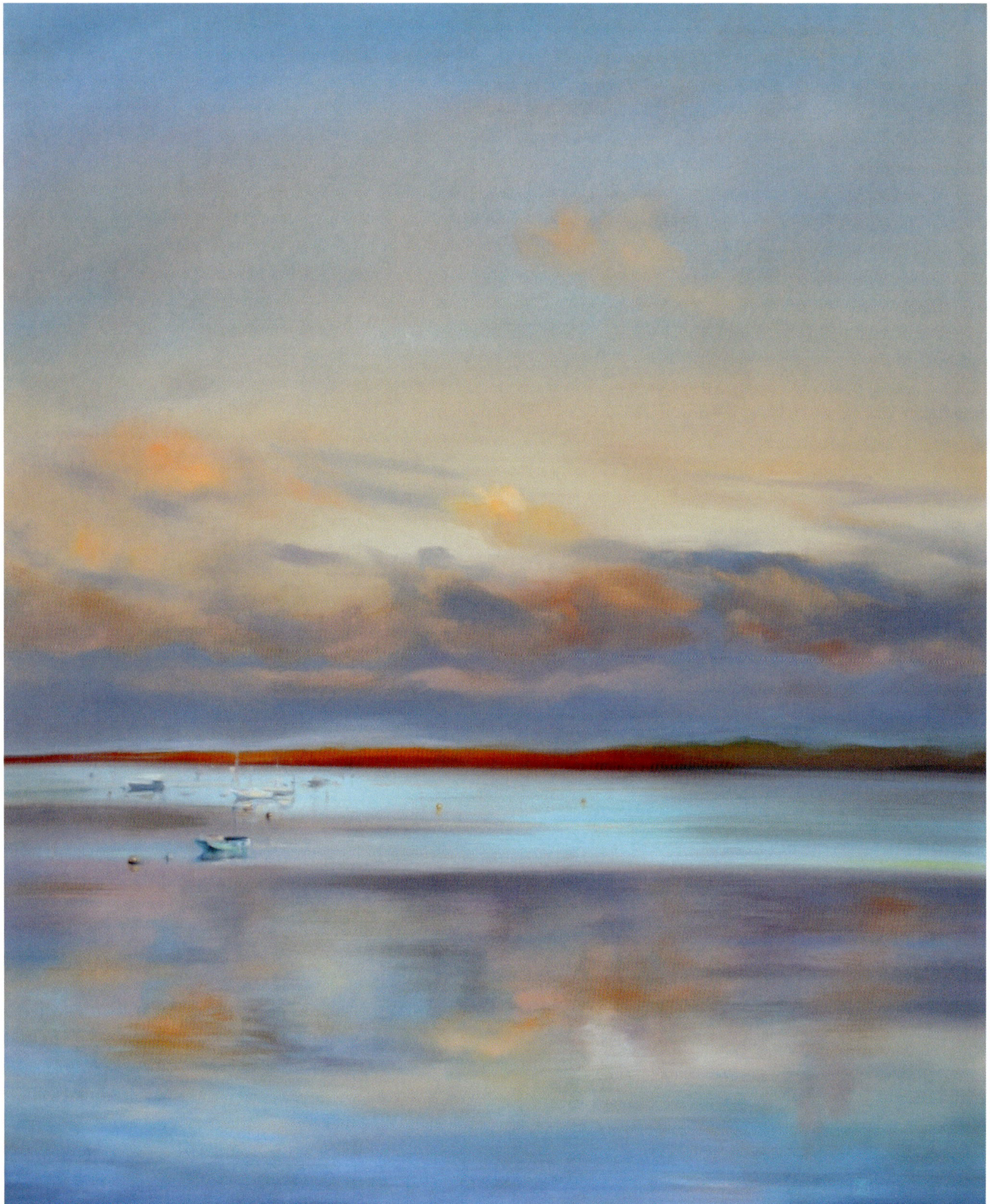

19 August

This morning I woke early as I always do on sunny days, the light seems to switch on my brain. Vic and Jon are already opening up Picnic Fayre Deli and busy organizing their day ahead. Vic proudly shows me with a sweep of her arm the new lino on their kitchen floor. The smell of Vic's fresh baking fills the air and I can't resist buying some cake for breakfast.

As I drive towards Wells, I can see the day is shaping up to be something spectacular and I can't wait to get to the harbour. I'm able to while away many hours here, especially as I can park right up to the harbour edge and sit in the warmth of my car to watch the ebb and flow of the tide. This beautiful morning had enticed many others to see the stunning view. We all stood against the harbour railings, silently looking out. Normally people would be crabbing or throwing their spare chips up for the gulls, but today was different. A police car pulled up beside me with four uniformed men inside and I remembered that I hadn't put a ticket on the car - no matter, they were only interested in the view. Out came their sandwich boxes and off came their jackets. The opalescent colours deepened, there was a silent feeling of camaraderie as we shared the same view, nothing needed to be said.

I decided that the painting of this scene had to be a very large one. The view I had seen was so immense and enveloping I wanted it big enough to feel that I could swim in it. I had to lower my easel to the ground to reach the top of the board I was painting on. Unlike my other work, I built the layers up in glazes to capture that smooth, opalescent light.

Wells Harbour Dawn
oils on board 150x90 cm

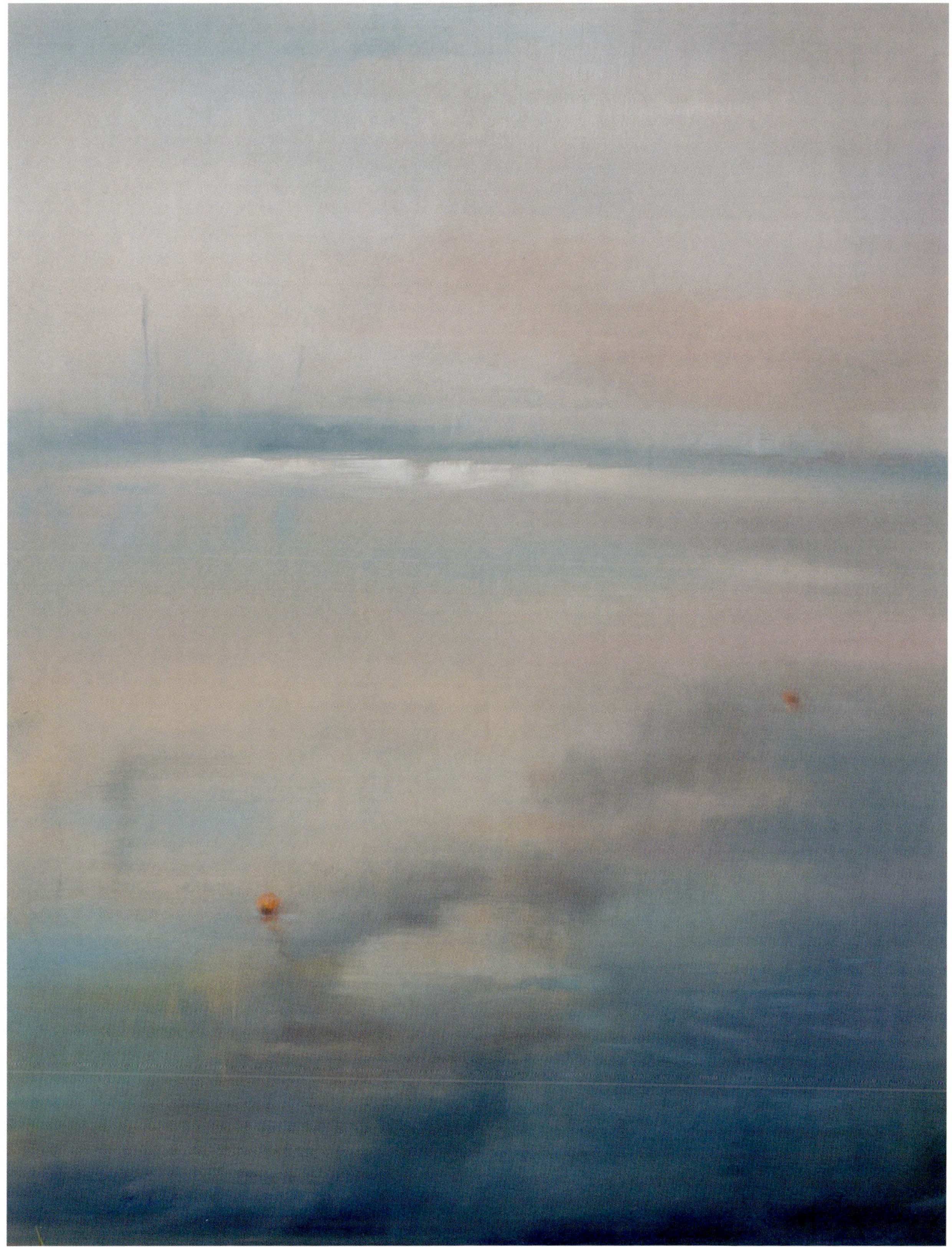

Harbour Mist
oils on board 105x75 cm

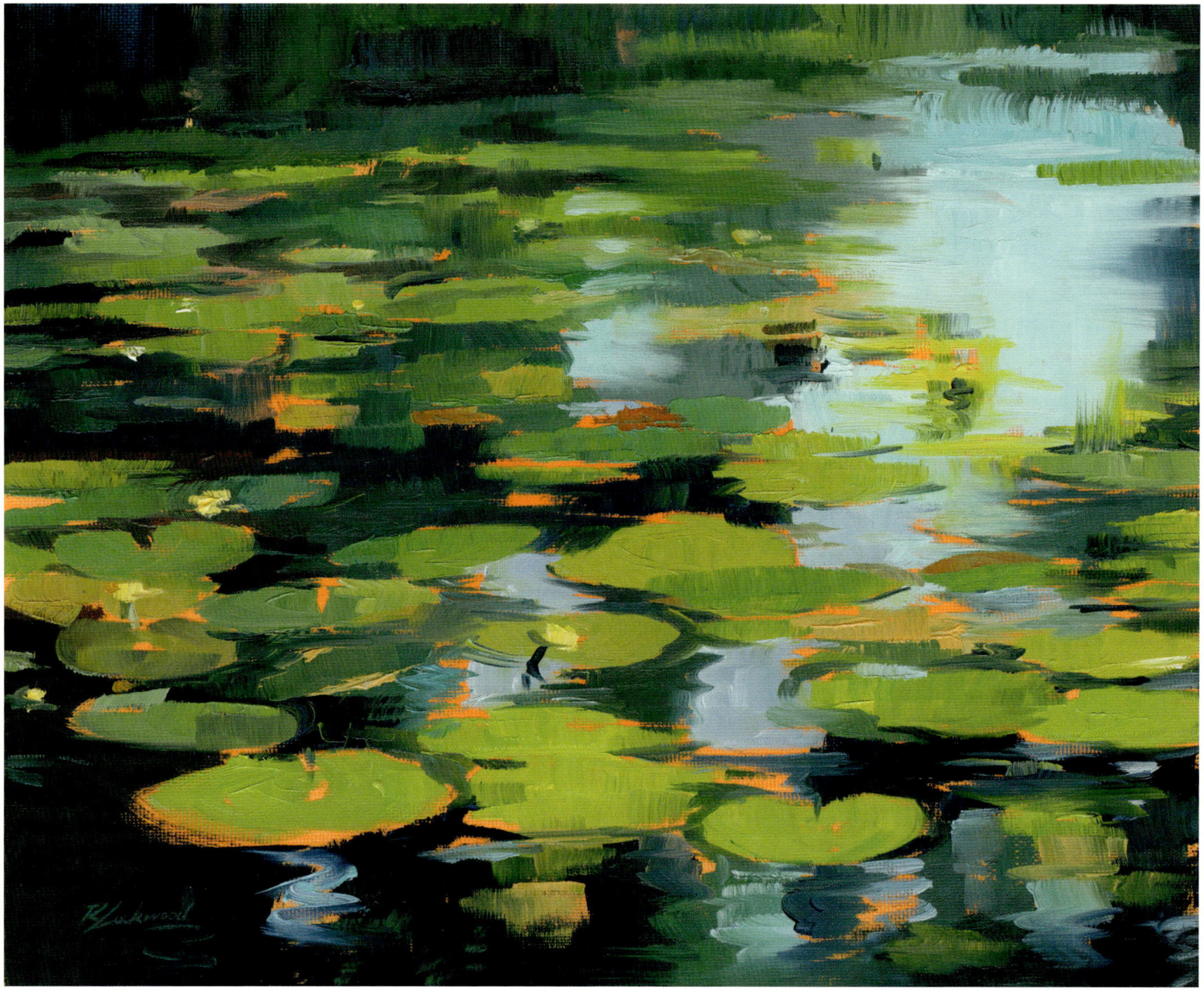

Gooderstone Water Gardens
oils on canvas paper 28x23 cm

24 August

In a never-ending search for more watery scenes, I went inland to Gooderstone Water Gardens today. This was once an ordinary boggy piece of land that someone transformed into an amazing environment. A trout stream passes through feeding the pools bringing in all kinds of wildlife, such as Pike, Kingfishers and dragonflies. You would never know it was in the middle of a village. The feeling of stillness and tranquility also comes from the tall trees surrounding the secret gardens.

There are many Monet-type scenes to be painted here, but one scene that caught my eye was a willow tree swinging its pendulous foliage on the water's surface (opposite). Just a simple thing, but what I wanted to do in this painting was capture that feeling of movement.

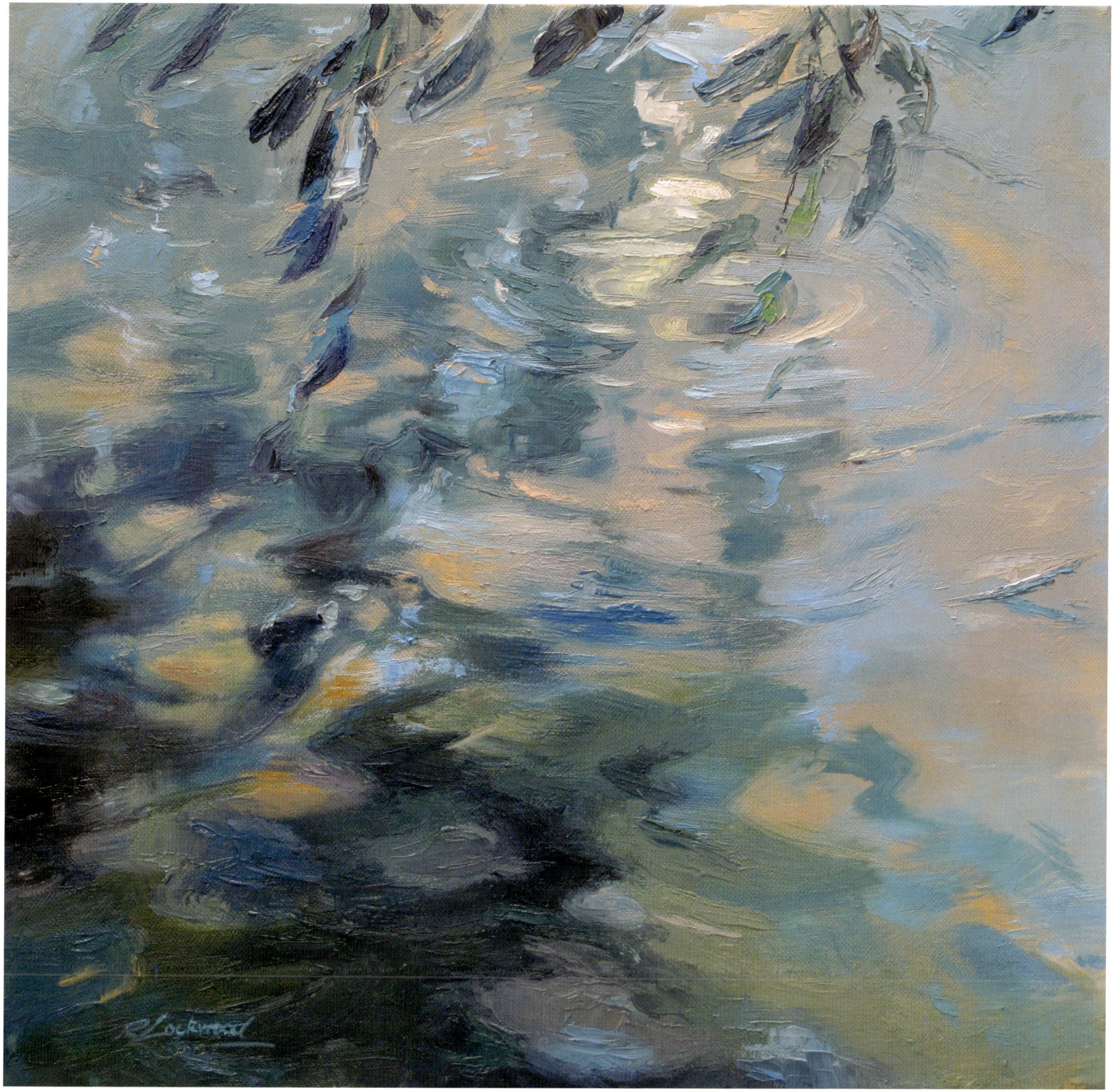

Swaying Willow
oils on canvas 50x50 cm

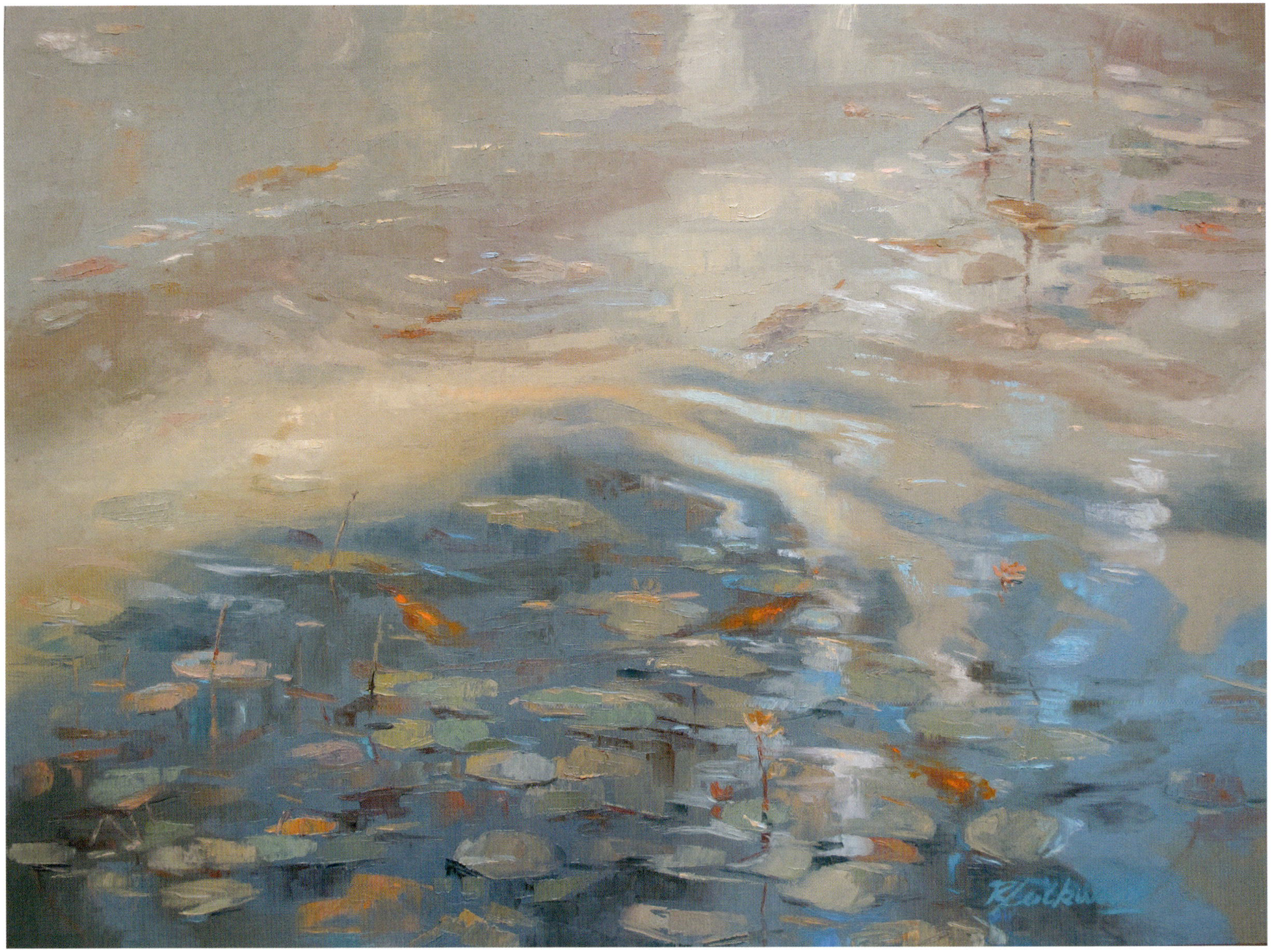

Summer Pool
oils on linen 90x120 cm

26 August

As often happens when I'm about to fall asleep, an idea for a painting will start to brew in my mind. The excitement can sometimes make it really difficult to sleep and by morning I'm eager to get to my studio and begin. Frustratingly this morning I didn't have any canvases prepared, so before I could do anything, I had to knock the frame together and stretch the linen over it. I prefer making my own supports, because to me the whole process becomes part of the picture. It allows time to think and plan and for some reason, there's something about feeling the linen that kick-starts the whole thing for me.

It's very rare to find the perfect pool that shows all that I love about water. This large painting was a combination of all kinds of things I'd seen. In my mind I had an overall idea but no real plan. However, my subconscious mind was far cleverer and as soon as I began this painting, it seemed to have an idea of its own. It began with a milky pond that I'd seen recently, combined with a pool of bistort lilies from elsewhere. The marriage evolved and felt right as it poured out onto the linen. I've since tried to create a similar painting, but it seems to have had its magic moment and then gone, never to reappear.

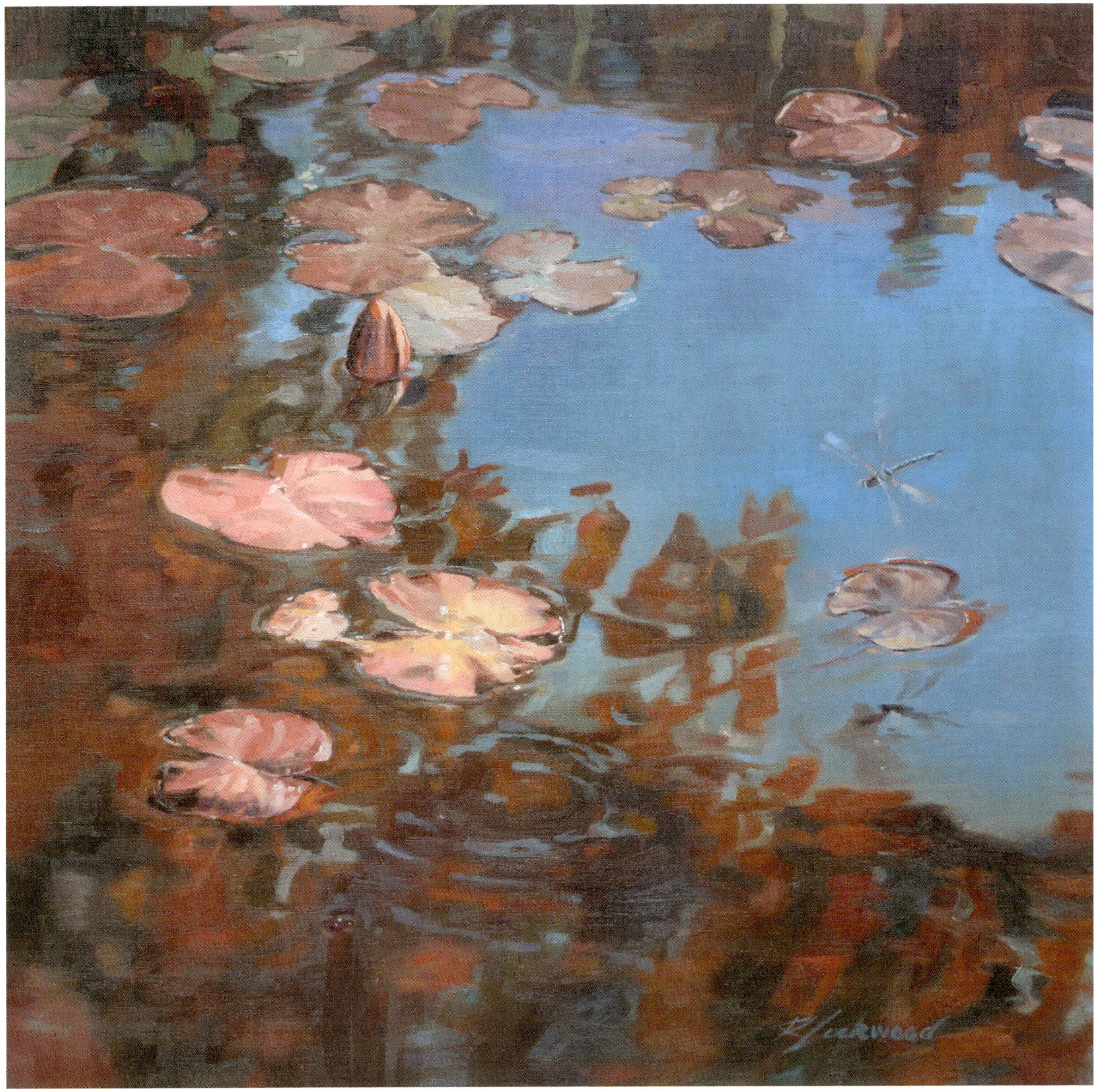

Joy's Pool
oils on linen 90x90cm

This is a painting inspired by a beautiful summer's evening in my mother-in-law's garden; wine, barbecue and Blackbirds washing themselves in the shallow waters of her pond. The evening light lit up the Copper Beech leaves that reflected on the water's surface. I was mesmerized by the shimmering rich red and blues that made the pond feel as if it was alive and excited. The scene looked bizarrely oriental in amongst a classic English cottage garden.

I couldn't get Joy's pond out of my head, pictures of it kept me awake. I think it's the unusual reds reflected in the water that are drawing me in. I decide to go back and spend a few days watching this pond, plus the temptation of Joy's cakes made it hard to resist. Making quick oil sketches at my easel sounds idyllic but with Joy's two over-excited terriers as companions, disaster was inevitable. Luckily it wasn't me that ended up in the water - although it was close, but Dolly wasn't so fortunate. The worst thing was that the beautifully calm lily scene I was in the middle of painting now resembled a sludgy quagmire.

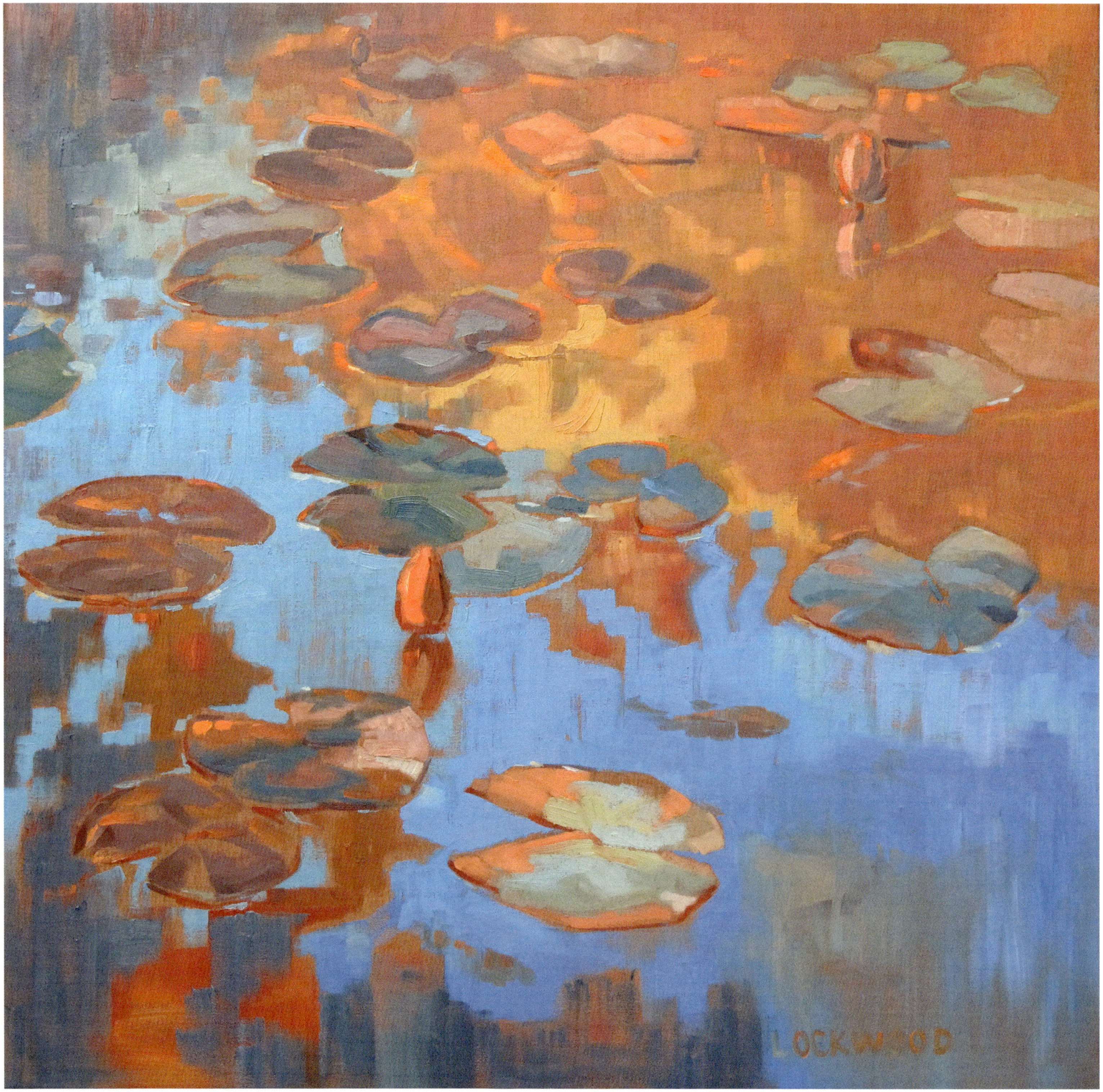

Gold Pool Lilies oils on linen 100x100 cm

28 August

With *Gold Pool Lilies* (left), my intention was to paint a similar picture as the previous page, but as I was drawing it out I already felt that this picture was going to go its own way. As soon as I started to put down marks with the paint, I realised it was going to become more angular and block-like in finish. I didn't want to stop this development and was intrigued to see where this would take me. I'm fascinated by how my work is beginning to evolve, it seems like a natural process, something that is inside trying to escape. When I stood back and looked at what I had painted, I was pleased with the end result as it seemed to have captured in essence the linear reflections of that day.

However, I was so inspired by Joy's pool, I've decided that the only thing to do is to build my own pond. Then I can watch the light throughout the day and view the lilies as they grow and change throughout the year. Also, this will create an additional area for wildlife.

These two paintings on the right are a further development of the style that took over on *Gold Pool Lilies* (left). My mind thinks quite mathematically and the shapes I'm seeing are becoming intriguing.

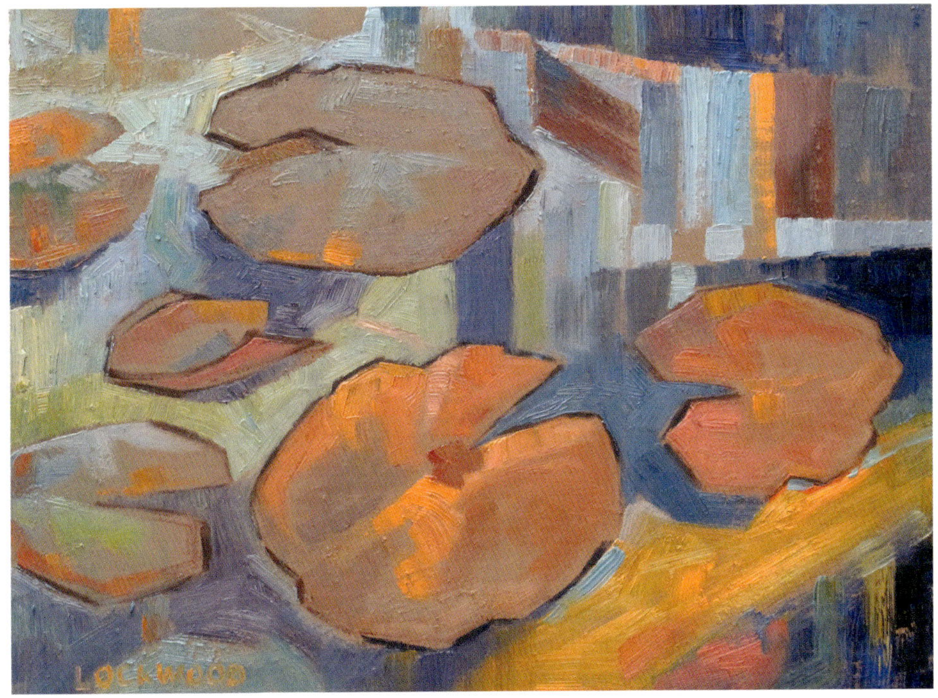

Studio Pond Study oils on canvas 80x100 cm

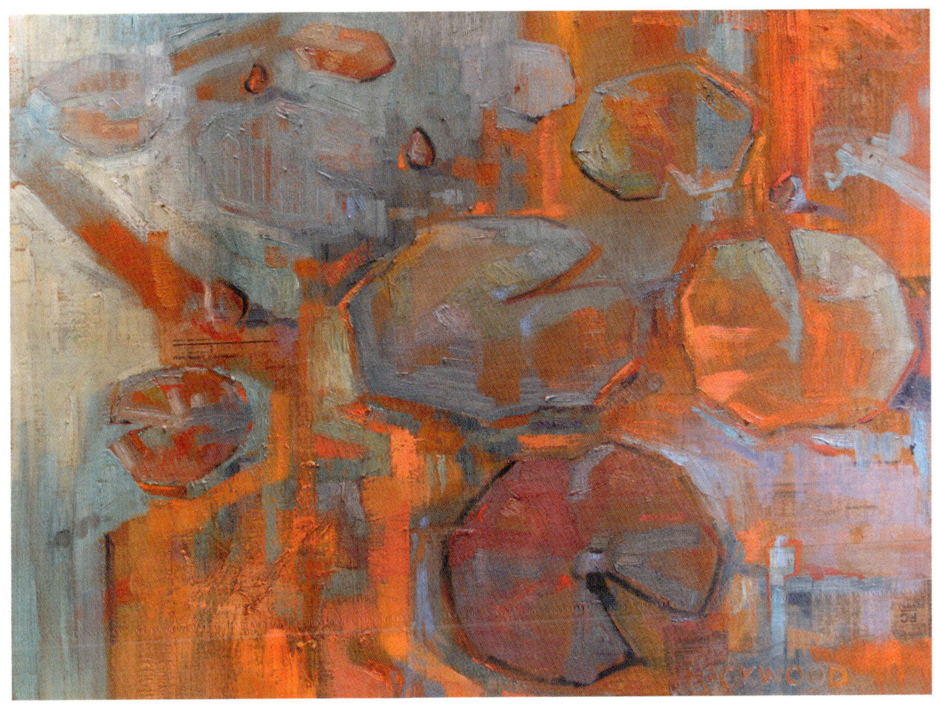

Evening Light Lilies oils on canvas 80x100 cm

30 August

It was raining hard first thing this morning, but I knew the weather was going to improve, so I decided to drive over to Snettisham Deer Park. I know I shouldn't admit to this but I love the fact that I can get really close to the deer here; so close in fact that you can feed them. I know I'm lucky in that I can see wild deer near to where I live, but it's really useful to be able to sit down with them and observe their movement up close.

On my way there I came across a pond near Stanhoe with a new brood of ducklings of the Heinz 57 variety. Some were just hatched and others were around three days old. I think there were around twenty ducklings clambouring over my toes and dropping into the water. Who wouldn't stop to adore these wonderful creatures? One thing led to another and paintings began to form in my mind. But I was torn, they were so cute and in my head a battle was brewing. Awful things were happening in the news, countries around the world becoming bankrupt, the markets crashing and many people's lives being turned upside down. Why was I here looking at fluffy ducklings thinking happy thoughts? What a contrast. I go to work in a world of my own, a little bubble of wonderful things. And then I thought, well maybe we all need the benefit of this, no matter how awful it is in the world, there is always something to smile about. So I continued with this theme and a series of duckling pictures began to develop. A contrast of a beautiful simple life of a duckling compared to a disastrous world we sometimes create for ourselves. I decided to mix in text from current newspapers as I'd done before on a previous series, essentially to provoke thought and perhaps a wry smile.

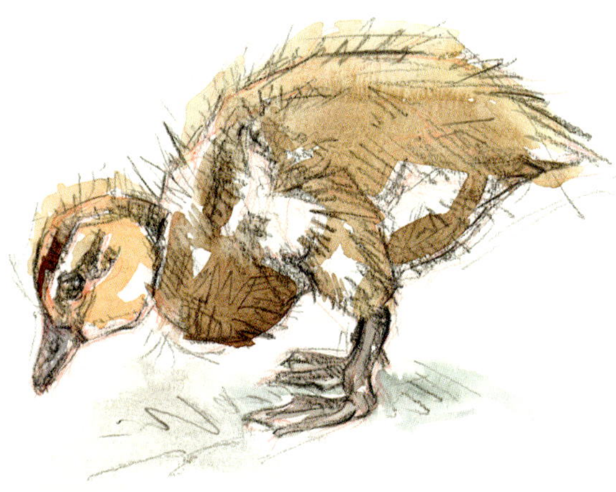

Duckling Sketch
pencil and watercolour on paper

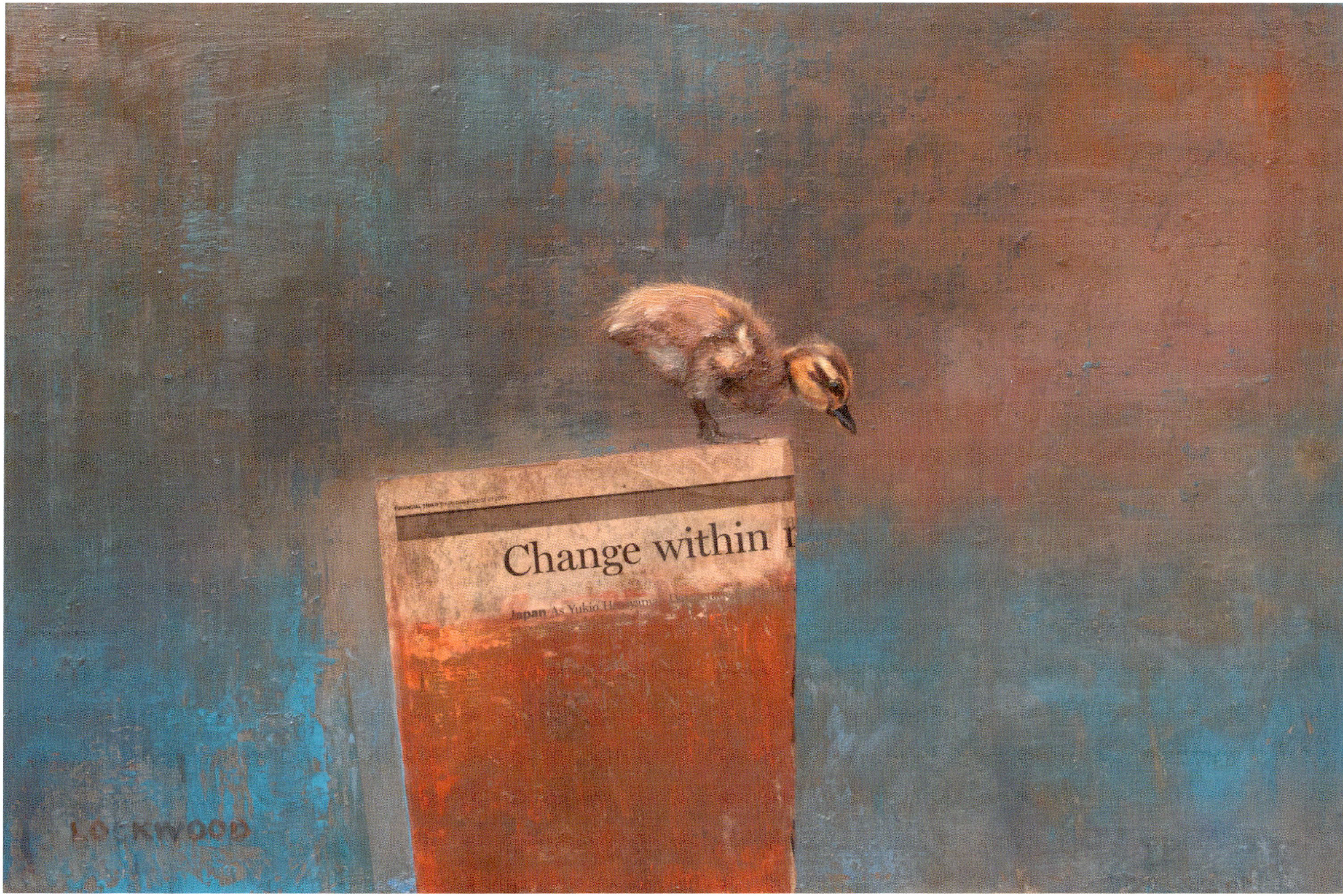

Change Within mixed media and oils on linen 50x70 cm

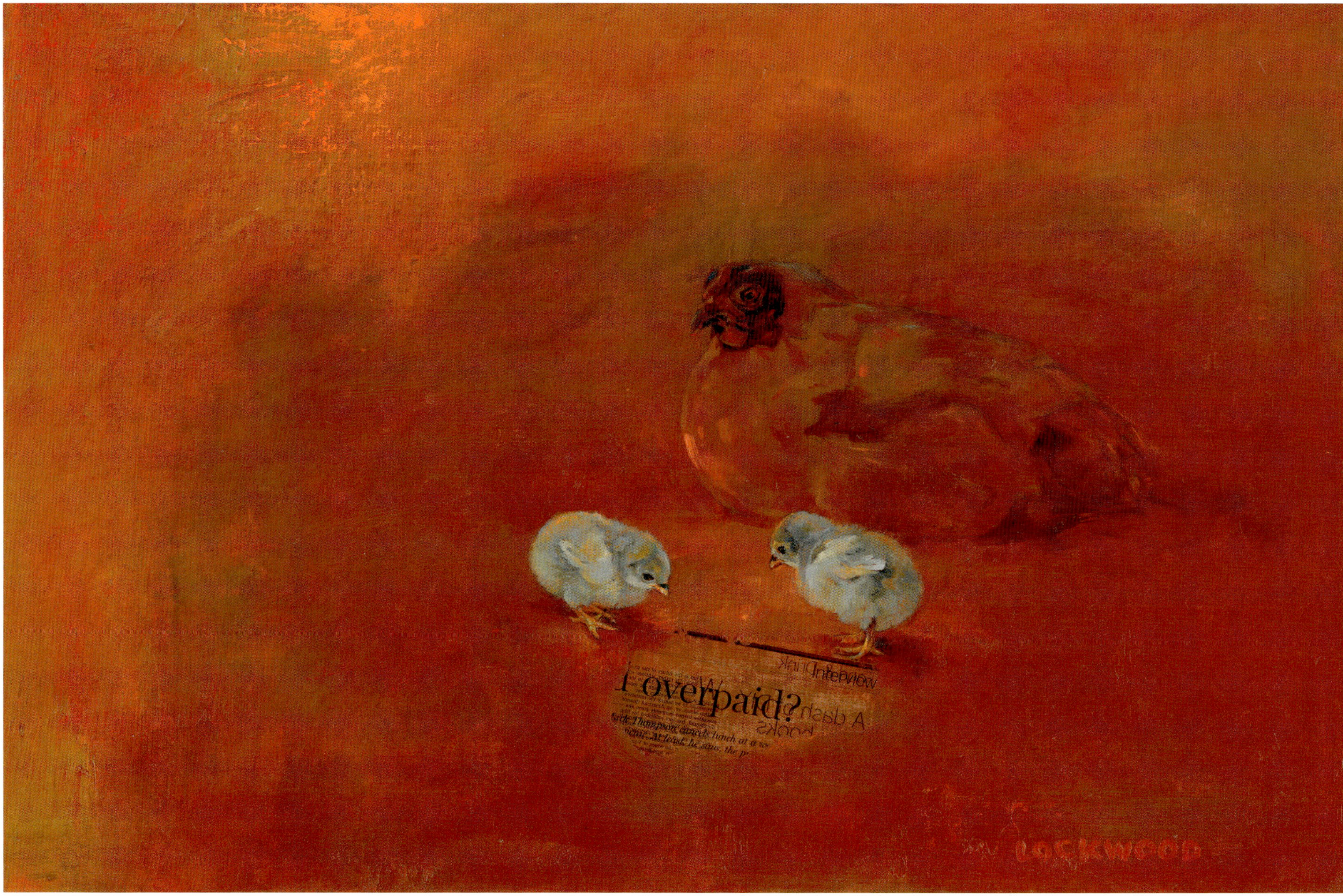

Overpaid mixed media and oils on linen

30 August

When I finally reached Snettisham Park, there were baby animals popping out everywhere: calves, chicks, ducklings and kids! I spent some time following the chicks around, watching their busy and focused routine of foraging and learning from mum - they were comical to watch as they busily wanted to learn about everything. One of the headlines in today's paper was 'Over Paid' and seeing this stressed mother hen with her wayward brood of inquisitive chicks made me smile, especially when I imagined them trying to make sense of our world.

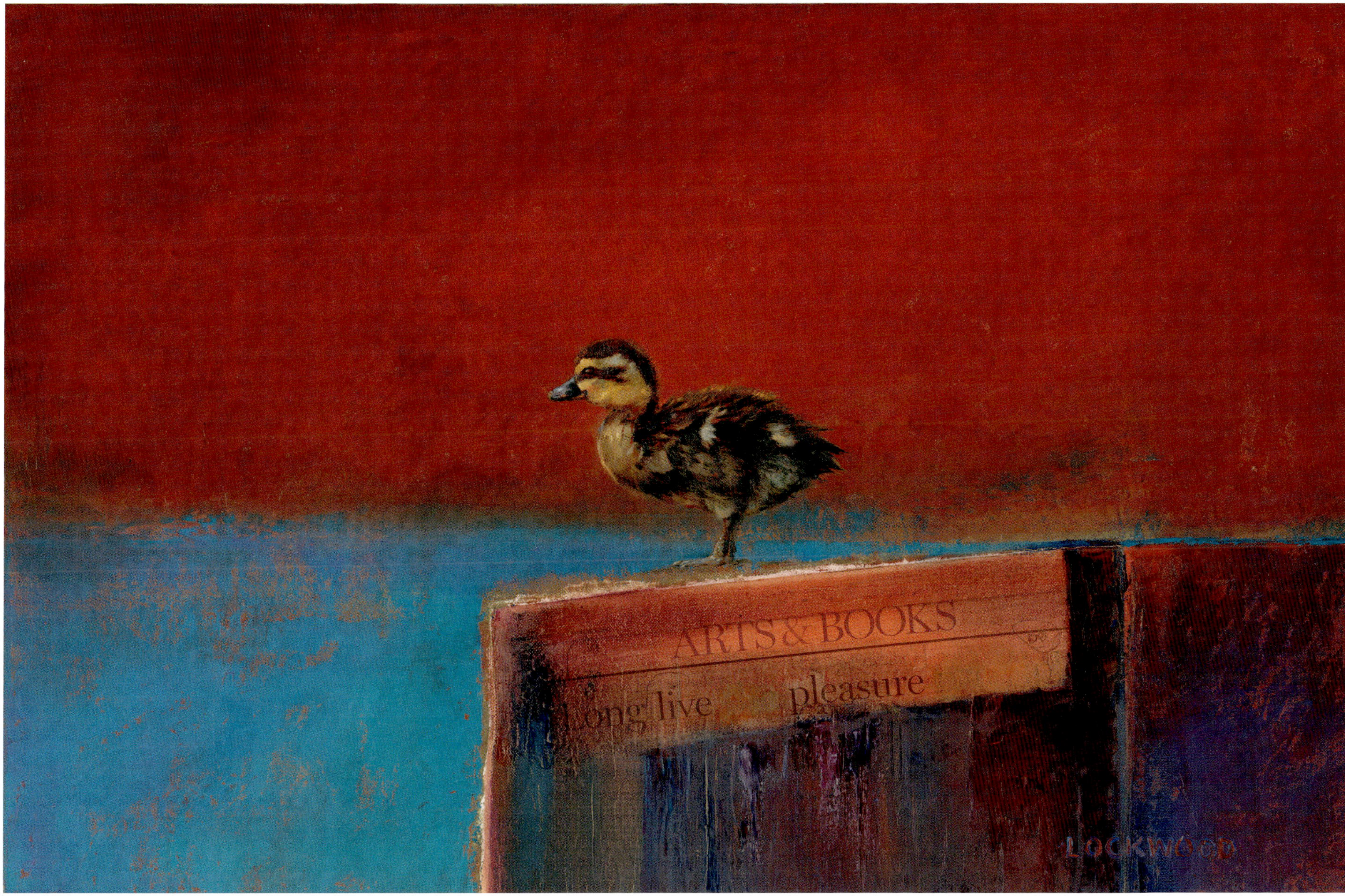

Long Live Pleasure mixed media and oils on linen

I September

While painting the duckling pictures, I remembered an incident from earlier in the year. I was sat on my studio step in the warmth with my cup of tea when I was distracted by a commotion over towards the track. It was two Shelduck ducklings flapping and running away from an eager Magpie. I realized they were in distress from the Magpies attention. They ran back and forth, trying to wriggle into thick Couch Grass cover but the Magpie continued to look down on them. Their constant peeps would have given them away if nothing else. I walked over to the Magpie and it pretended to leave, only to return as soon as my back was turned. I went back again to try and find the ducklings but in their distress they'd decided to leg it down the track and into the wood behind, zigzagging and crying all the way. They soon disappeared into the forest but I decided not to follow as I didn't want to push them further in. A minute later and the parents were quartering the sky and calling for their brood. There was nothing I could do but hope they would reach the ducklings. I don't know how this ended, I returned later to see if I could find them but there were no calls, no feathers, just silence in the wood.

Beautiful Orange is a nod to that memory. I wanted to capture the innocence and vulnerability I saw in these creatures. I wanted to emphasise this duckling's smallness in a large world, hence the large area of nothing surrounding it.

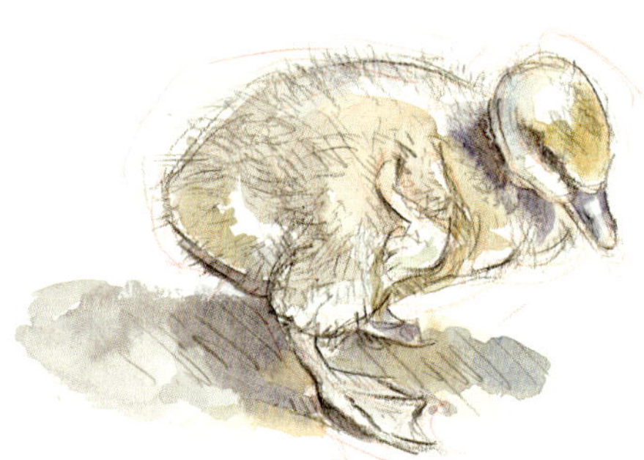

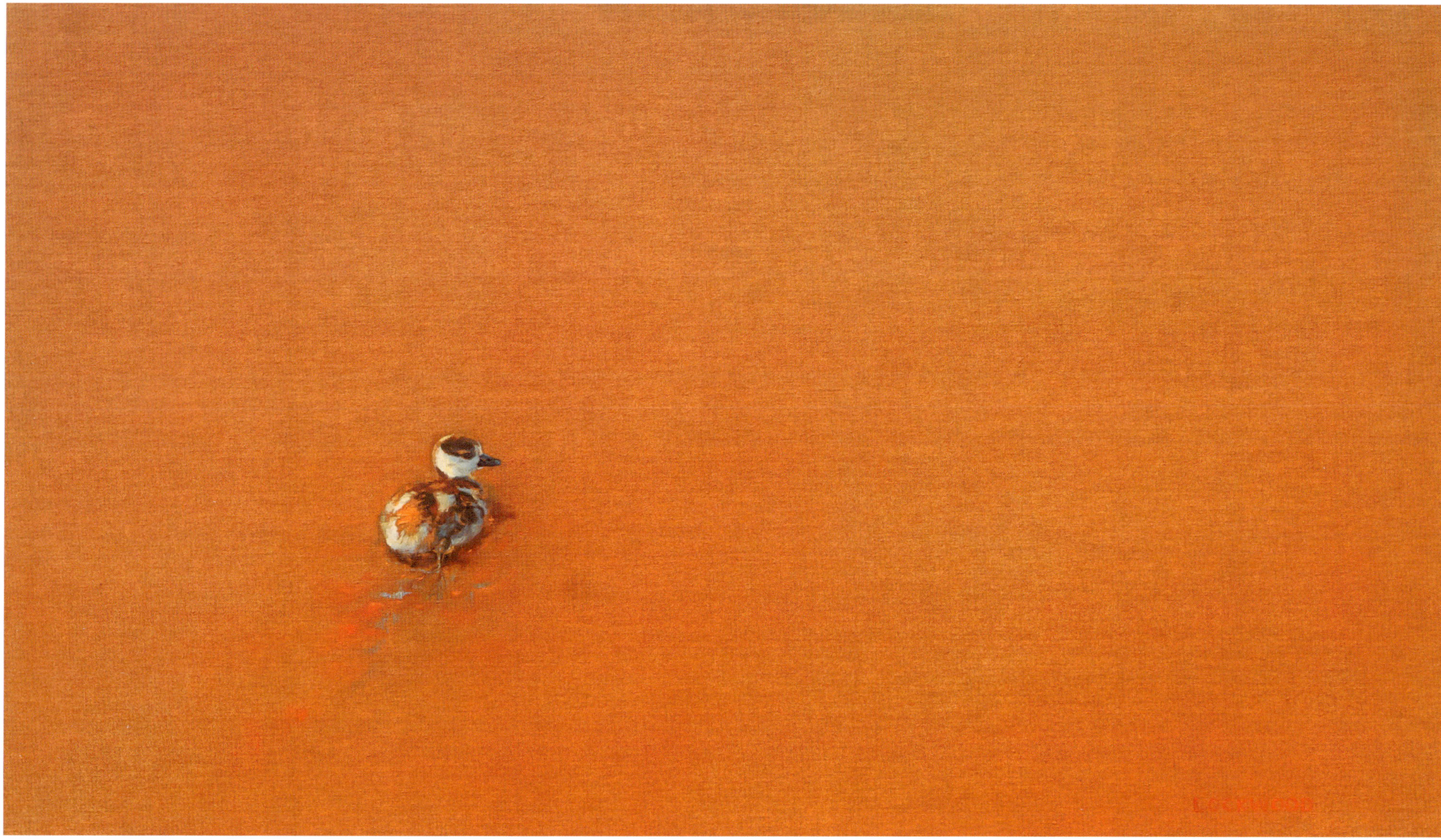

Beautiful Orange oils on linen 70x120 cm

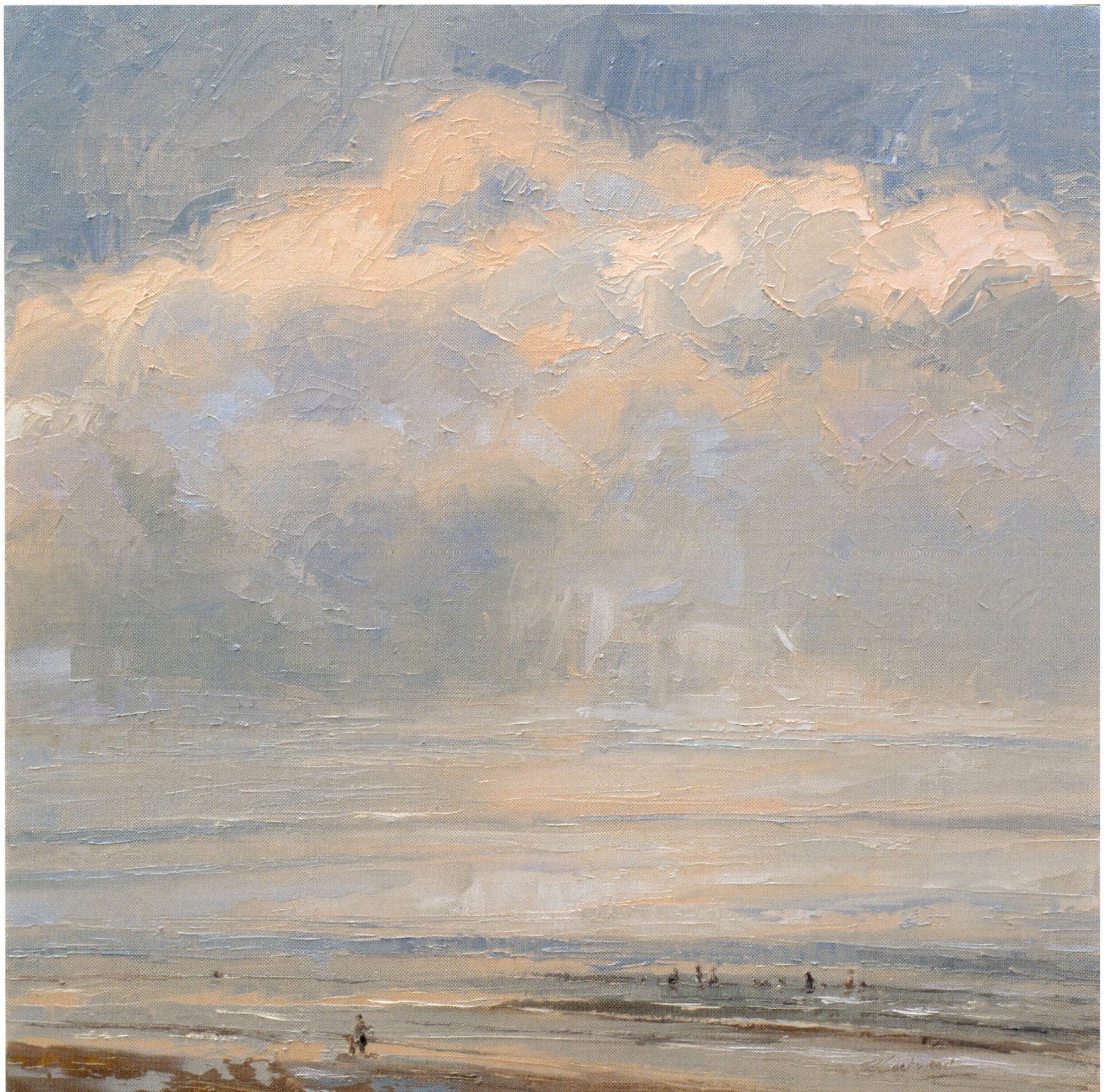

Hunstanton Bathers oils on canvas 50x50 cm

4 September

We wanted to take our friends Penny and Robin away for a birthday surprise, so we decided to head further west along the coast. We settled on Old Hunstanton as I'd never been there before but had heard from Sarah how beautiful it was. We stayed at Le Strange Arms, a hotel that almost sits on the beach. It's front lawn runs down to sand dunes and then on to the wide, open sea. We picnicked in the sand dunes in the blazing heat but before we'd even reached dessert, thick heavy clouds started to roll in from the sea. Instead of walking eastwards to Holme, we decided it was safer to head away from the clouds towards Hunstanton. However, the storm moved much quicker than we thought and we only just made it to a café when giant hailstones pounded the promenade. We watched the mini golf course turn from green to white and instead of drinking ice cold drinks, opted for hot chocolates and lattes.

The storm quickly passed, leaving steam rising from the pavements. We went down to the beach and walked back along the tideline. The whole scene had changed dramatically, now the pinkish red cliffs had turned dark red, the sea glistened and seemed to be exceptionally pale. These two paintings are really a before and after memory of that weekend.

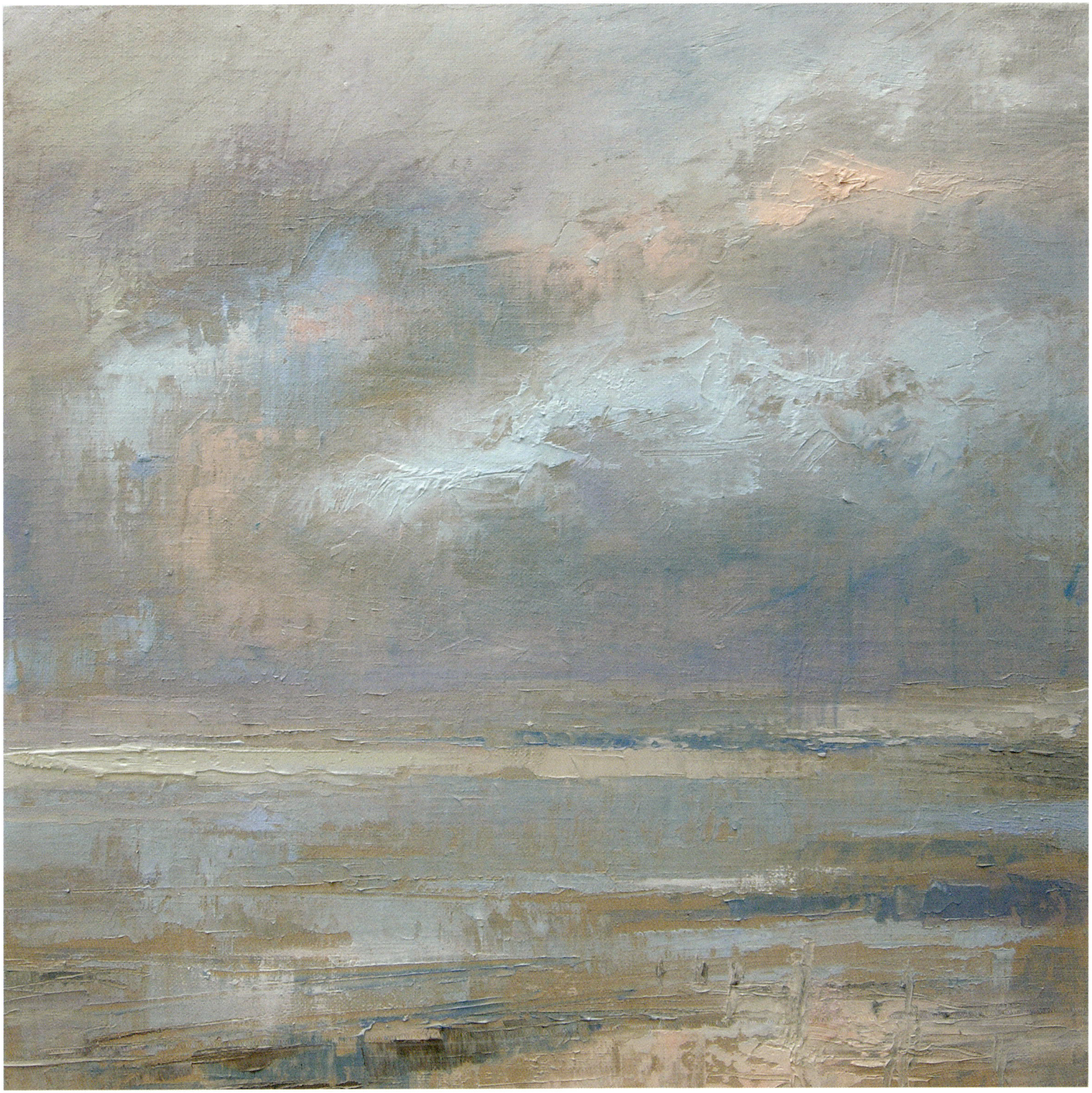

Hunstanton Haze oils on linen 40x40 cm

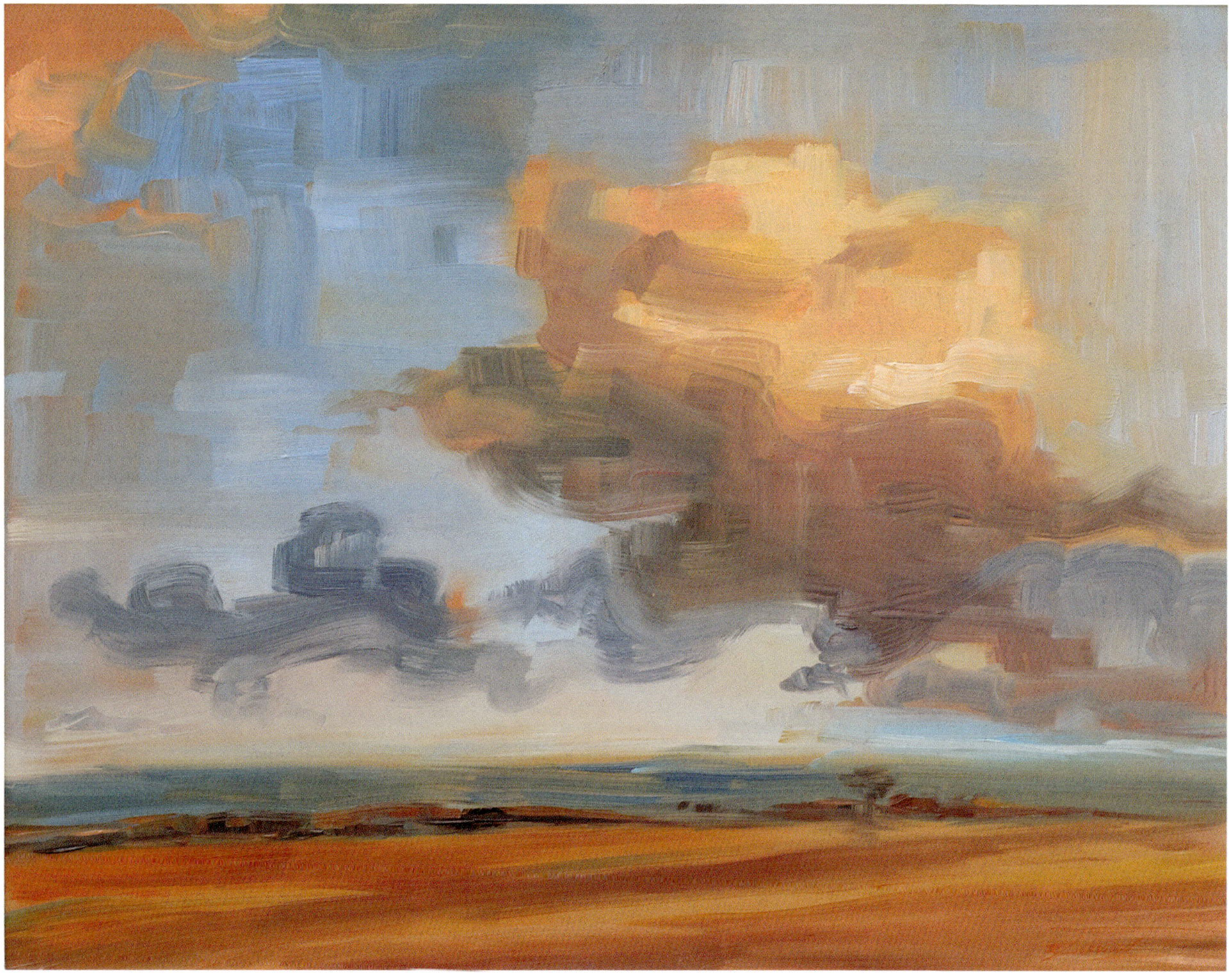

Summer Cloud, Weybourne oils on canvas 50x35 cm

6 September

I spend a lot of time throughout the year watching the sky as I have become a bit fixated with clouds. The changeable weather at the moment is great for me as it means sunshine and great skies. When I see a good evening sky beginning to form, one that has a few clouds to bounce the light off, I rush out to gather as much information as I can. It's very hit and miss - I know it sounds hard to believe, but for me finding the perfect cloud is harder than you might think. In this painting the emphasis is obviously on the cloud; I considered it perfect and worthy of a whole picture. I painted it very quickly using loose brush strokes, I didn't want to make it solid and heavy as clouds like this can move and change so quickly.

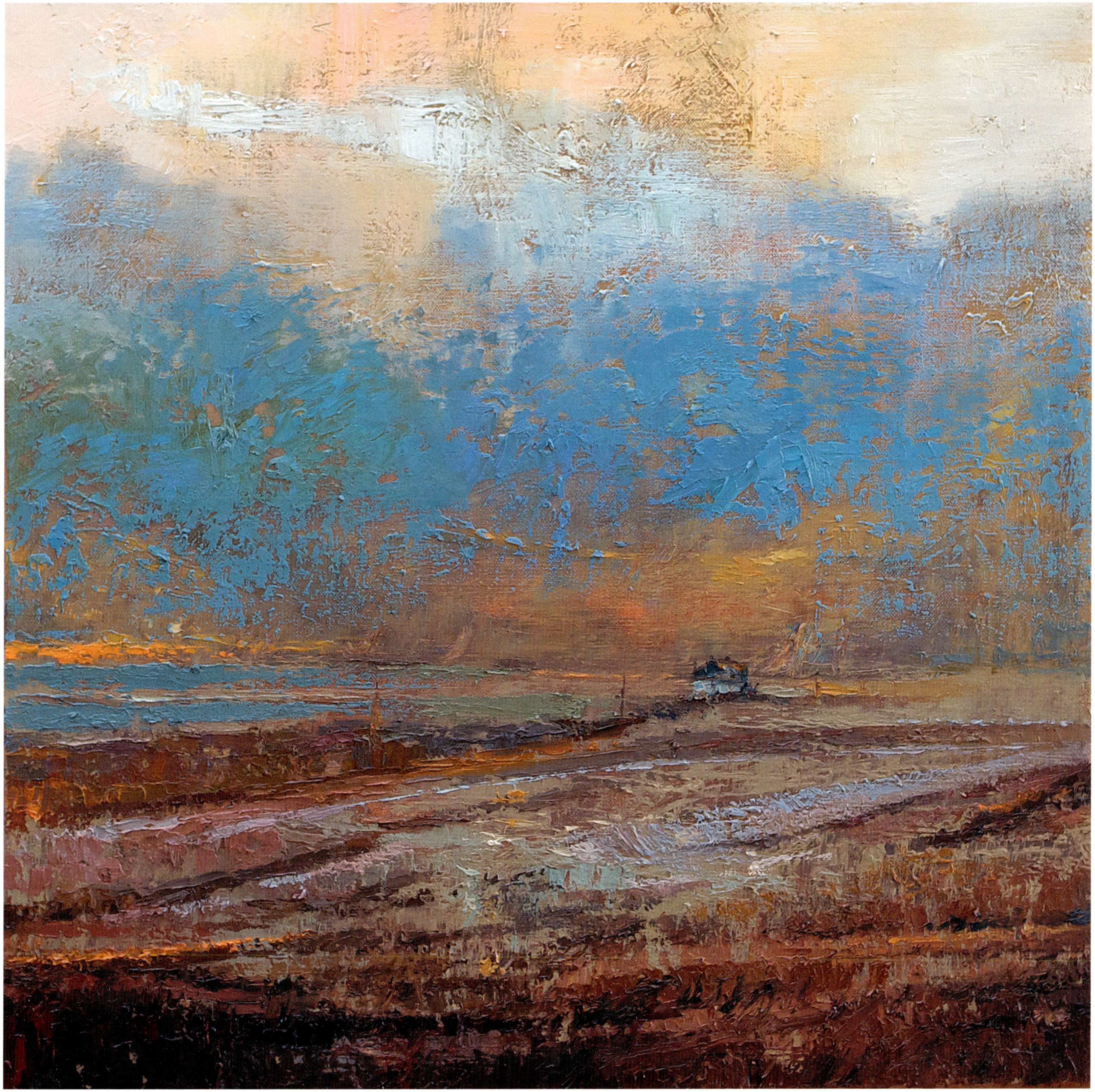

Summer Evening, Weybourne
oils on linen
60x60 cm

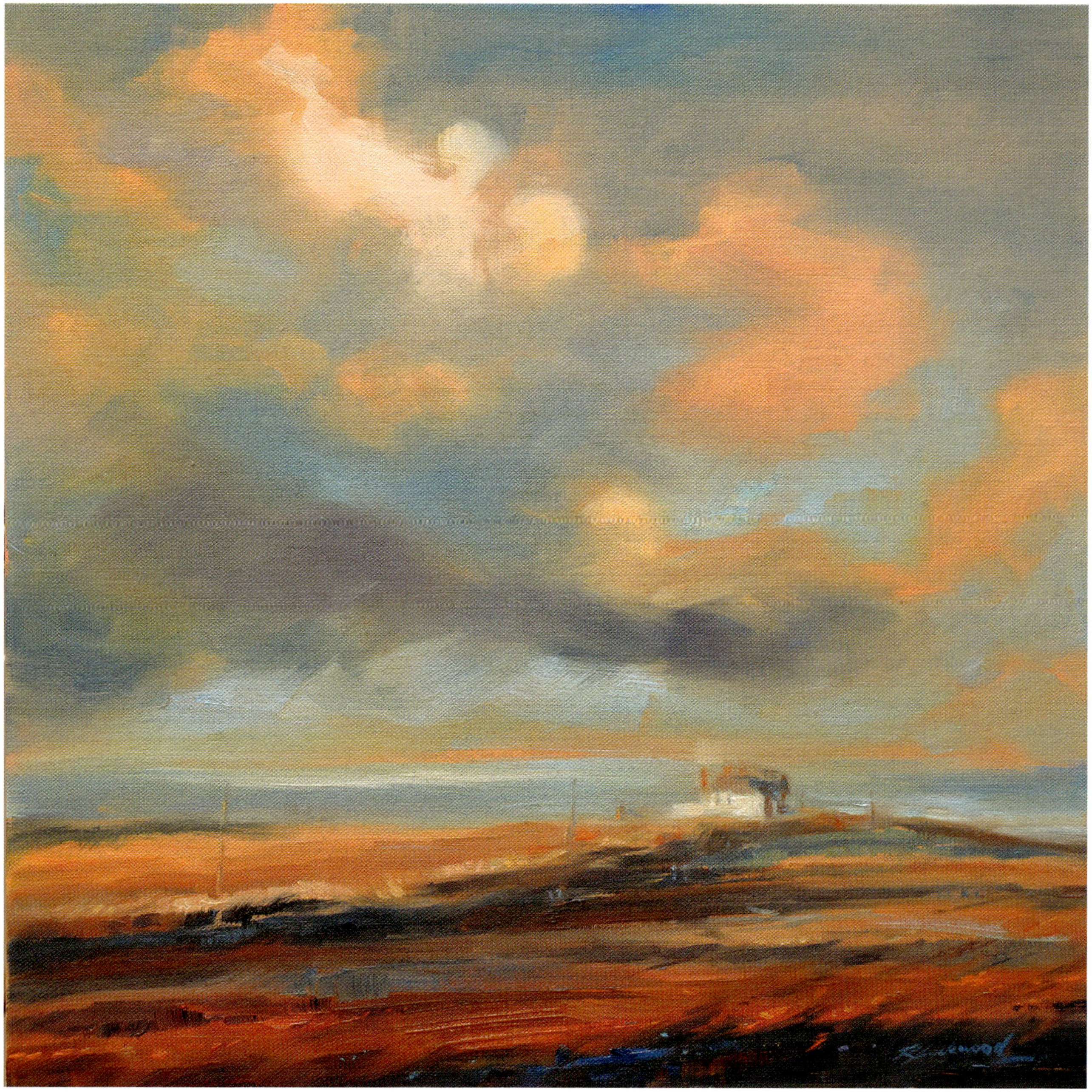

Coastguard Cottage, Weybourne
oils on canvas board 40x40 cm

7 September

When I had my studio in Sheringham, I'd either drive every day from Cley or catch the Coast Hopper Bus. Sitting on the bus meant an even better view as you're raised up just enough to look over hedges. I've always been intrigued by the Coastguard cottages just outside Weybourne. These isolated cottages are perched right on the edge of the cliff, only a few metres from the sea; sometimes I drive past after a storm and wonder if they will still be there. For some reason, the evening light just at this spot is nearly always spectacular; there have been many times when I've had to stop and get out of the car just to stare at the sky and sea. This combined with the cottages creates a story that takes me back there again and again to paint.

At the time I didn't know anything about these buildings, so I called them Fishermens' Cottages because of the village's strong association with fishing. However, I've since discovered they were built for coastguards to guard against the illicit smuggling that used to run riot along the coast from Sheringham to Weybourne.

I always think of this panorama as somewhat cinematic, like something from the amazing technicolour films of the 1950s. The combination of colours from the sea, sky and land seem to react with each other to make it glow.

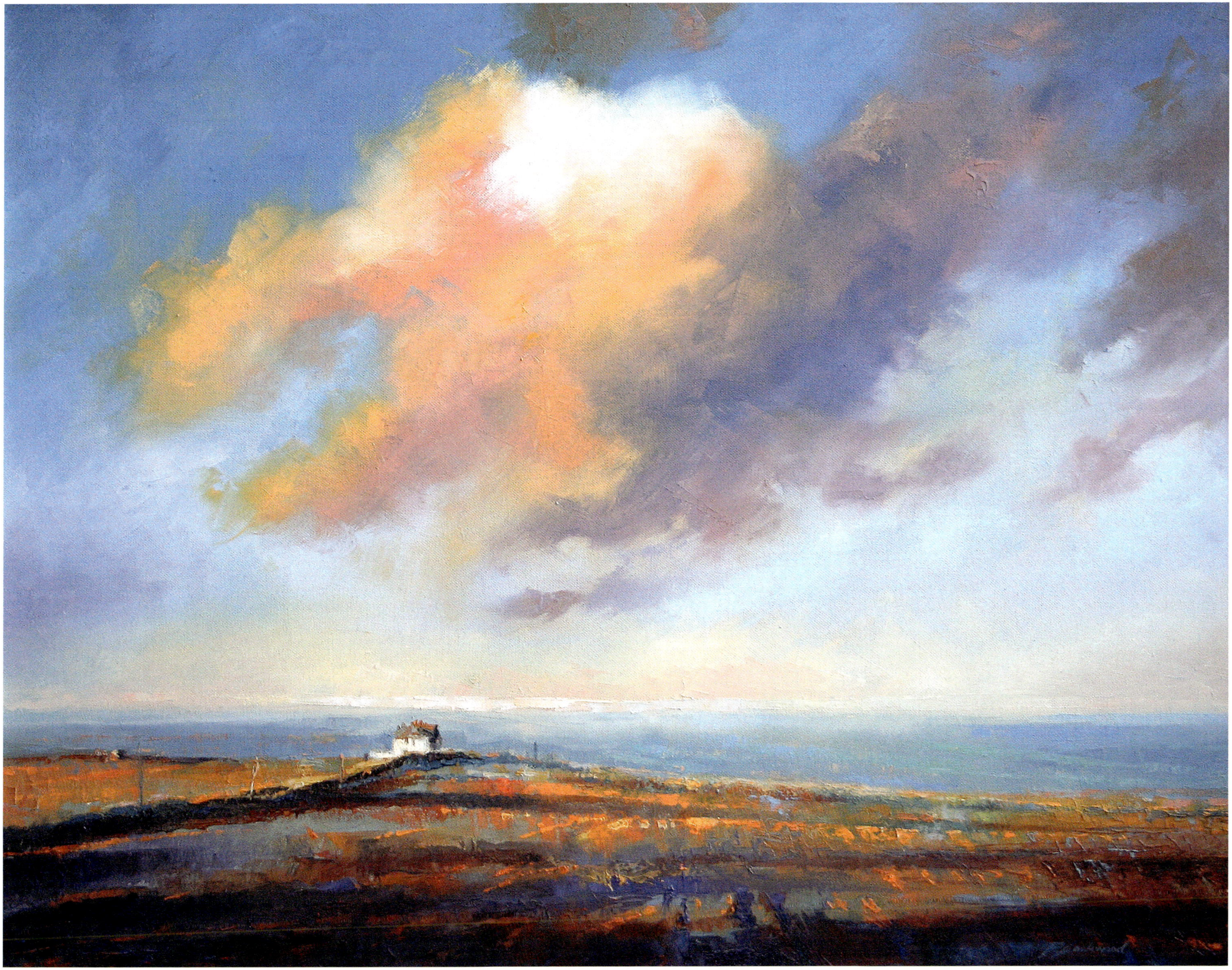

Fishermens' Cottages, Weybourne (Coastguards Cottages)
oils on canvas 60x80 cm

8 September

Sarah and I took ourselves on a mini tour of local roads we'd never really been down before – the hinterlands of West Beckham and routes east of Bodham. This is Norfolk's version of the Bermuda Triangle; once you've entered these roads, it's hard to escape. We managed however to zigzag our way back and somehow ended up at Salthouse.

We pulled over to watch hoards of boisterous gulls annoying each other. You could see they had their hierarchy, adults were scolding juveniles but it didn't stop the juveniles from annoying the adults. When people arrived with their fish and chips from the take-away across the road, the show began. A cloud of gulls silently criss-crossed above the duck pond, biding their time for the first scrap to be thrown. Their heads flicked and twisted watching every movement with their sharp eyes. When the first chip went up, the noise of aggressive squawks scraped the air. I watched them as they agilely weaved in and out, like a ballet in the sky, there was never a collision.

With *Chips Are Down,* I found my inspiration when the gulls had got hold of some newspaper and were looking into it expectantly. That mixed with the current news about banks becoming bankrupt sparked off an idea.

The painting on the opposite page was inspired by that evening. I wanted the movement I felt when watching them to come through in the painting. Slashing and sculpting with thick paint helped me to do this.

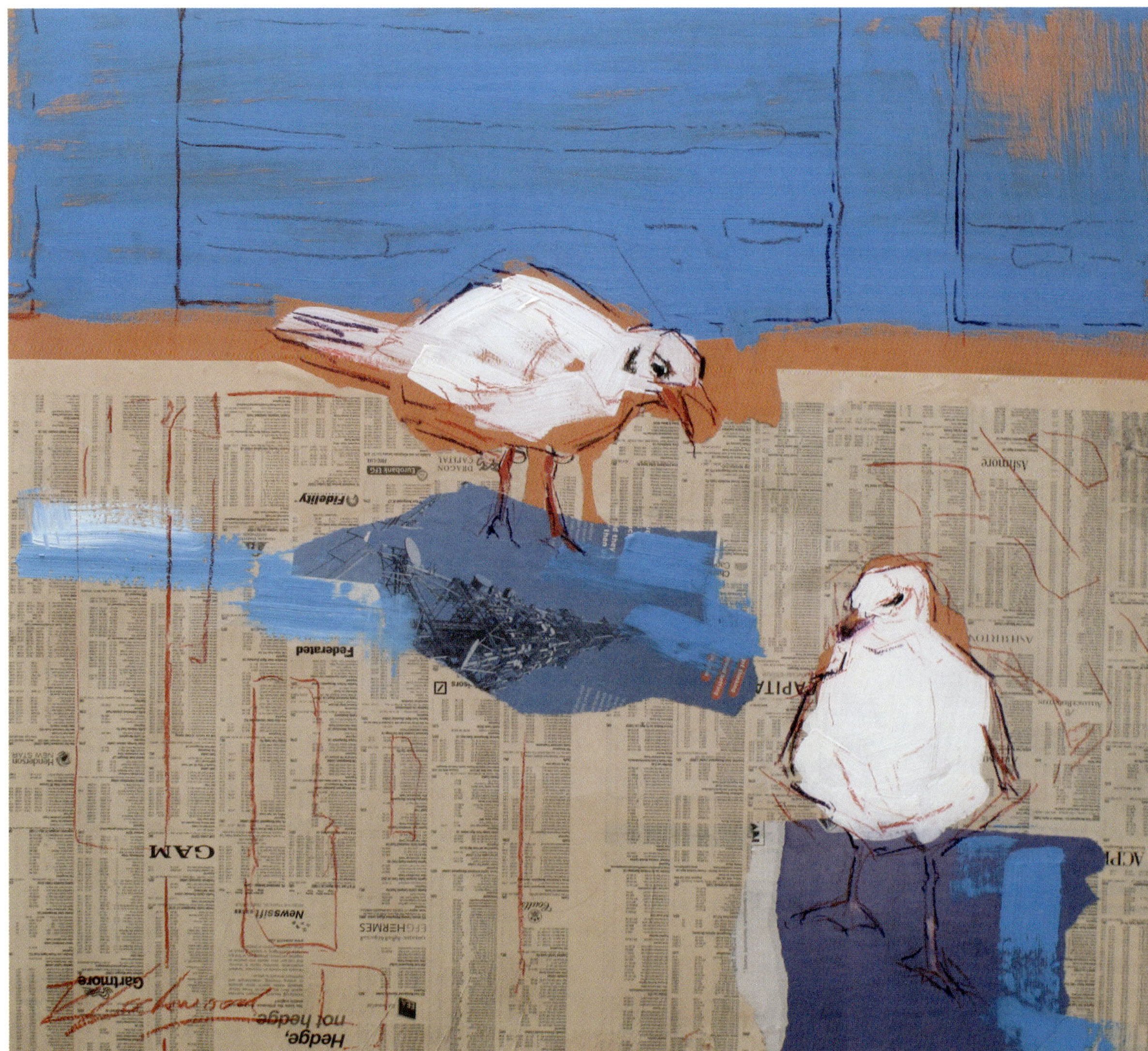

Chips Are Down
mixed media on board 50x40 cm

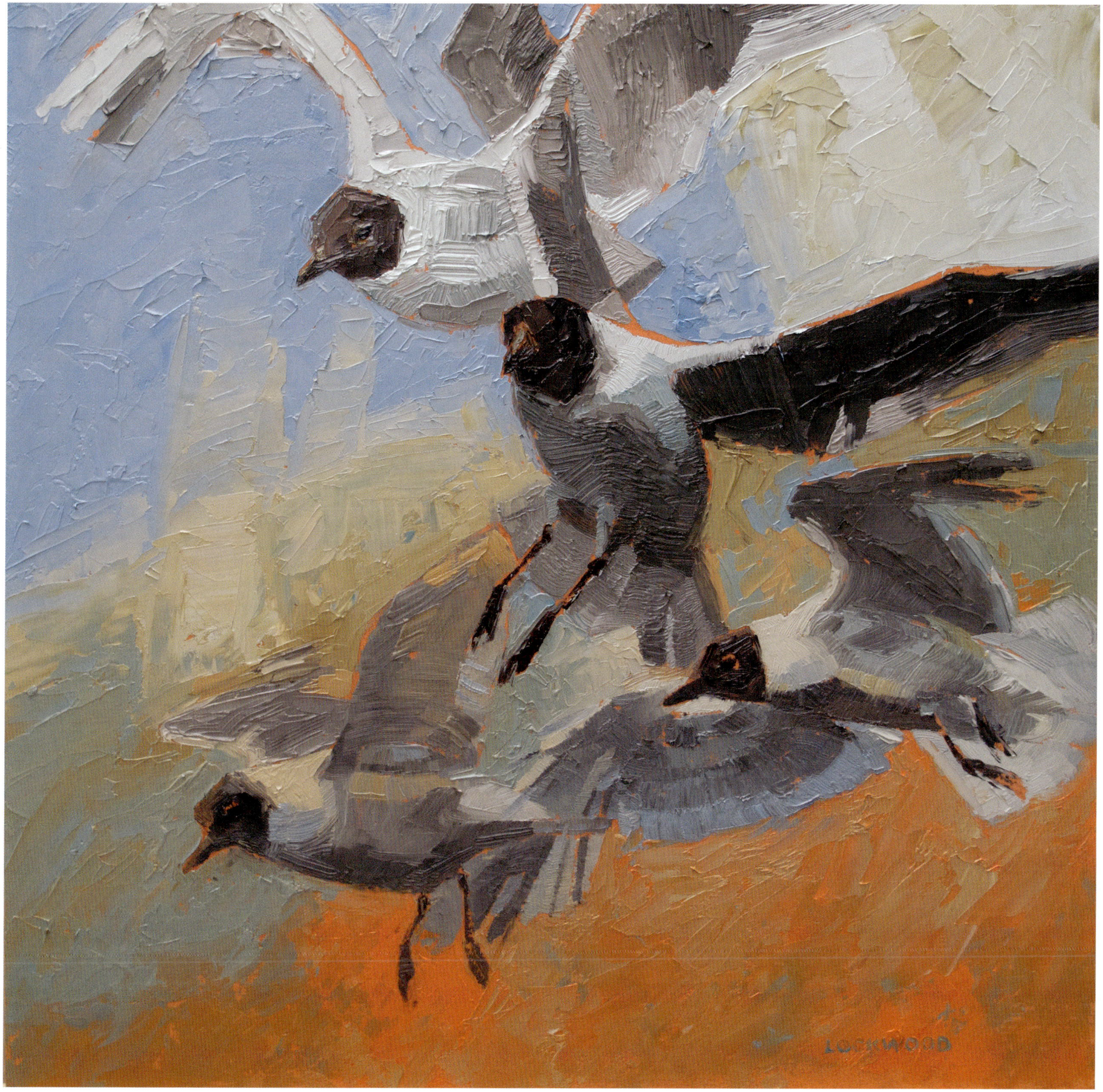

Salthouse Gulls
oils on board
100x100 cm

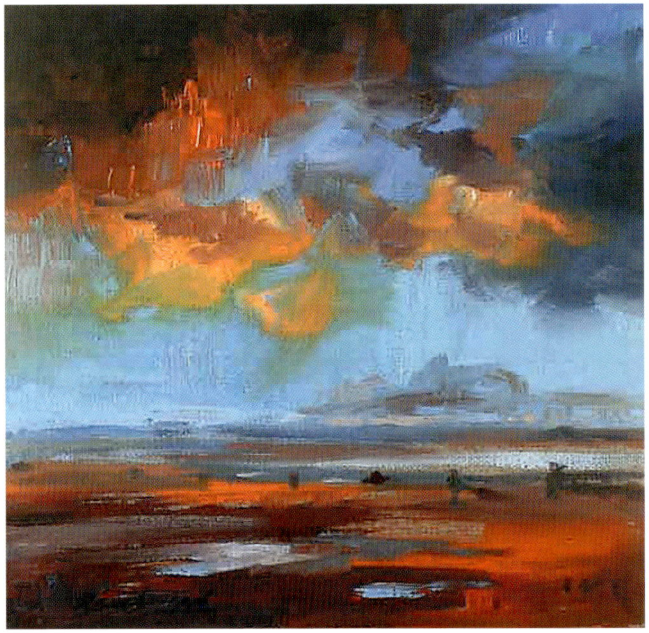

Storm End, Cromer Beach
oils on canvas board
20x20 cm

9 September

Searching for gulls again today brought me to Cromer, but as ever I quickly became distracted by the storm clouds that blew in. The heavy rain that washed down the beach made it a perfect surface for reflecting the sky. The pier was hidden in the drizzle, softened and subtle. A quick flick with my oil-laden brush was all I needed to hint at this iconic landmark in the distance. This was only a small painting so I had to be economical with the amount of detail I showed. Next I took my palette knife to capture the sharp breaking light of the clouds. Pictures like this don't always work, but I'm relieved when they do. Sadly, others end up being painted over at a later date.

Another trip out to Cromer coincided with a perfect afternoon tide just right for leaving reflections of the pier across the sand. I liked the marks the stanchions were making, as they cut through the waves. I decided to concentrate on a small area of the pier, just enough information to hint at what it was, then I could make a study of the light that was glistening on the beach. I used the raw linen to do some of the work for me here, by leaving areas bare of paint, which I think added to the feeling of it being sand.

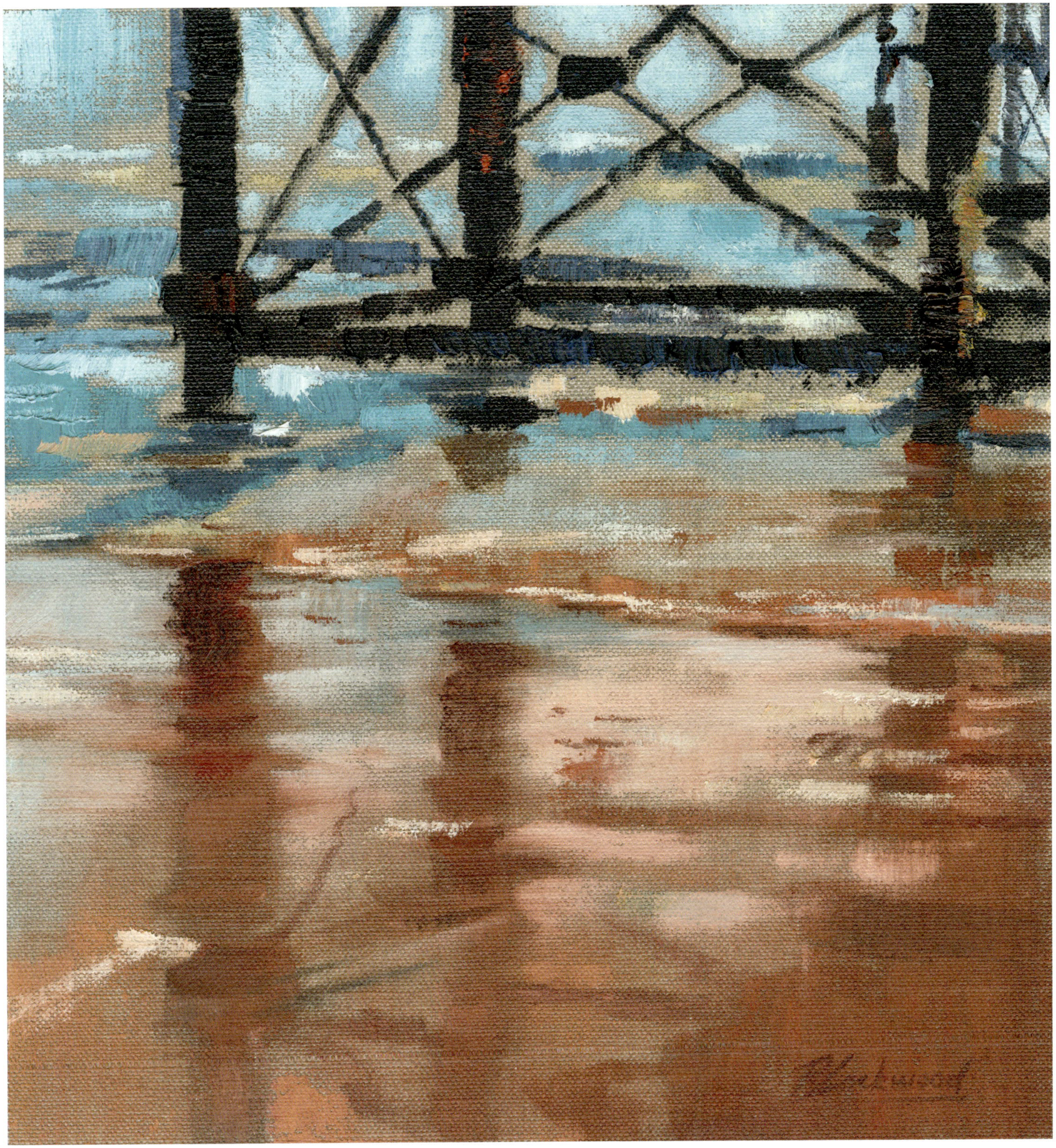

Cromer Pier, Wet Sand
oils on linen 23x21 cm

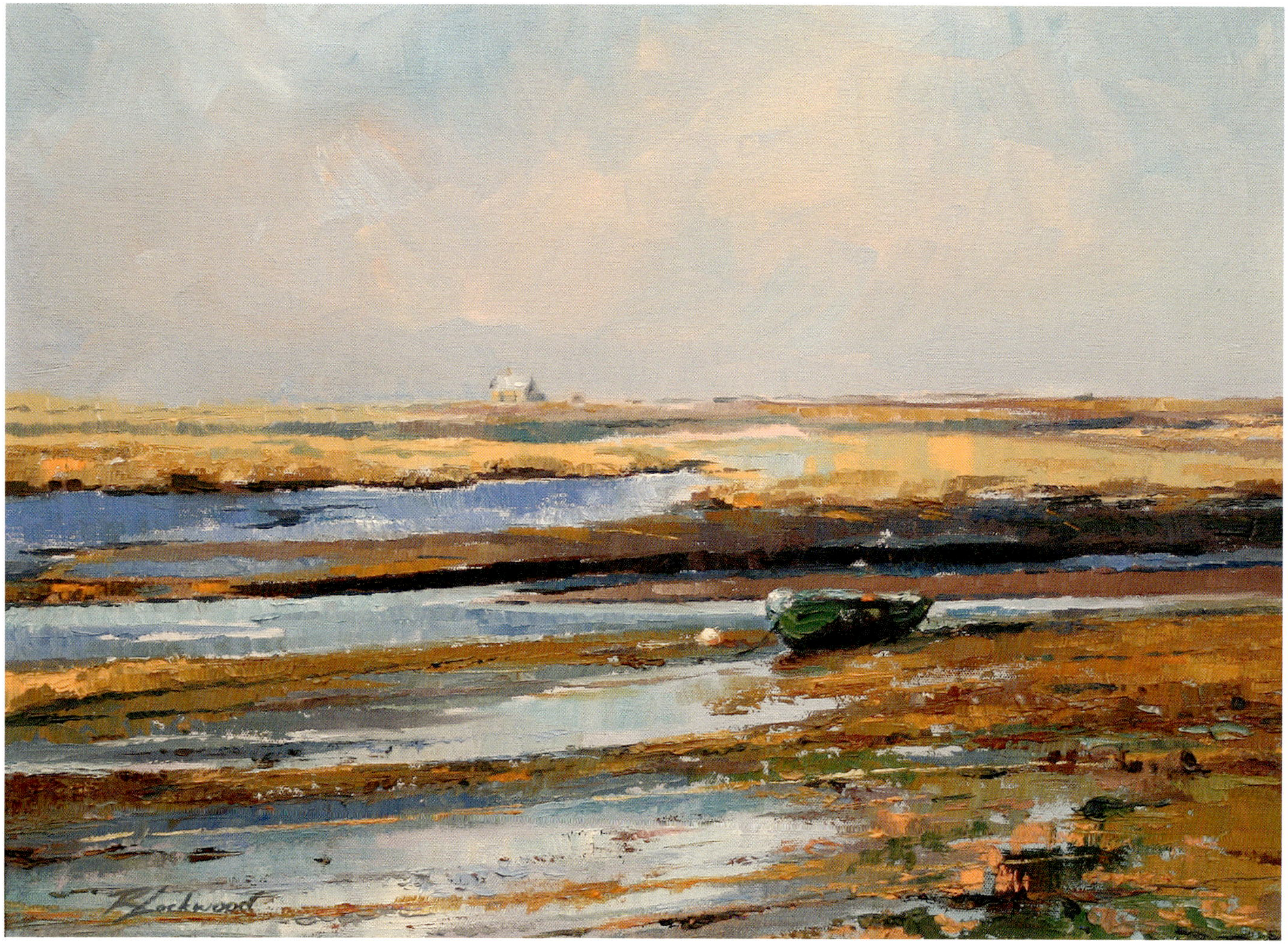

Blakeney Quay,
Halfway House In Distance
oils on canvas 30x40 cm

12 September

I felt a change in the air this morning, nothing I can put into words but something I wait for that marks the change of season. The air felt different, and also the light – almost metallic and cool is the only way I can describe it. I miss the swifts flying over the marsh and the sounds of their scraping and squeaking in the ceiling above my bed where they nest. Although it marks the passing of summer, there is something else to look forward to in the landscape; the colours that autumn brings.

There is a house on the marsh between Cley beach car park and Blakeney Point. I call it Halfway House as I didn't know the name for it when I first arrived, all I knew was that it lay betwixt the two. The name stuck with me, but it is known locally as the Watch House. It sits alone on a shingle bank overlooking the sea and is empty most of the year, apart from rentals in the summer months and a meeting place for the Scouts. It conjures up many images in my mind, a scene from Wuthering Heights, a mysterious place to end up at in a storm. A brick body waiting, watching at the edge of the sea. It draws my attention constantly with strange imaginings. And in an otherwise even landscape, it is a marker that tells you exactly where you are. I have painted it many times, through different weathers, seasons and angles. It will not leave me alone.

Autumn is my favourite time though for painting here. Longer, cooler shadows begin to creep across the land but the air is still warm. Seedheads from marsh plants crackle; their warm colours of purples and pinks light up as the sun drops.

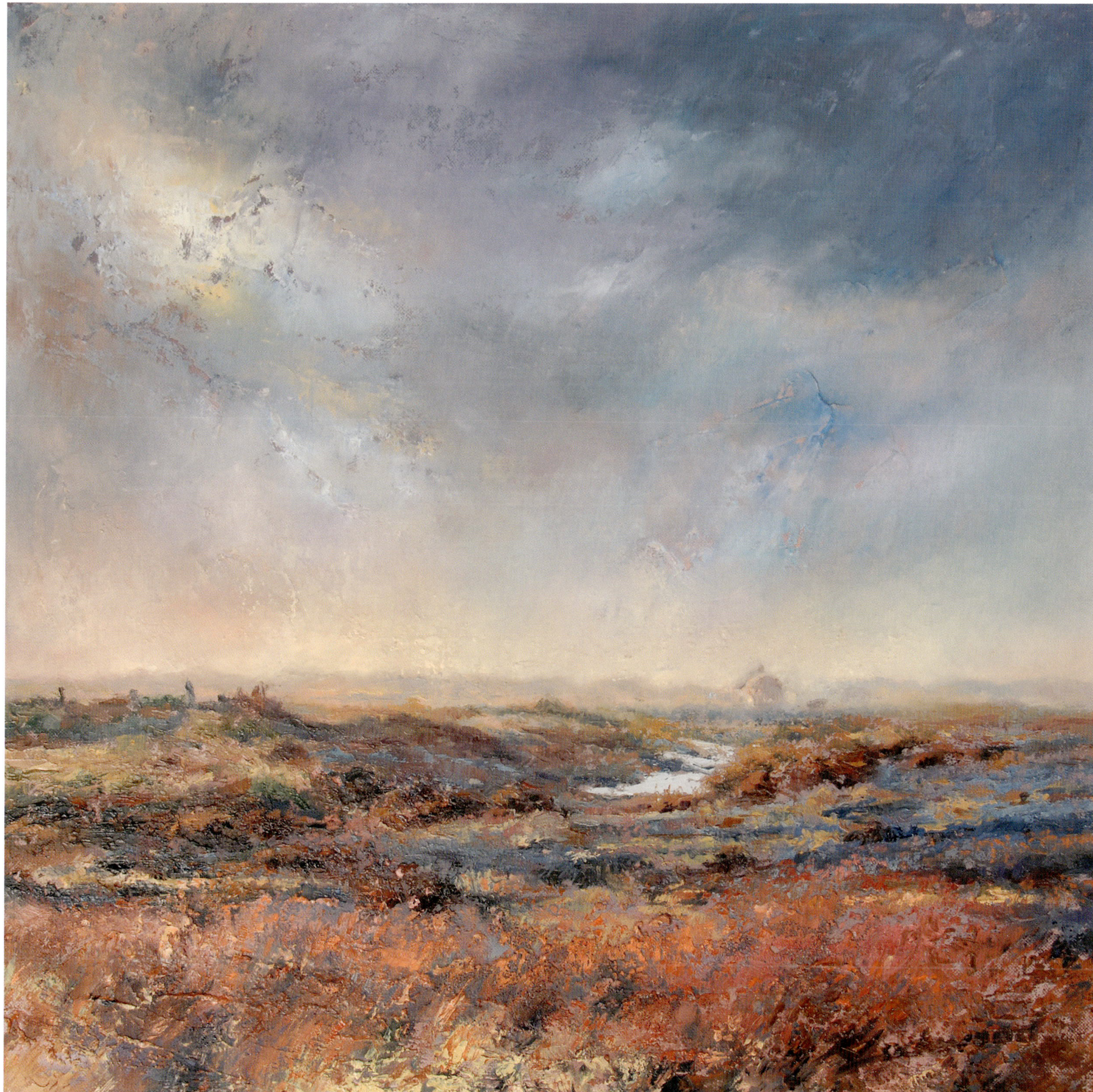

Halfway House, Blakeney
oils on canvas
80x80 cm

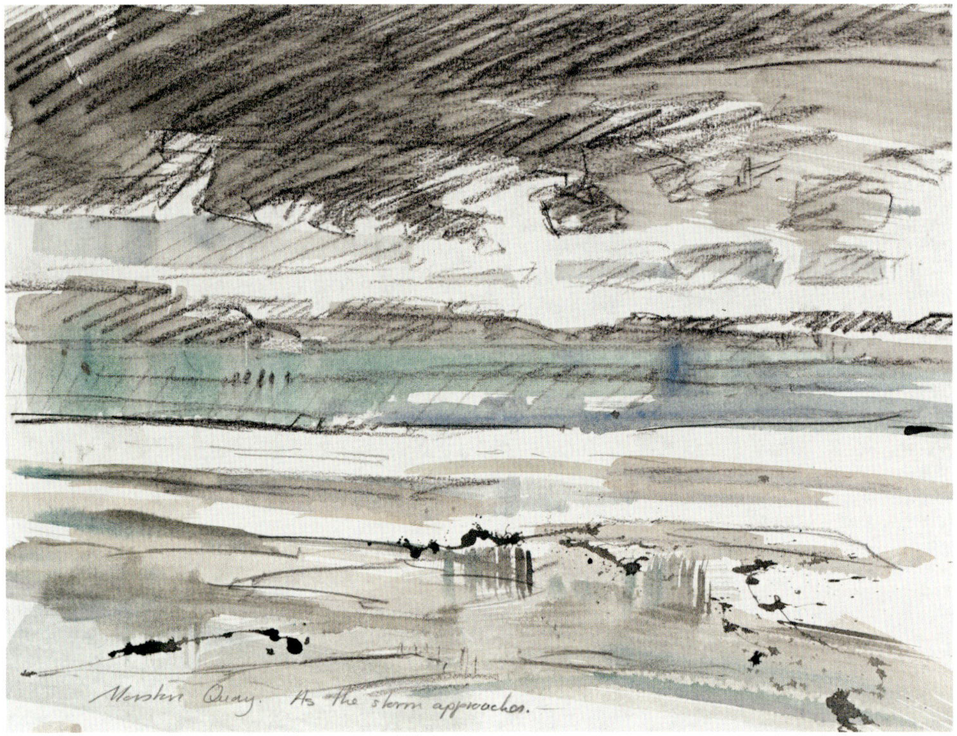

Morston Quay watercolours on paper
Sometimes if the weather is too bad I sit in the car and sketch.
I have a few favourite sketching spots along the coast where I can
get close to the water - Morston Quay is definitely one of them.

18 September

A passing storm at Blakeney Point provided a strong contrast in the landscape today. When the sun finally broke through it hit the pools with a powerful intensity. The painting began much lighter than this, but layer upon layer of darkness went on to achieve the strong contrasting light I saw. I tried really hard to work the paint into making the land look wet and glistening.

Sometimes it takes my eyes a while to adjust to a painting I'm working on, and occasionally it can turn in to a battleground for me. This was one of them. I'd feel like I'd finished it then walk away, come back an hour later and realise that it just wasn't there. I'd go over the painting again, pushing it further, darker and darker, but again I'd come back and it wasn't enough. It came very close to being thrown out, but eventually I reached the contrast I wanted.

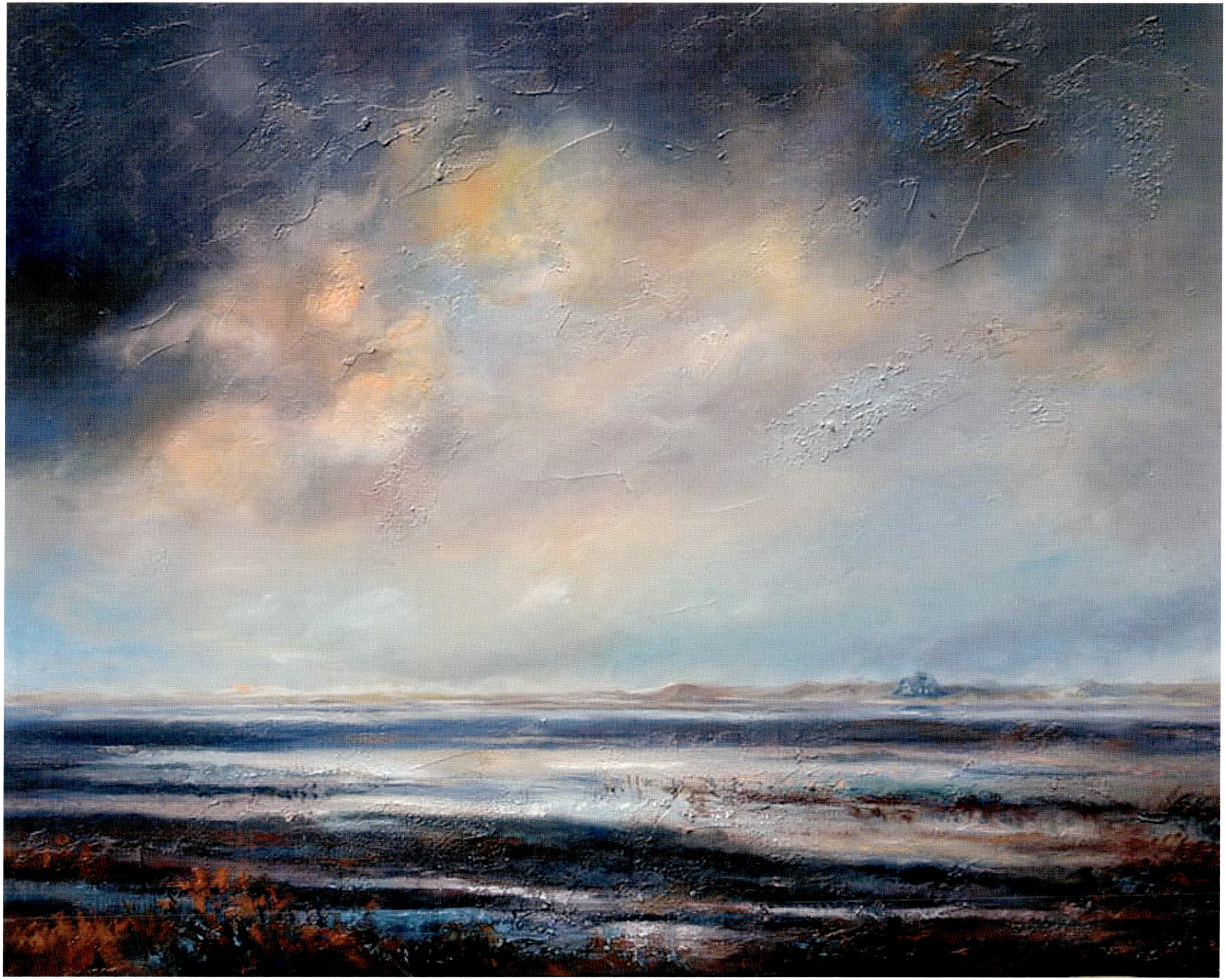

After the Rain, Towards Blakeney Point oils on canvas 60x80 cm

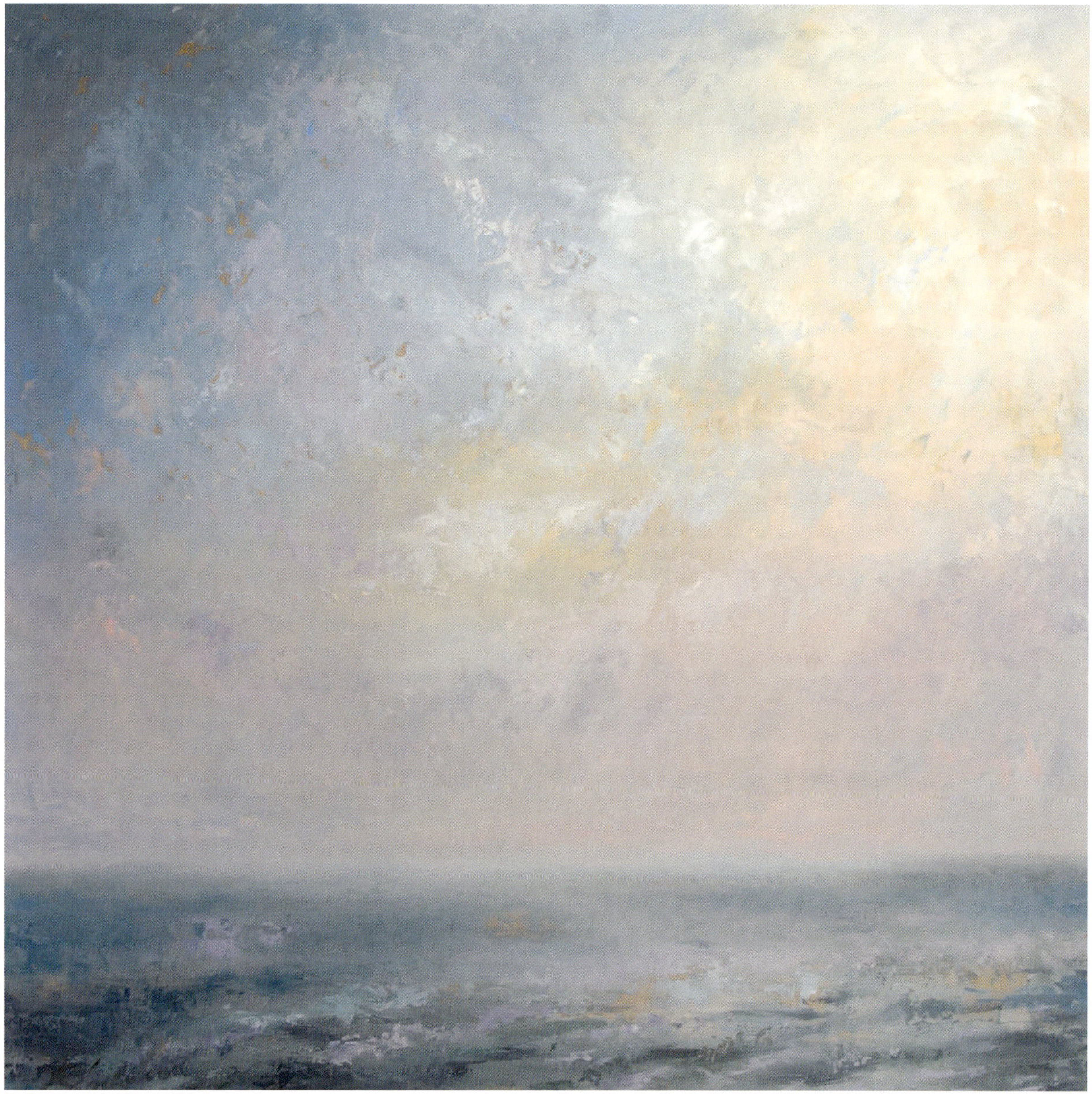

Dawn, Sheringham
oils on canvas 100x100 cm

20 September

I watched the sun rise over the sea today and knew it was going to be a day for spending by the water. The light is perfect. It feels like summer has returned. I went down to Morston later on and sat and watched the clouds move gently over the bay. Hardly a breath of wind - not a good day for sailing. After finishing the painting on the right, I decided it needed something else, so I added the boat, then took it out as I wasn't happy with it, then put it back in again. I still can't decide if it was the right decision.

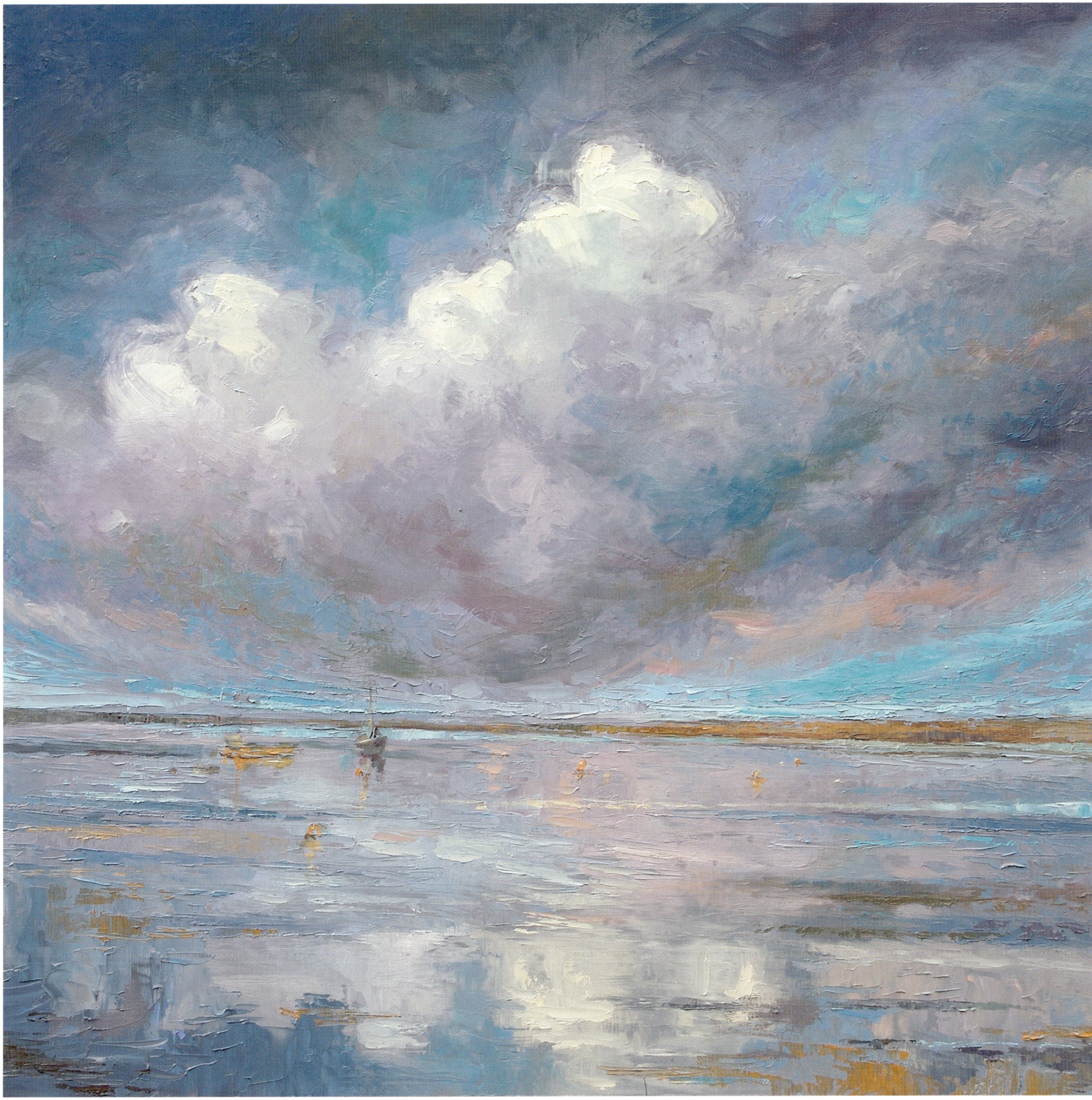

Blakeney Bay
oils on board 70x70 cm

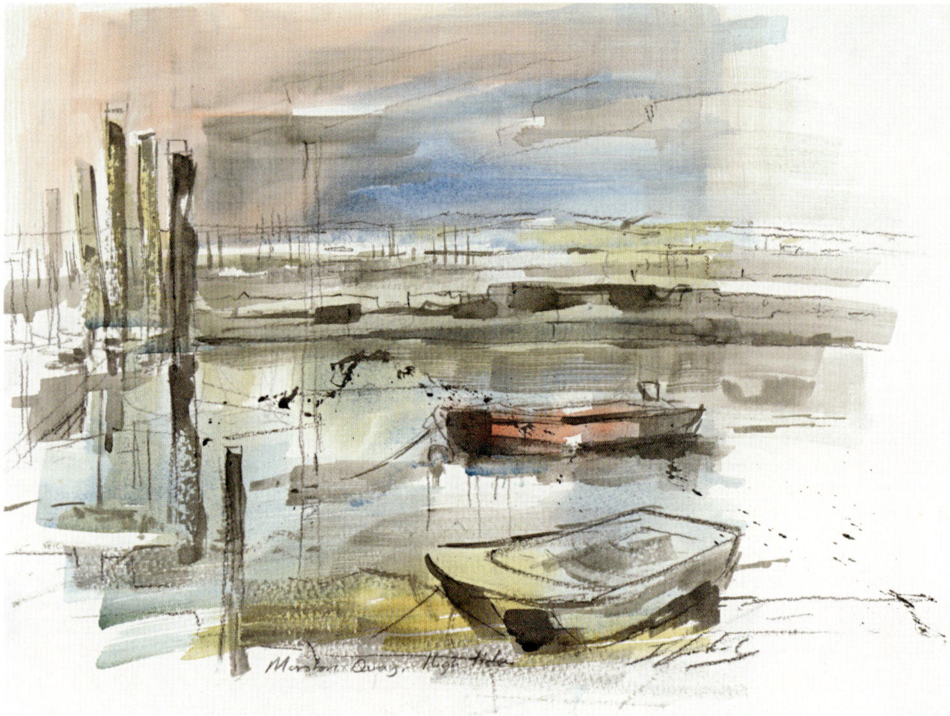

Blakeney Harbour Sketch
mixed media on paper

Sketches reveal more about what I'm thinking, there's no pressure to make the perfect painting, instead a lazy hand takes over. Here I'm able to record a moment in time, relaxed and meandering, without the worry of having to make it work. The lines of this sketch have developed, becoming even more of an important feature of the scene.

22 September

I've realised that constantly seeing the same images again and again have left their imprint on my mind. Again the linear theme is present all around me. The stanchions, reeds and trees seem to be appearing in my work more and more; there's something about the strong vertical lines contrasting with the softness of nature that I find fascinating. This painting was done in my studio and is a mix of reference from my sketchbook but more importantly it's simply the over-riding memories of the scene. It's how I remember it. The landscape broken up into blocks and lines with the odd unnatural curve of the boat. The shape of the boat is seen in full but I've filled in the gaps because that's how my mind reads it.

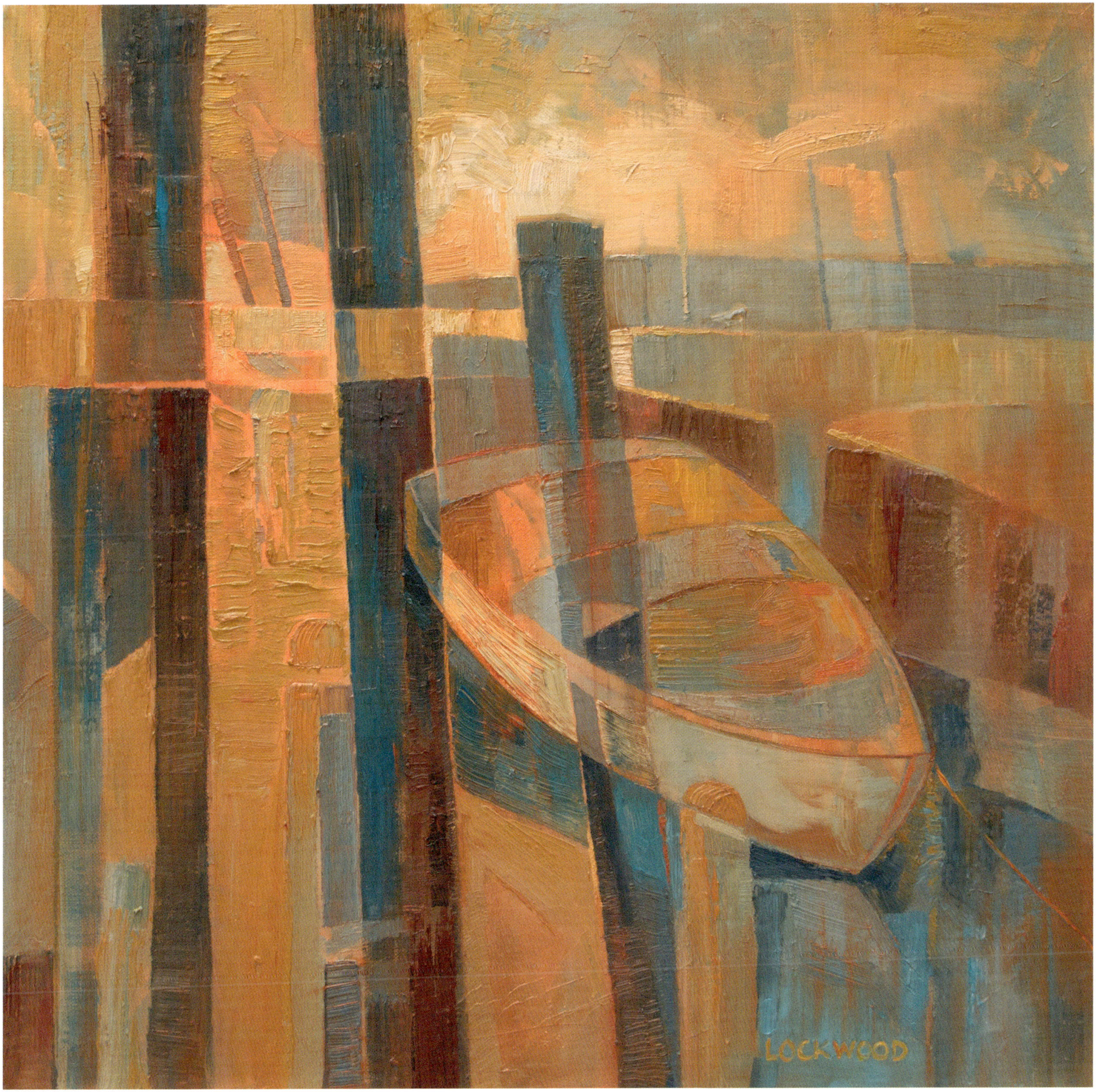

Blakeney Harbour
oils on canvas 60x60 cm

Moving Boats
mixed media on paper

25 September

Grey, dank weather has come. I find it challenging when there is no break in the light to create a focal point or cast a shadow. Today is just a blanket of muzzy, grey flatness.

Finally by lunchtime the sun pushed through and started to dry the marsh grasses. As my eyes became accustomed to the light, subtle colours began to emerge in the landscape, undulating layers of texture led me in and my palette knife began to scrape and sculpt the canvas. Damp air blew by and at some point I thought it might rain, but once the rhythm of the picture had begun it was hard to stop. It was frenzied, and each new layer and mark balanced and unbalanced the picture in its unsteady journey towards capturing what I saw and felt. Then the rain finally came and I had to pack quickly, I had paint everywhere as I'd caught it on my sleeve and down my trousers and even on the car bumper; definitely an improvement on the mud that was covering it. I left the picture overnight in my studio to 'cure' the paint a little, and over the following days I let my memories of the view help me finish the painting.

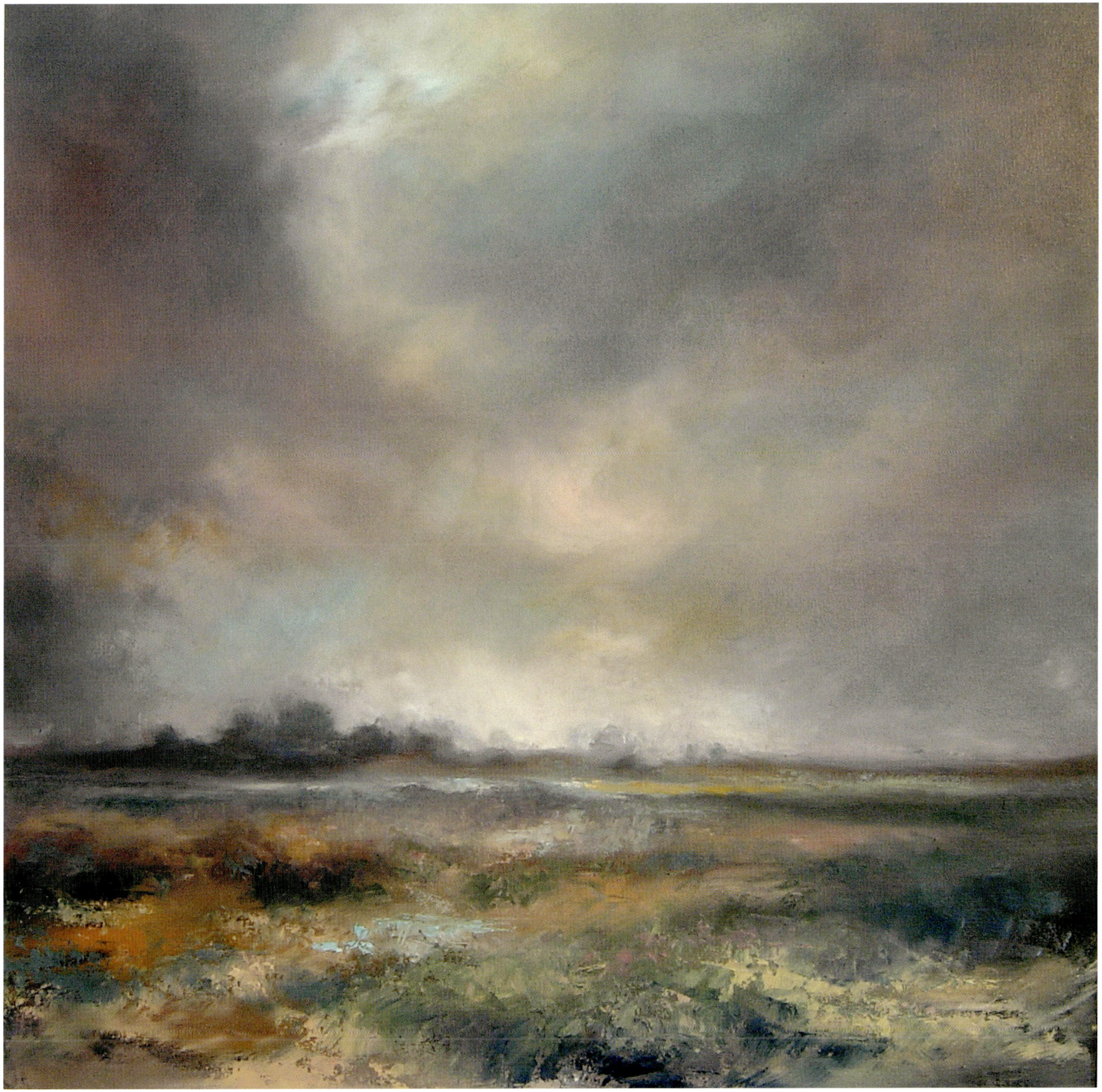

Stiffkey Marshes
oils on canvas 60x60 cm

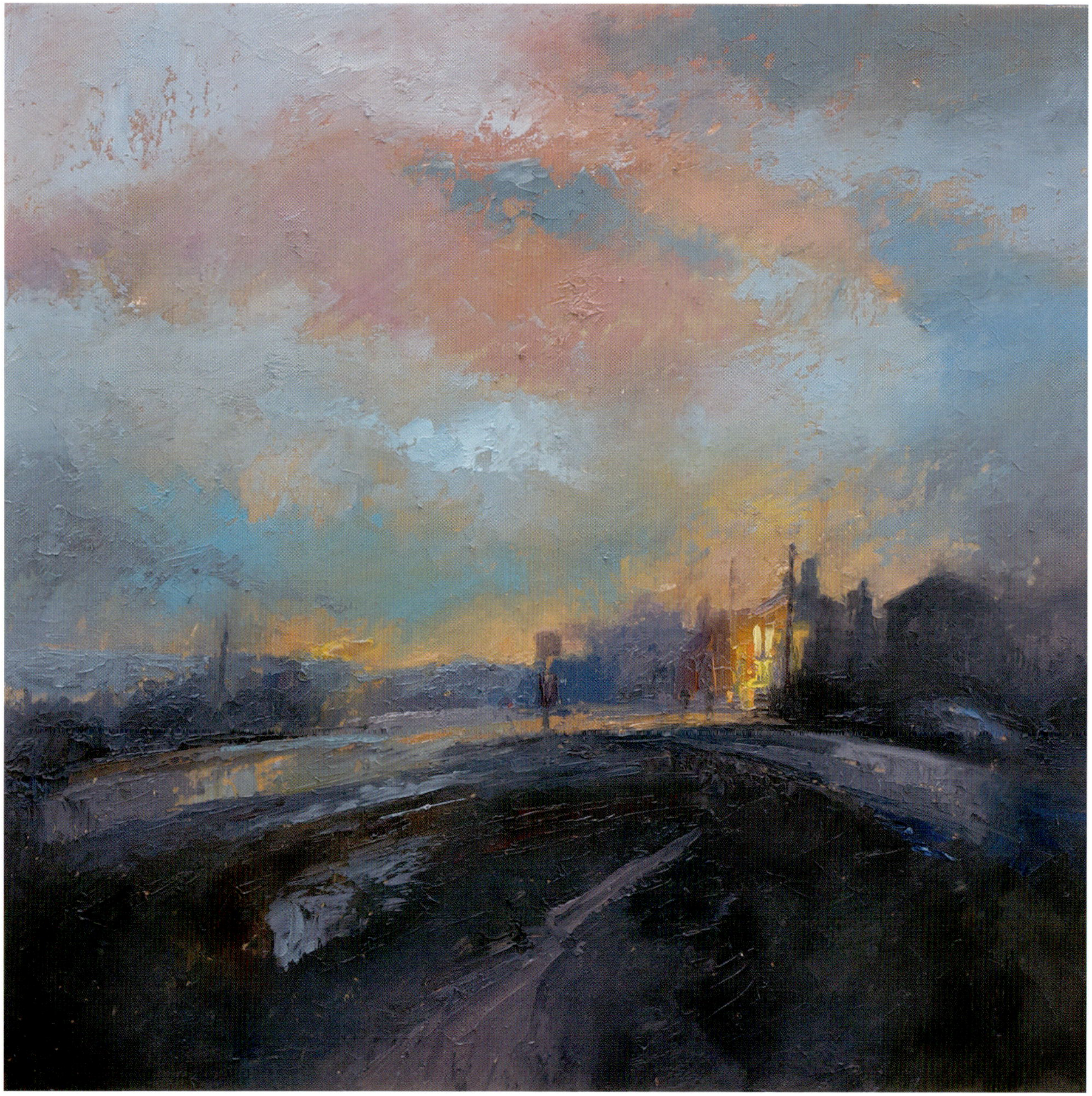

Three Swallows in the Mist, Cley
oils on panel 60x60 cm

27 September

A thick mist and a welcoming glow shone out of the Three Swallows pub. At the time of writing, this painting sits in my studio far from being finished. I had a battle with my partner who wanted to put in into the book as it was, even though it was unfinished. As you can see, I lost. So here it is, an unfinished piece. It could be completely different when it's finished – these are just the bones that capture in essence what I saw.

30 September

Walking home tonight I saw Cley's resident Barn Owl meandering silently over the marsh and meadow near Bramble Flap. The rain had been pouring down and now the air was just damp and still. The temperature dropped and the sky had become hazy. The owl passed by again and again, like a spectre appearing in the mist. The light from the moon shone and spread through the thickening haze and lit up the river flowing through the meadow. It was pretty much like a dream. I painted this in my studio, but I'm really not sure how I did it though. But I do know that I had all of the previous night's feelings in my mind.

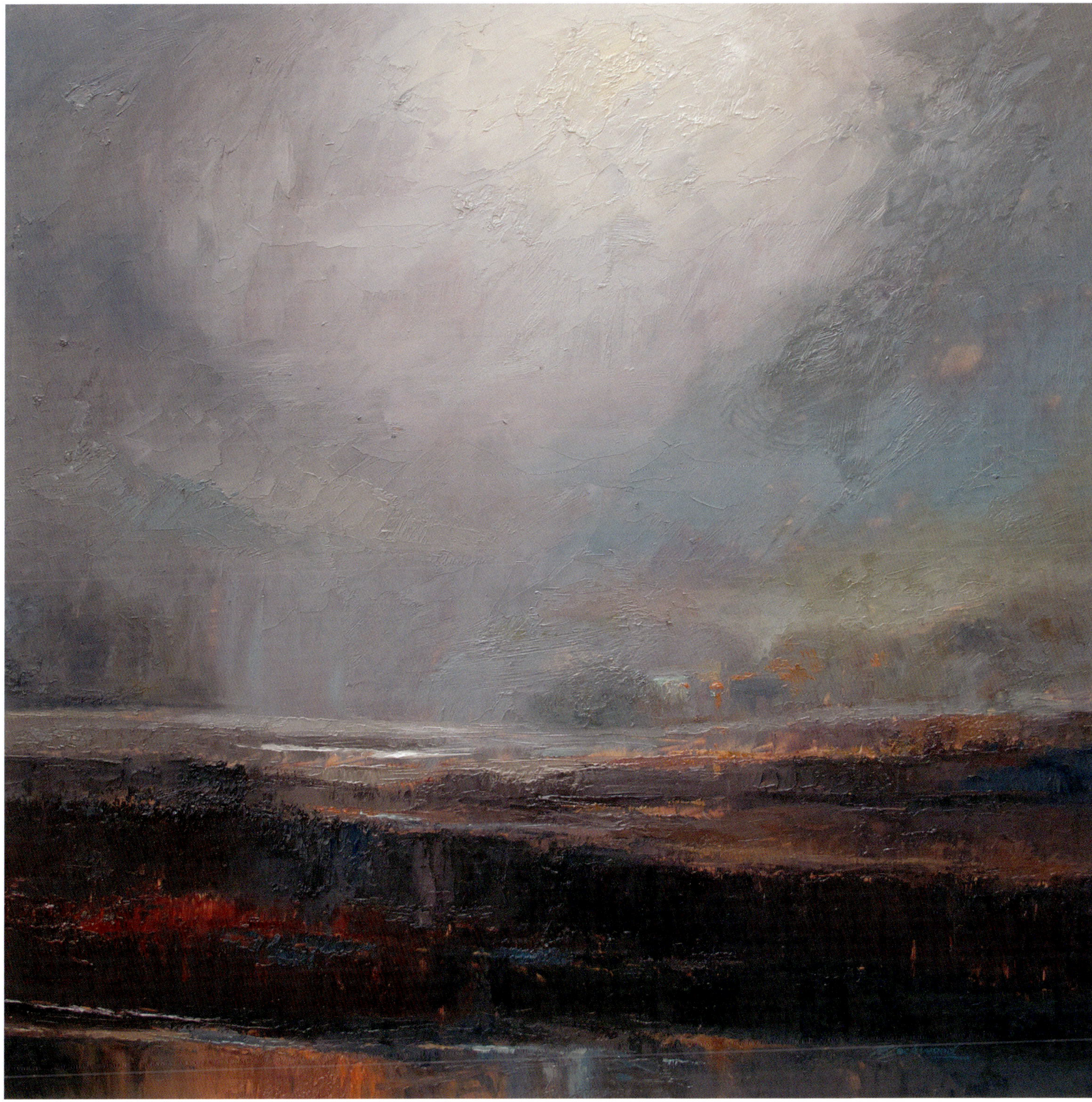

Mist Over The Moon, Cley
oils on canvas 70x70 cm

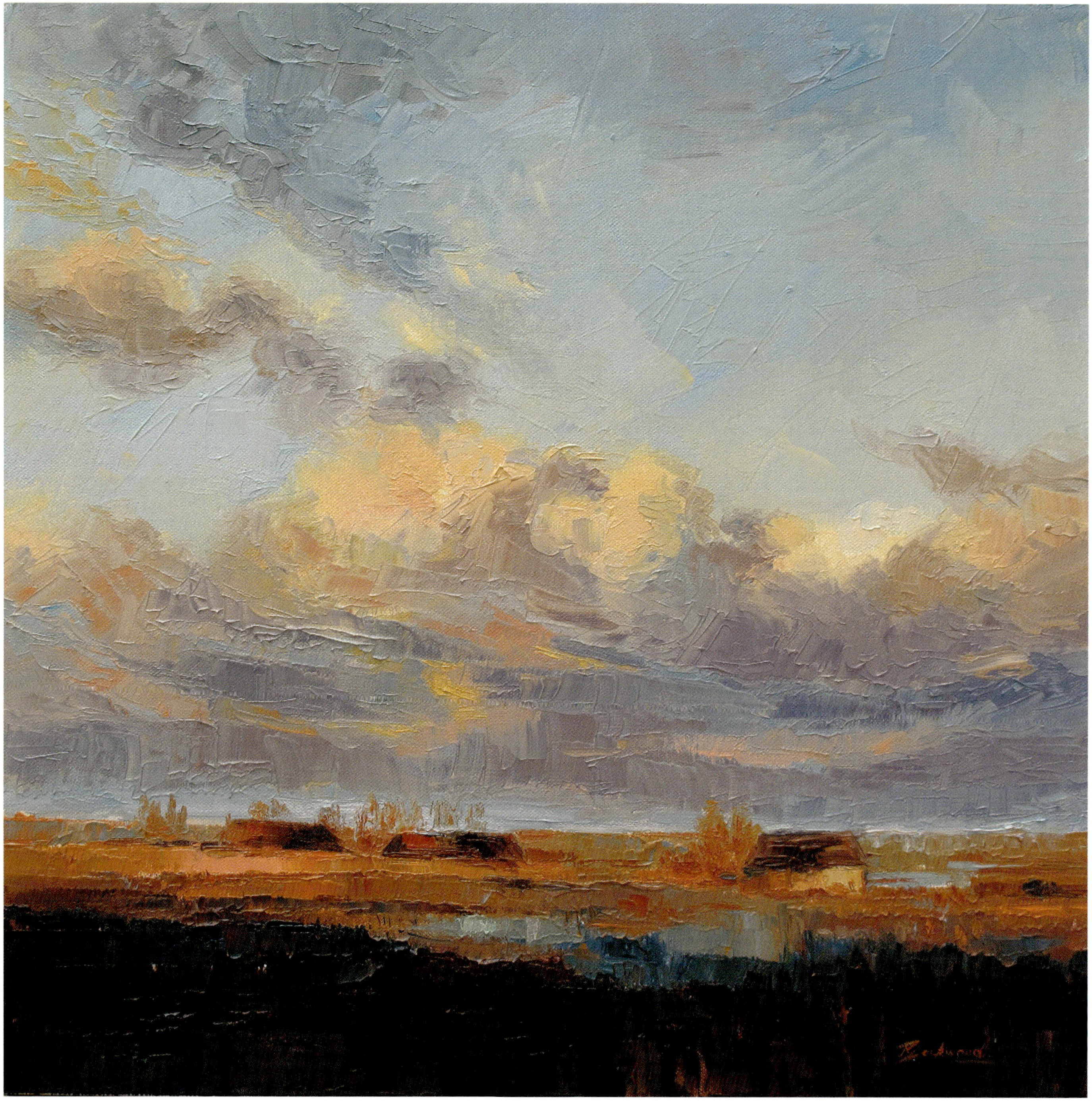

Cley Bird Hides II
oils on canvas 60x60 cm

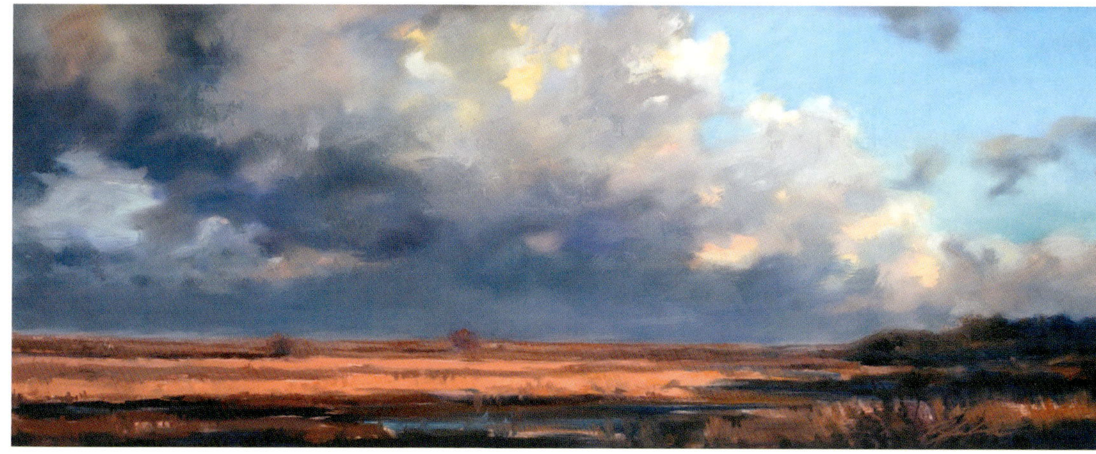

Over Cley Marsh
oils on canvas
40x80 cm

1 October

I wanted to see the late afternoon light on the reeds tonight, so walked the long way home, down Old Woman's Lane and on to the reserve. I disturbed a Muntjac as it fed on the verge and a clamour of Rooks noisily left the fields for their roost. I wasn't disappointed when I reached the reserve, the evening light lit up the reeds with a golden glow, and I knew what I would be painting tomorrow.

These paintings are born through the hours I spend pounding the marsh around Cley. The bird hides on the reserve are something I see every time I walk the long way home. I think living in the landscape you paint is so important. It allows you to experience every slight change, it's as if it's now in my bones. Over the years of being here, I feel more in tune with the landscape, I always have one eye out looking to see what its doing. To be honest I'm surprised that I ever get any work done, the slightest hint of an interesting sky is enough to prise me from my studio.

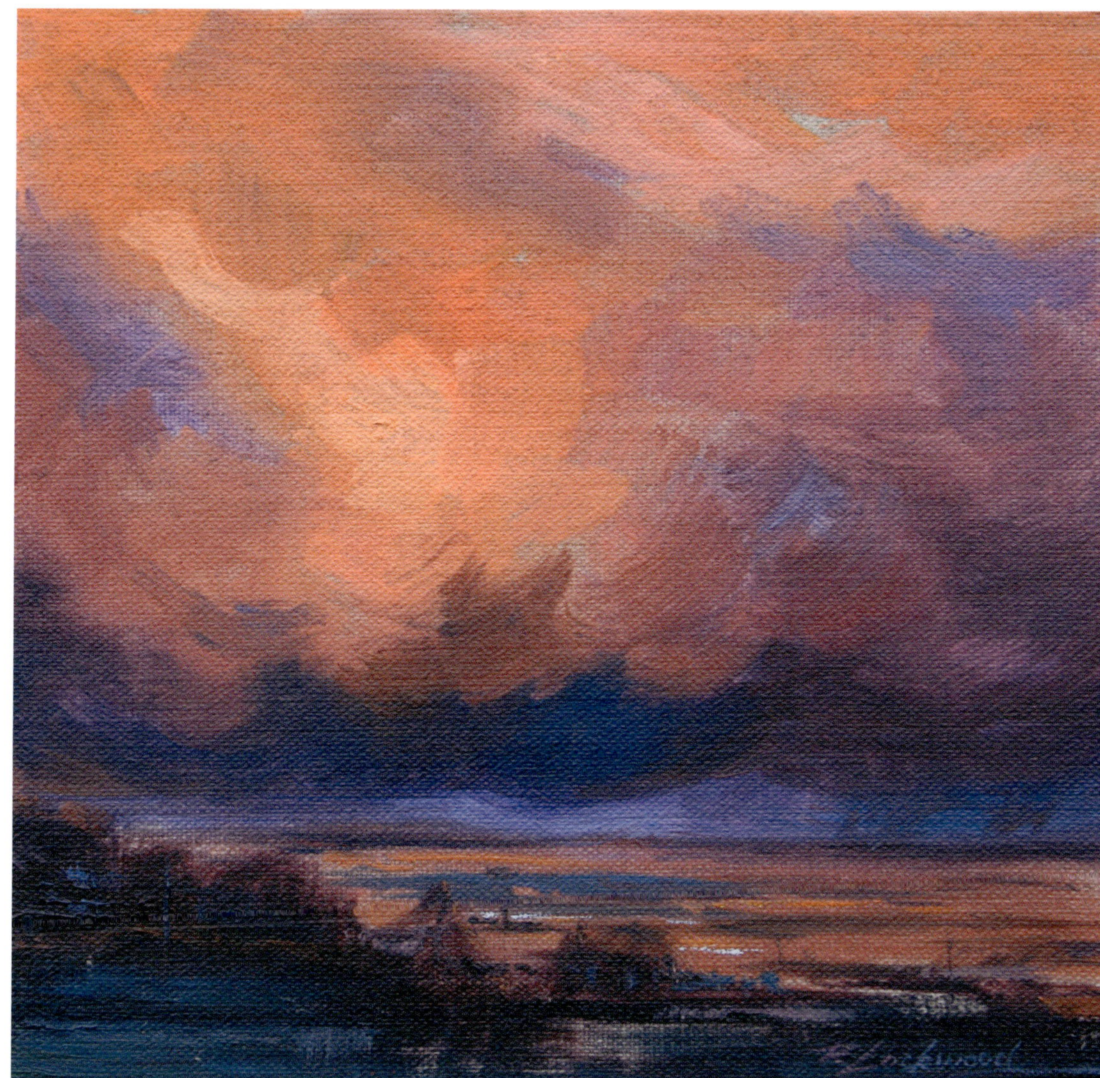

Old Woman's Lane
oils on canvas
20x20 cm

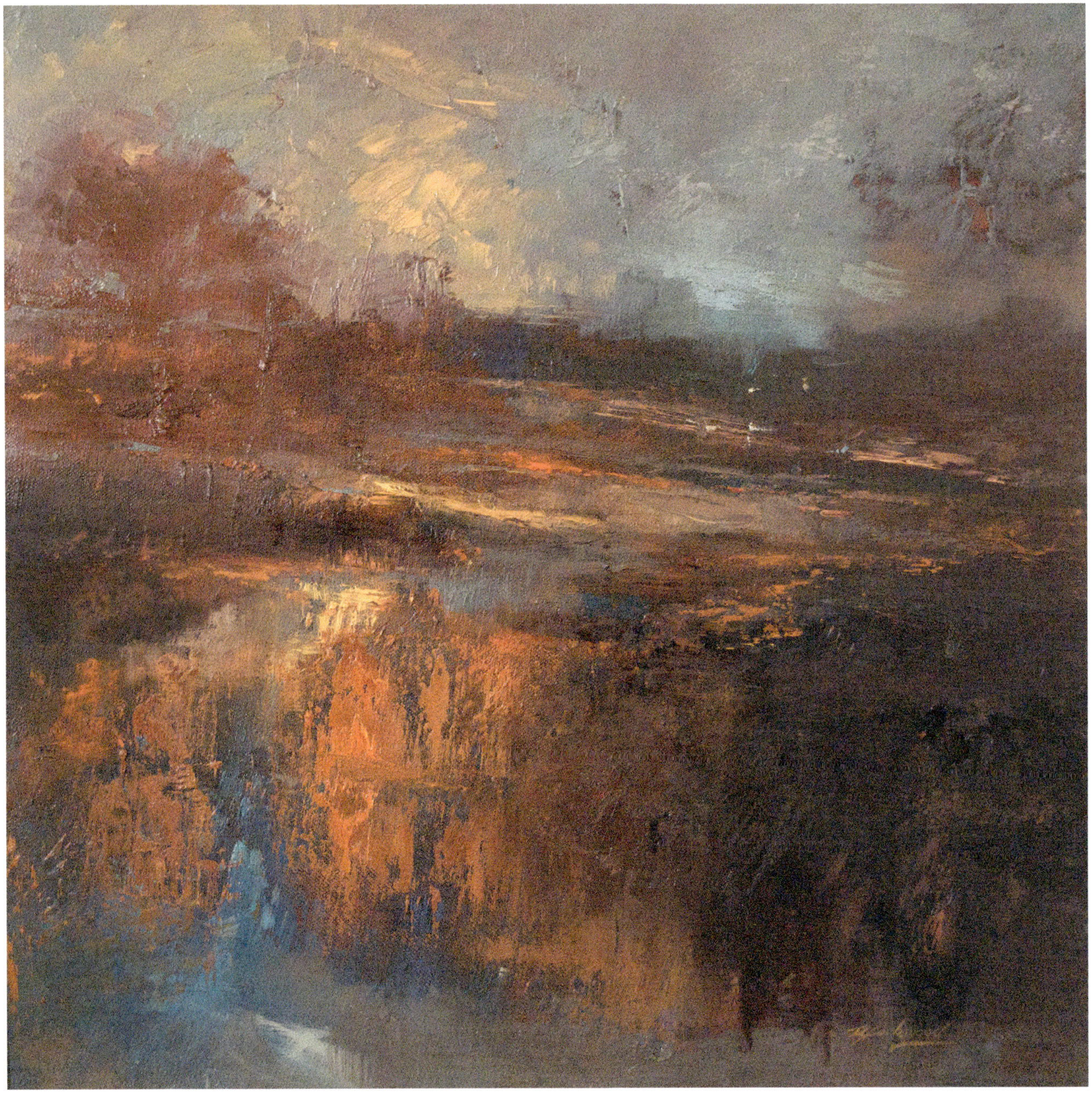

Evening Meadow oils on linen 50x50 cm

I October

I worked late tonight, battling with a painting that wouldn't let me go. It put me in a bad mood so I decided to take a slow walk home in the hope that I'd cure myself by the time I reached the flat. Although it's almost dark, there's a strange light over the Glaven Valley, I can just see glimmers of oranges and soft reds through the gloom. This painting turned out to be far more dramatic than the actual scene. I fear my brooding mood may have stepped into this picture.

3 October

Early Sunday morning, my favourite time of the week. Cley is quiet and still. The curtains at the Three Swallows are still closed, its wayward wonky signs resembling last night's customers. I take a little detour to look over the beautiful Glaven Valley; two trees cast shadows of blue, I make a note for a future painting. The heat from the sun is surprisingly strong today and the air still. So many birds can be heard across the meadow: Curlew, Mistle Thrush, Collared Doves and flapping Pigeons.

This is another time of year I get excited about; there's still just a hint of summer in the air but you just know the season is changing. I walk on up the hill, past a garden full of sculptured heads that watch me walk by, the only inhabitants that seem to be awake this morning. Onwards I go, blinded by the low rising sun. I arrive at the studio and find that my freezer door wasn't quite shut, so it's defrosted salmon for the stray cat today.

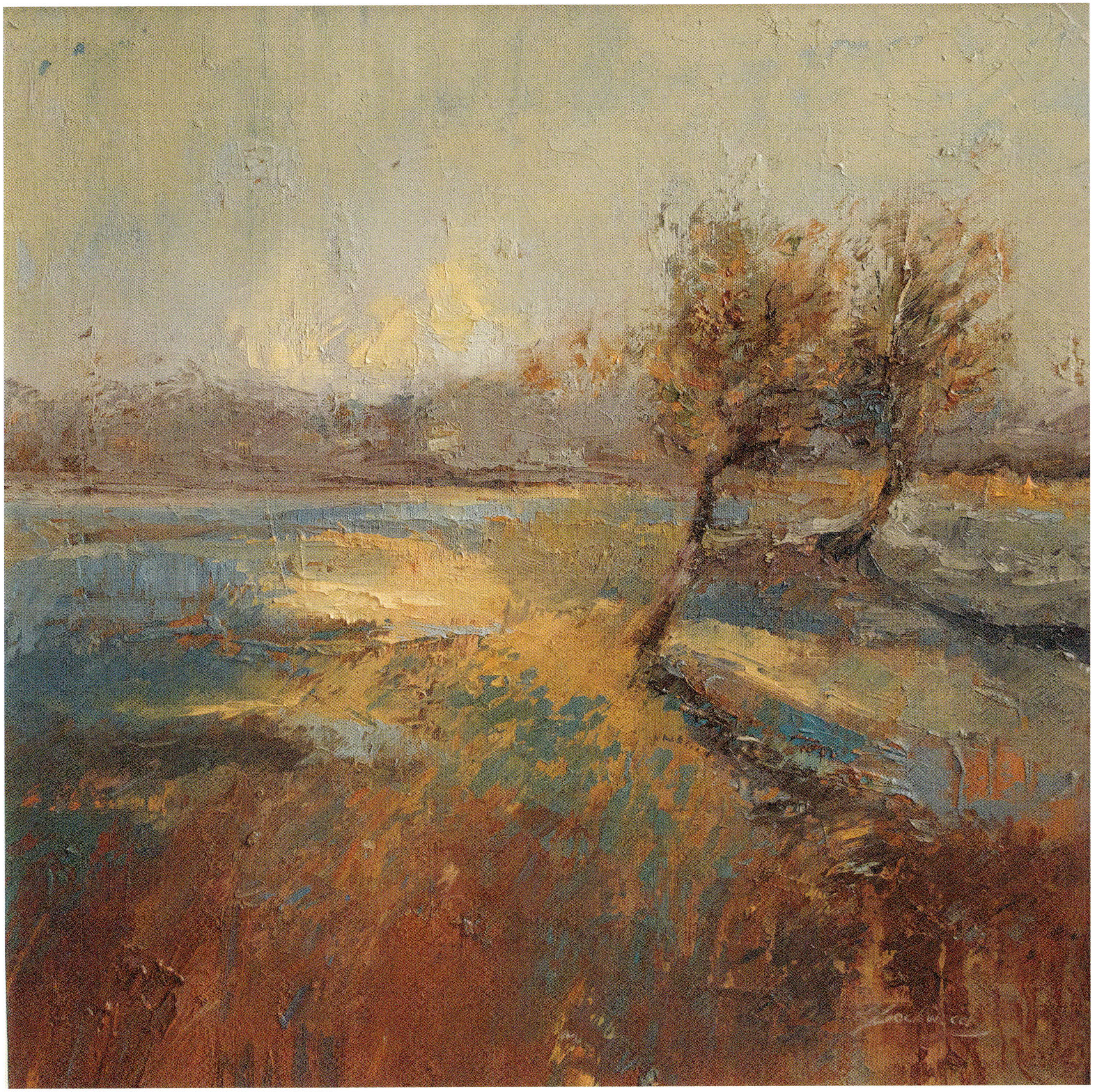

Glaven Valley Trees oils on canvas 60x60 cm

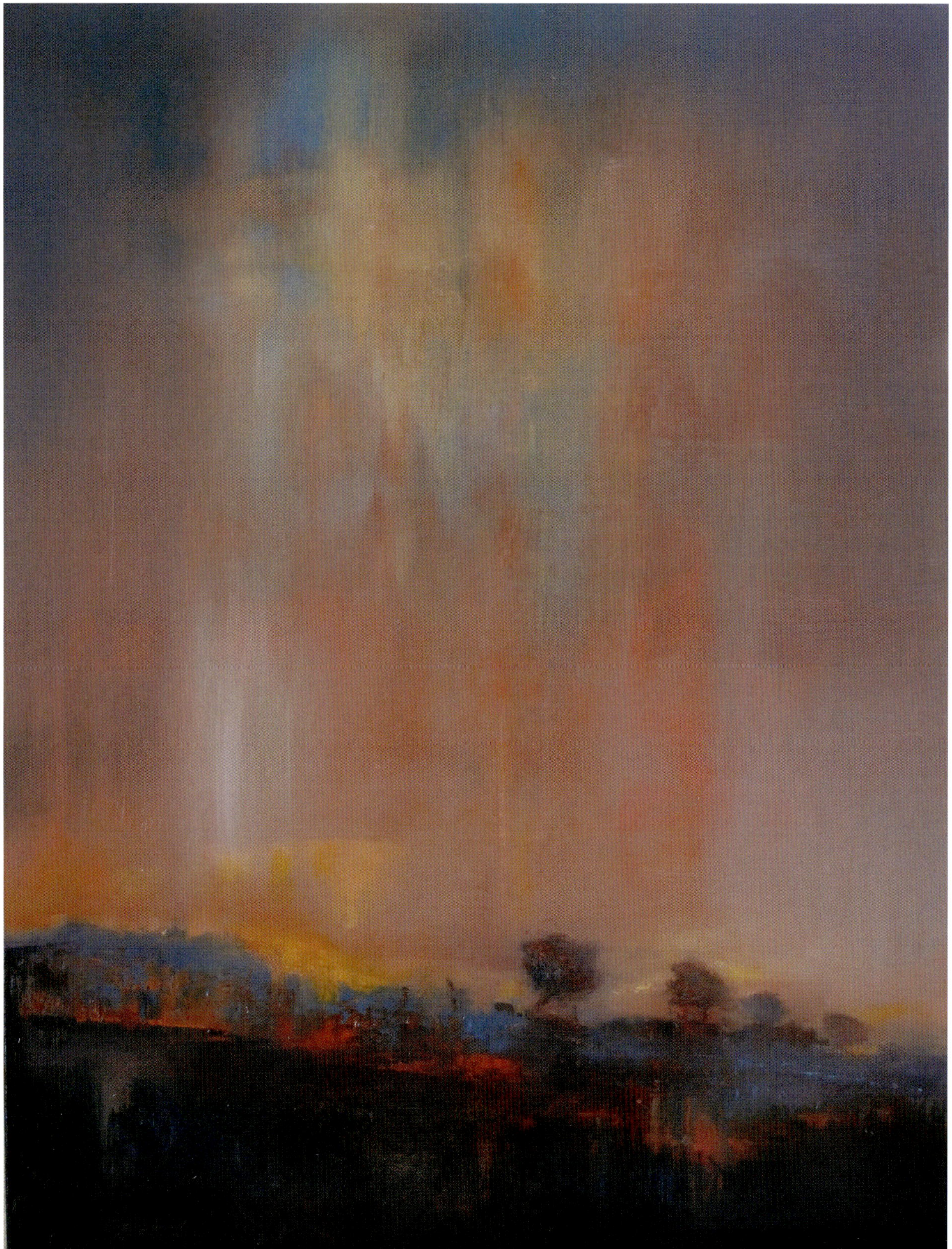

5 October

Went back to Cockthorpe today to see Chris, Anna and their two fantastic children Emma and Ben. They're always ready for an adventure when we meet up and although we were meant to be having dinner, it had to be put on hold while we went off on another jaunt down the valley.

As the sun dropped down, the light in the valley changed dramatically. The colours became richer and the air felt still, it was as if there was a drum-roll in the sky, preparing us for something spectacular to follow – and it did, we were treated to an amazing sunset. The Crab Apple tree on the horizon caught my attention again, I painted it earlier in the year when it was in blossom but now it looked completely different. Yet again, it had to be the focus of another painting. I remember it being lit up like a gem in this landscape that had been gnawed by sheep and rabbits.

Cockthorpe Valley Walk
oils on canvas 80x100cm

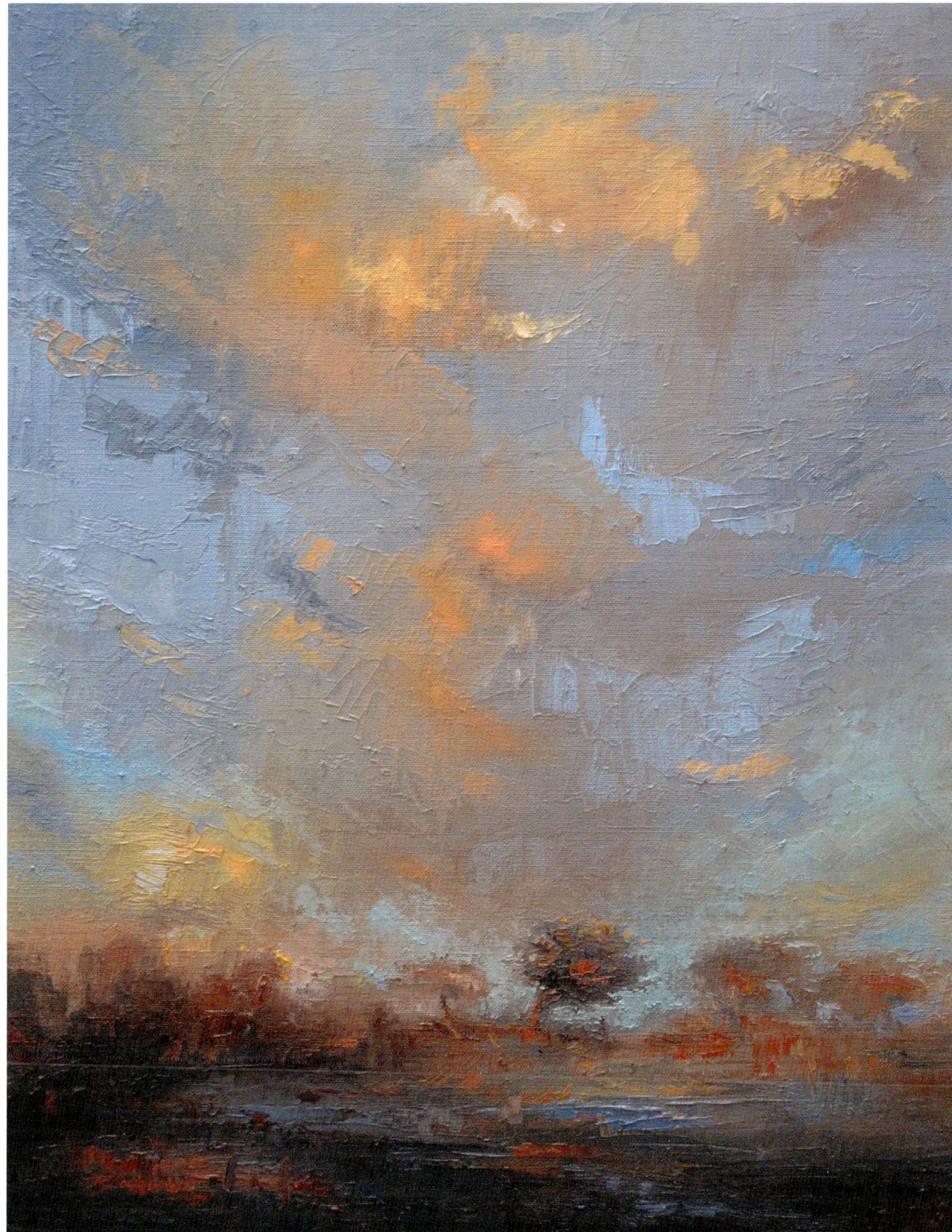

Cockthorpe Crab Apple
oils on canvas 50x35 cm

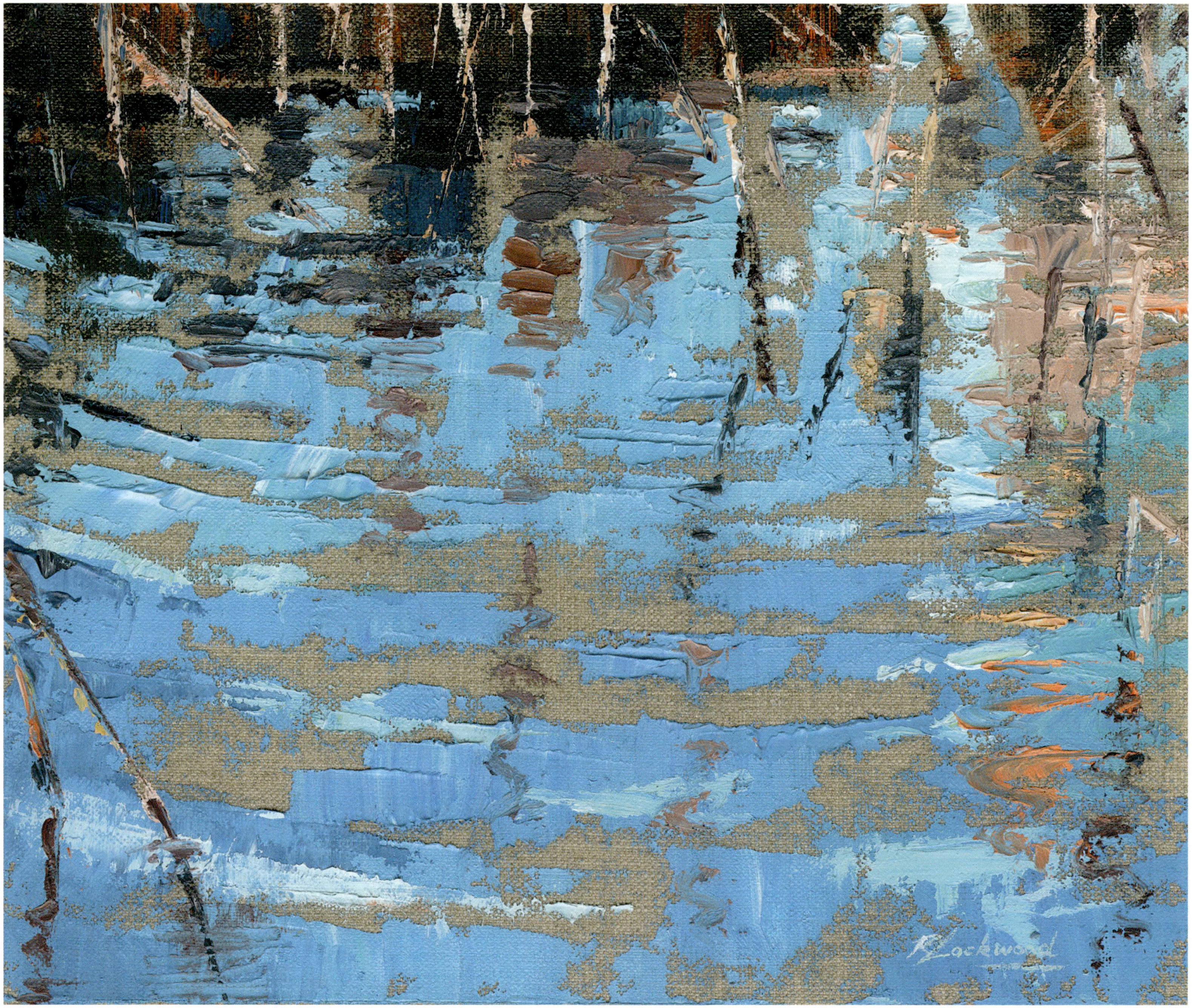

10 October

Cley Reeds at Water's Edge
oils on linen 20x24 cm

While walking down to the bird hides in Cley, the waterways that edge part of the reserve catch my eye and I see that the low light of autumn has intensified the colour reflected on the water. It sets me off on a trail to revisit my favourite watery places again. I've been distracted by painting landscapes and have realised that this would be a missed opportunity if I didn't make the most of this amazing light.

11 October

I did a lot of walking today. I went to one pool then another, visiting areas of receding lilies, a lot in decay now rotting, stagnant and slimy on the surface of the water. There was nothing quite right until I came across this pool in Kelling Park. It was early evening and an intense gold light lit up the forest floor beyond the edge of the pool. Although it was only a small, subtle part of this painting, I used gold leaf on top of the oil for more impact. I wasn't the only one standing by the pool tonight though, as I looked up I noticed something staring at me, it made me jump it was so close. A Roe Deer had stepped out of the forest; we stared at each other for a few seconds before it leapt back in.

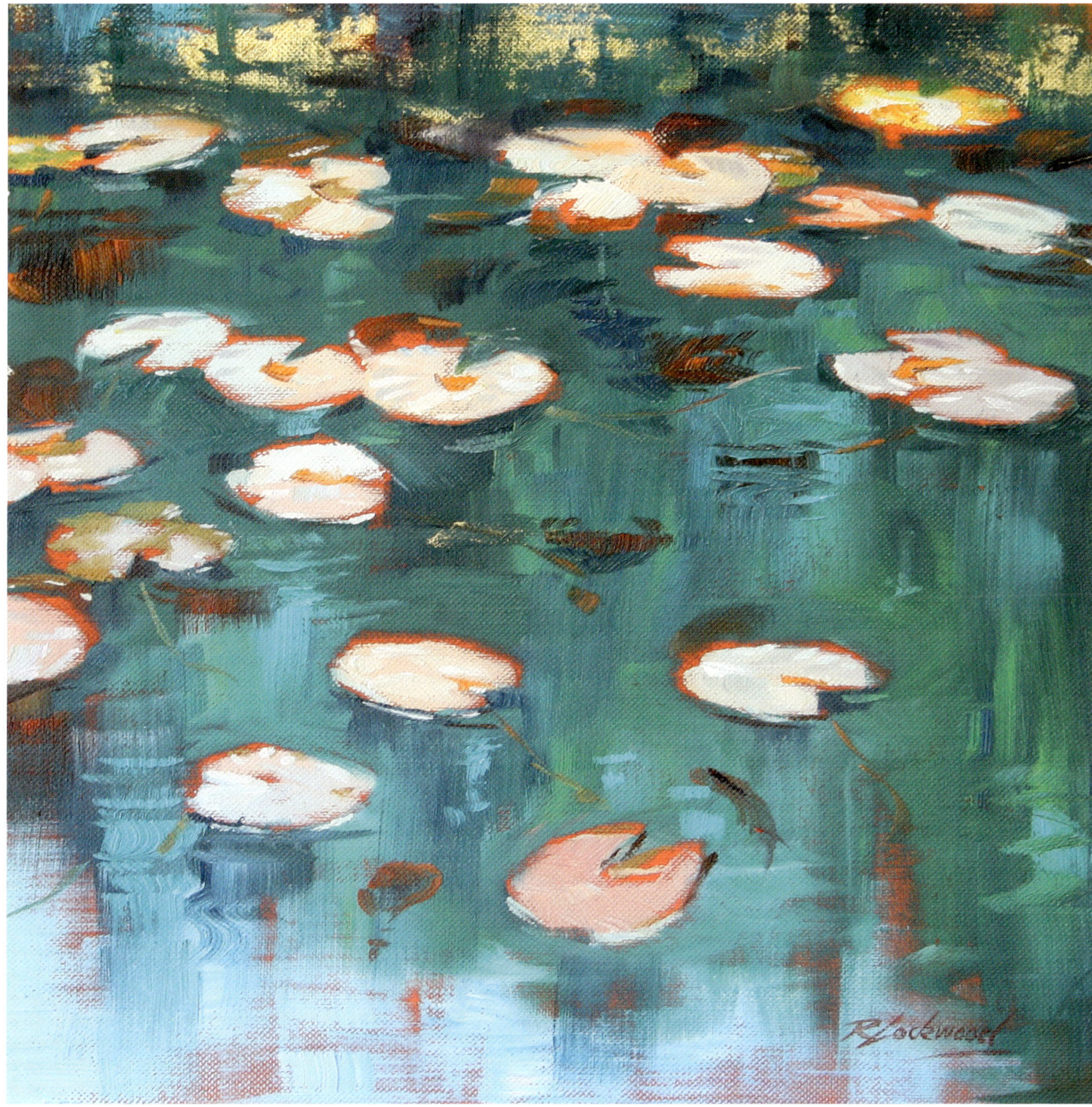

Gold Light
oils on canvas paper 20x20 cm

16 October

Standing on a public path surrounded by ploughed fields with dry dust blowing off the peaks of earth, I noticed a faint track cutting through the dirt heading towards a large island of trees and shrubs. As there was no one around, I decided to follow the path and entered a low forest of Silver Birch and Rowan. Deer tracks led me on under curved arches of branches and the ground became more boggy; I noticed reeds above a bank ahead of me and as I walked up the slope, a hidden pool sheltered by willow came into view. I stood looking at the mirror-like surface that reflected the evening sky. A ripple appeared and spread across the water's surface but I couldn't see what had made it. A few days later I began this painting. I had a great feeling of calmness throughout.

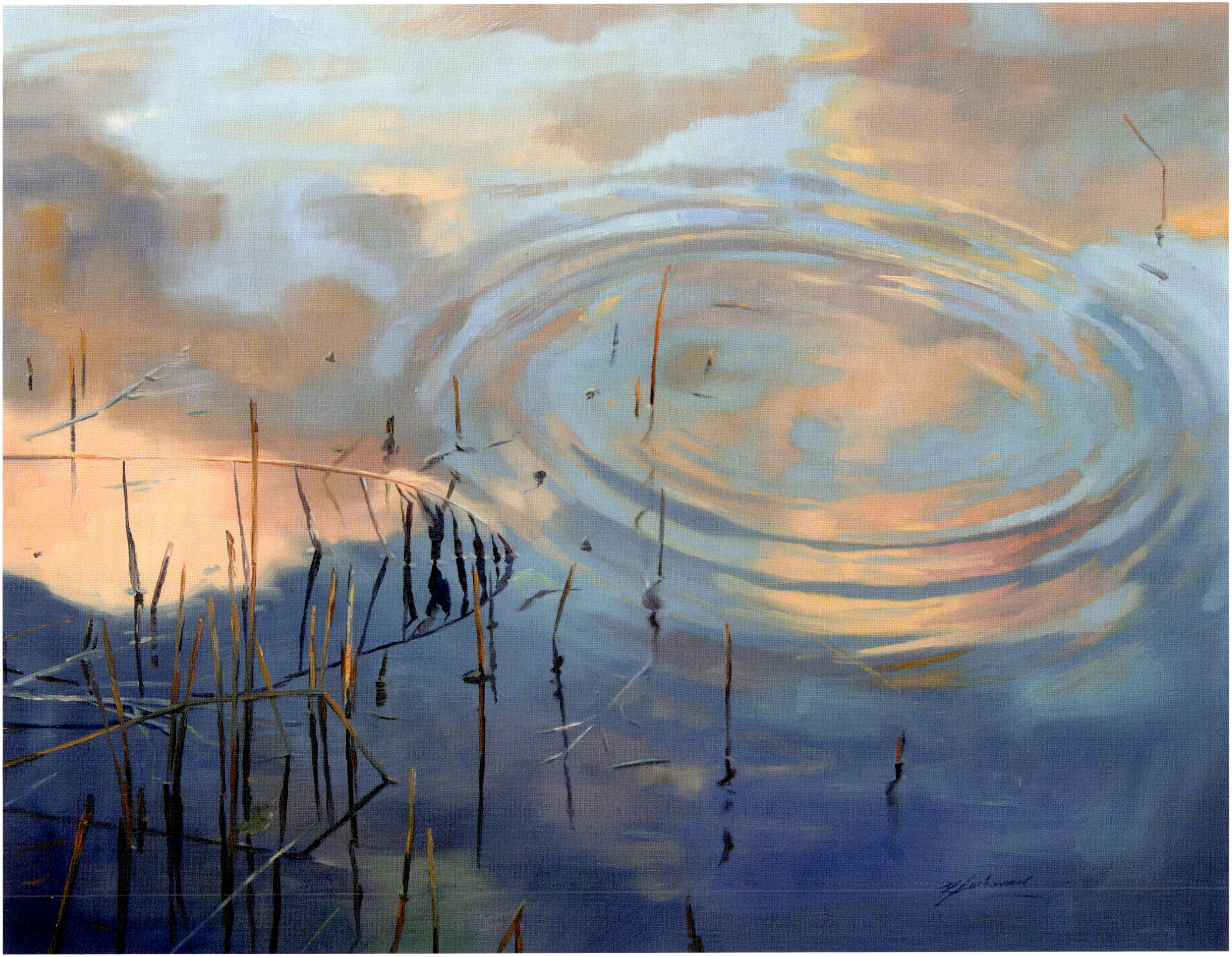

Hidden Pool
oils on board 40x60 cm

19 October

I had to go into Norwich today to pick a friend up from the station, which meant I wouldn't have enough time to start a new painting. But I knew I had to paint something today, some days are just like that. So I filled my thermos mug and walked down to Bramble Flap, which is just a stone's throw from the house. The autumn leaves had started to fall and were being snagged and collected by the brambles overhanging the water.

It's so easy to get carried away when you're captivated with a painting and you become completely oblivious to events surrounding you, such as the freezing cold weather! Even though I had several layers on and fingerless gloves, when I stopped I realized I was frozen to the bone. I couldn't wait to get into the car and warm up on the way to Norwich. The oil sketches finally led to the idea for this painting. In the sketches there were a lot more things going on in the water, the stream was full of leaves and tangled brambles. But I wanted to distill this scene, to tell a simple story. I picked out just one leaf and lost some of the brambles, this lack of detail also helped me loosen up in style – something I was keen to achieve after the very detailed paintings I'd been working on recently.

In experimental terms Bramble Flap is my 'control area'. I return to it again and again, monitoring the subtle changes in the seasons. It's one of those places that you either know of or you don't and I'm loathed to tell too many people about it as it's my secret spot. I've seen so many things from here, even though there's a footpath very close by. I've watched Water Voles, Reed Warblers, Minnows, Kingfishers and Barn Owls to name but a few. I think everyone should have their own secret place, I'm fortunate mine is right on my doorstep.

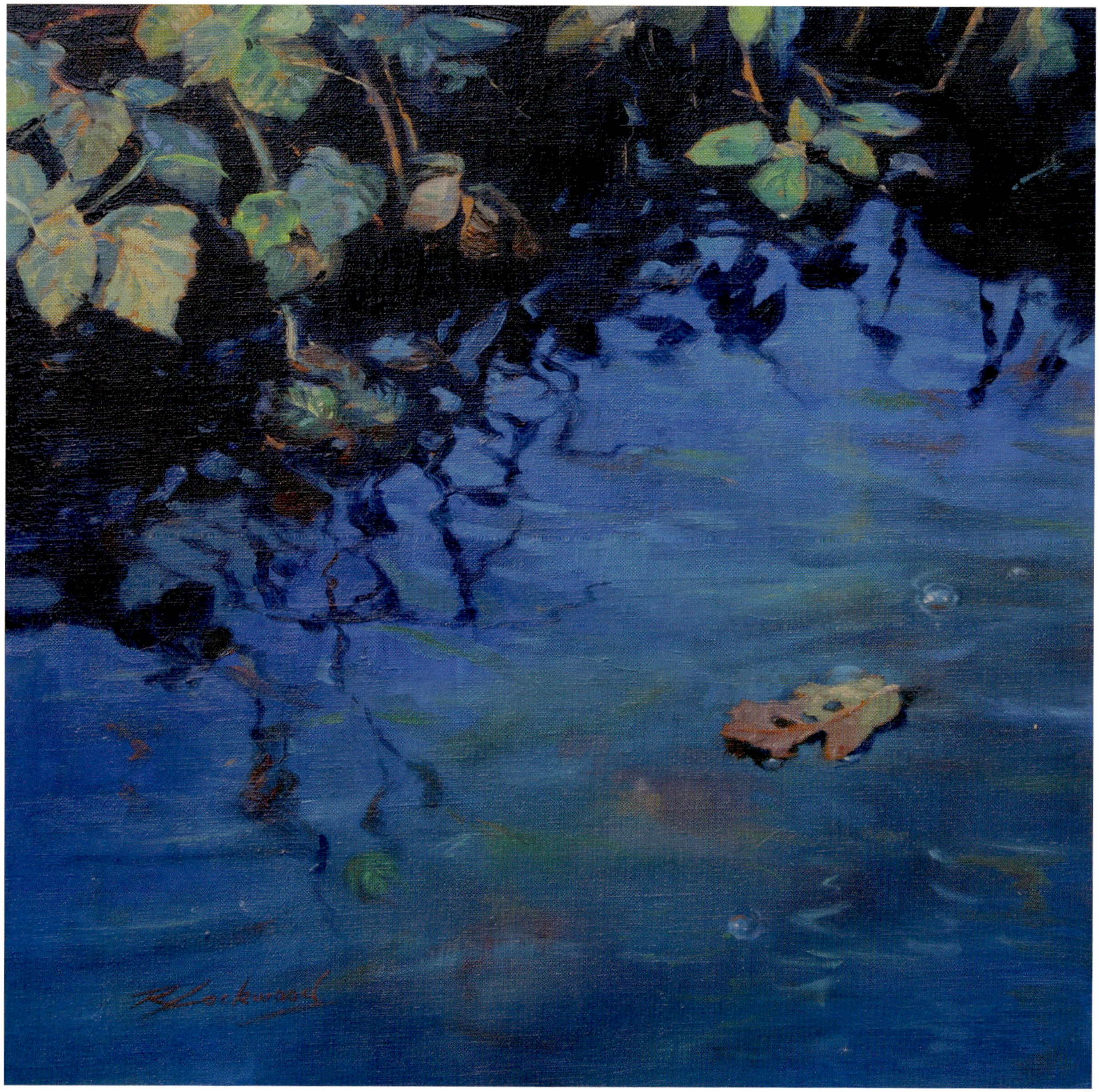

Oak Leaf, Bramble Flap
oils on canvas 50x50 cm

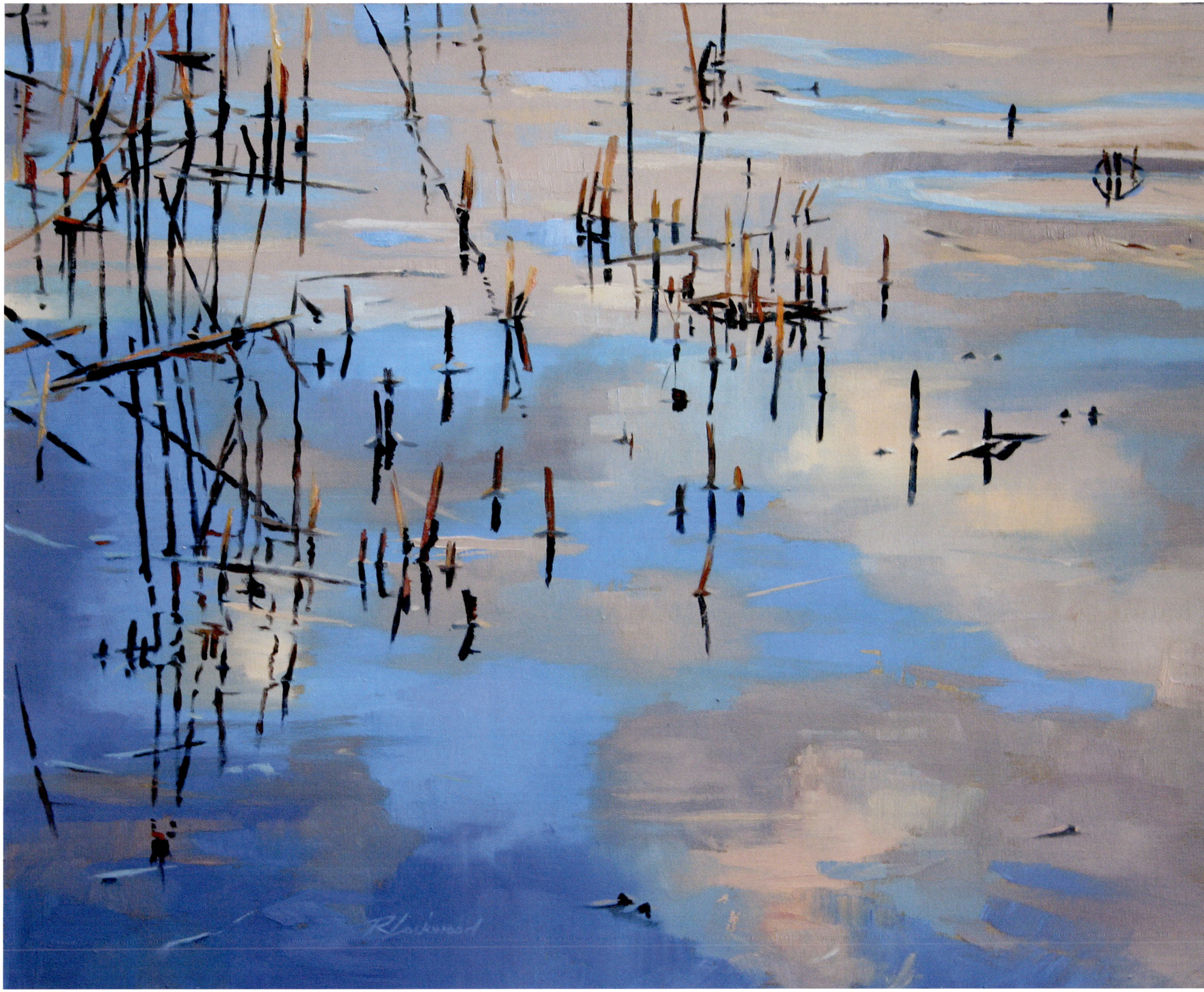

Reed Study, Bramble Flap
oils on board 60x40 cm

20 October

When I saw this pool it reminded me of a Japanese print. I've always loved the simplicity of Japanese art, but I believe there's an undercurrent of complexity that is hidden in its simple execution.

In this painting I was trying to keep the simplicity of space but tell a story by using the ripples. Originally I'd painted a fish towards the bottom of this picture but it completely ruined the overall effect I was trying to achieve. Without the fish, it immediately enabled the viewer to tell their own story and ask themselves what made the ripple.

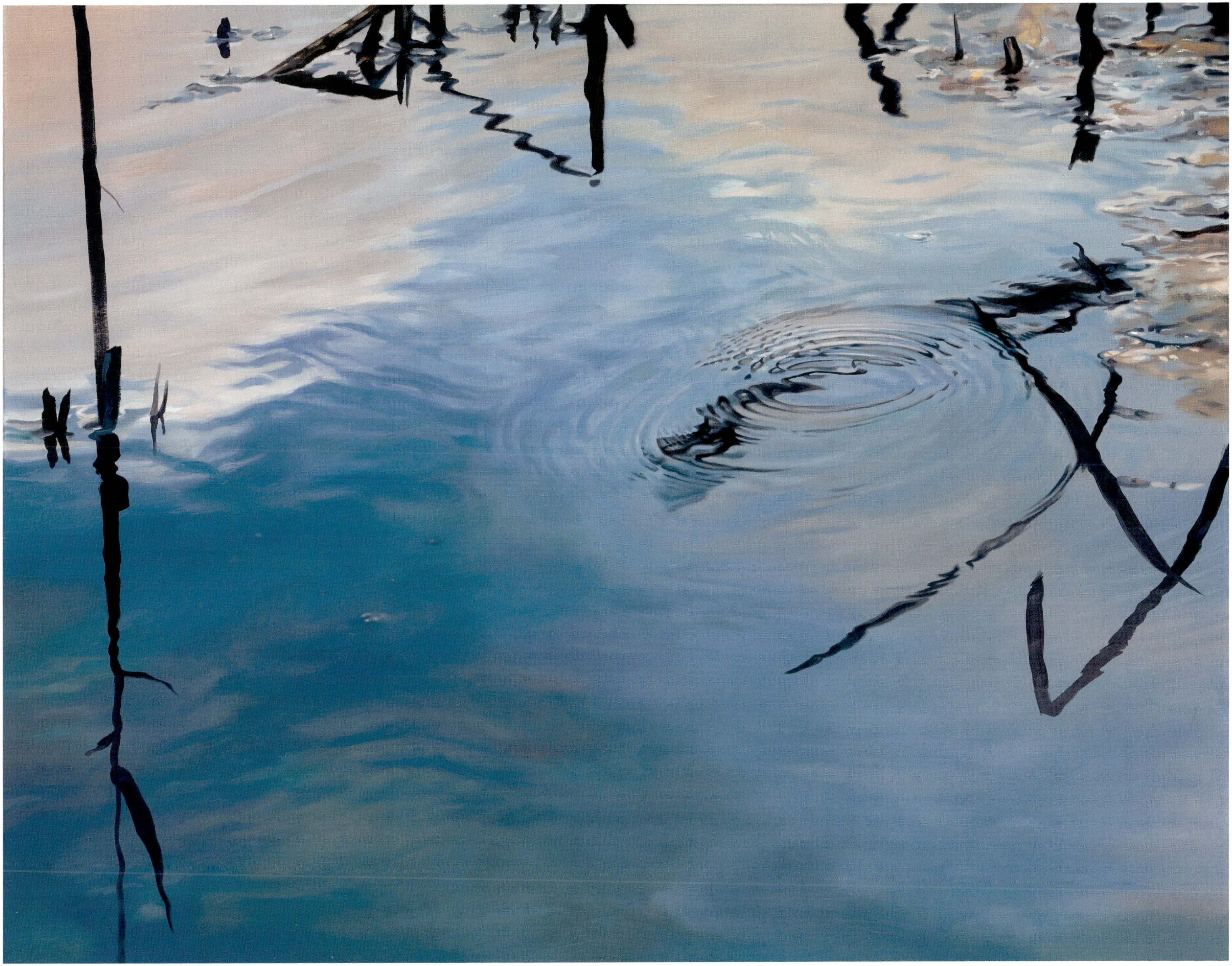

Black Reeds
oils on canvas 80x100 cm

25 October

For some reason I woke up very early this morning and immediately noticed more light than usual coming around the edge of the curtains.
The suspense was unbearable and I had to get up and have a look out of my window. There was a moonlit glow coming from the marsh. I quickly got ready and headed down to Cley Quay next to the mill. The combination of the moon and a thick frost created an eerie, magical light and the stillness of the air created an imaginary feeling of a film set. In this painting I tried to capture the iciness of the air, cool colours, a static landscape, frozen in time. The only movement was the sky as the mist rose. I needed to paint this scene large to create a cinematic feeling, so I picked out a metre by metre canvas to work on.

The lovely couple from Holt that bought the picture needed it delivering which enabled me to see where the picture was going to go. I still remember the fun of hanging the picture in their living room. It had to fit between the ceiling and the mantelpiece, it was a tight squeeze with only a few centimetres to spare but fortunately it looked like it really belonged in the space. I like creating a picture that you can almost walk into, bringing what I see indoors.

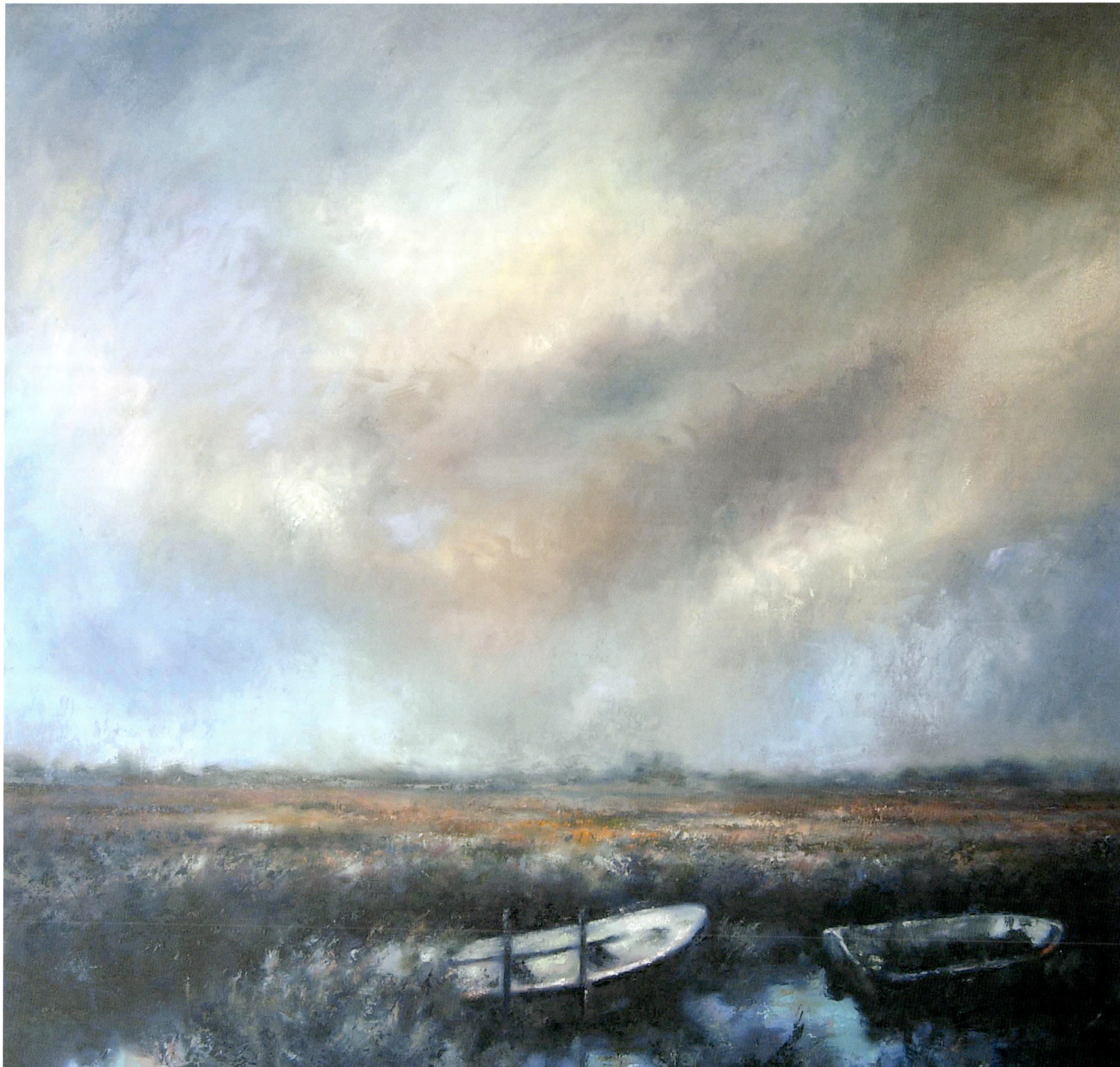

Cley Quay At Dawn
oils on canvas
100x100 cm

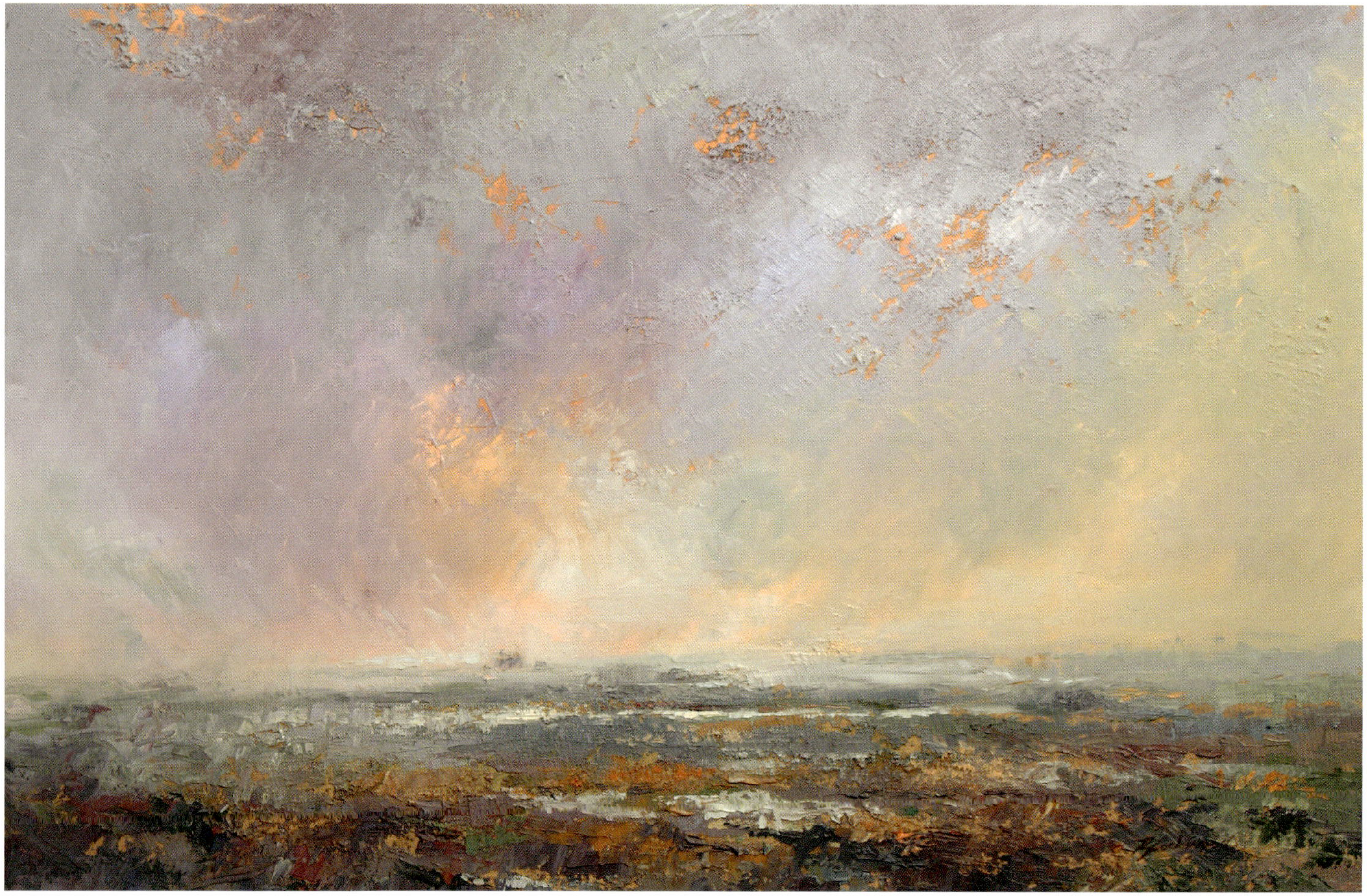

Halfway House, Blakeney
oils on canvas   50x70 cm

28 October

It's a grey, cold day today. The air is still and calm. The sky is full of multi-layers of various types of cloud, some look like they've been sieved – scattered thin strands, torn and tattered, and others solid and building from the horizon.

Even though I have a thermal suit to work in outside, I've found that some temperatures are just too painful on the hands. Instead I soak up the scene and gather reference. It's not far back to my studio where I light my fire and pour all that I've seen and felt down on to canvas. This view is my favourite again, Halfway House as I call it (everyone tells me it's called the Watch House, but old habits die hard). Like a desolatory 'figure' there on the marsh. Bitter winds scraping across it, scouring the land.

30 October

A battle commenced when I started the painting on the right. I began by putting down what I saw. I thought the simple landscape that was there before me would be enough to make a painting. So I began laying down the simple lines of reeds, with a pale frosted sky with the pale horizontal lines of Blakeney Point in the distance. But the picture was too flat for me. I wanted a way in to the reeds, a way of getting closer to the water in the distance. Days went by and the layers of paint gradually brought the reeds to life and began to give a depth to the sky, but I felt that there was still something missing. After fiddling with this that and the other, not really solving the problem, I suddenly thought boats, it needs boats. I know they are only small on the horizon, and not really what I saw at that moment, but for me they completed this battleground of a picture. The pleasure of being an artist – deception.

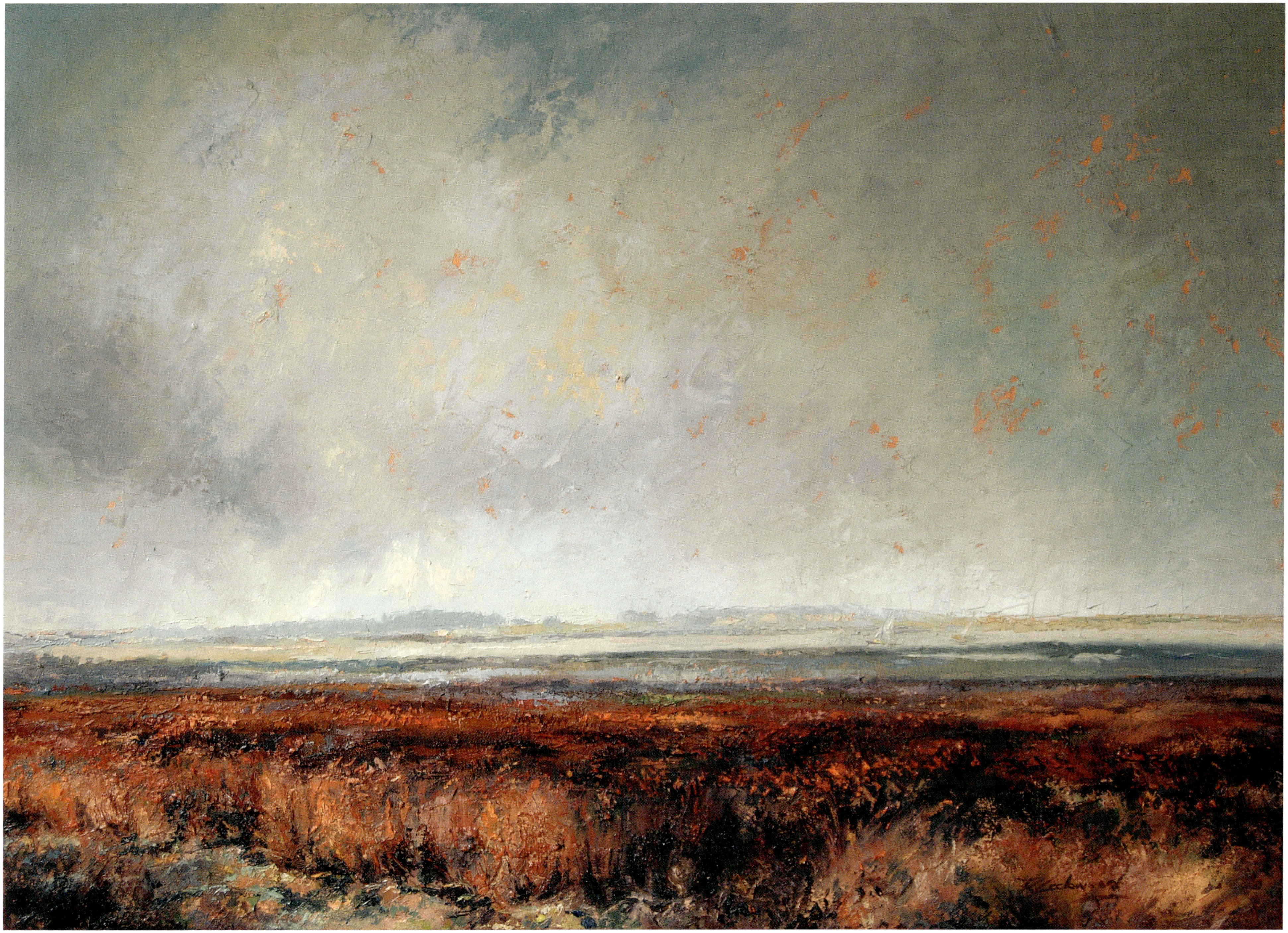

Towards East Hills, Morston
oils on canvas 60x80 cm

2 November

To be honest, some paintings are a painful process. Many times I've started paintings with a clear idea in my head and have ended up being taken on a completely different journey. I'm not sure if this is typical of most artists or whether it is weird and wonderful to me but it's the way it goes sometimes. It's like, yeah you've got an idea for a painting but something stored in your memory has a greater need to escape. At first I used to fight for control over these hijackings but now I've realized that if they have their way, they then leave me alone.

I can just remember how this painting began. It was quite a literal scene of sky and sea, a straightforward view from my old studio window in Sheringham that overlooked the sea, but from the outset it proved to be difficult. The clouds felt wrong and the sea wouldn't work, it was like I had a wooden arm, awkward and defiant. So I left the picture for a while, I just didn't know what to do or where to go with it. Then I thought I'd change the clouds and darken the sea. I planned it again in my head, trying to imagine the final painting, then I'd build up the courage to start, maybe have another cup of tea first, then run at it with bold sweeps of my brush. But I approached the canvas and started with a mark and something seemed to take over. One mark led to another, it flowed and weird marks made more sense than those I controlled earlier, and on it went. Now I realized what was happening. We'd been walking recently over at Holkham, I'd been showing an artist friend the fantastic open beach and neighbouring pine forest. This was the scene that was trying to come out of the painting. Now I knew what it wanted to be, I could relax into the painting.

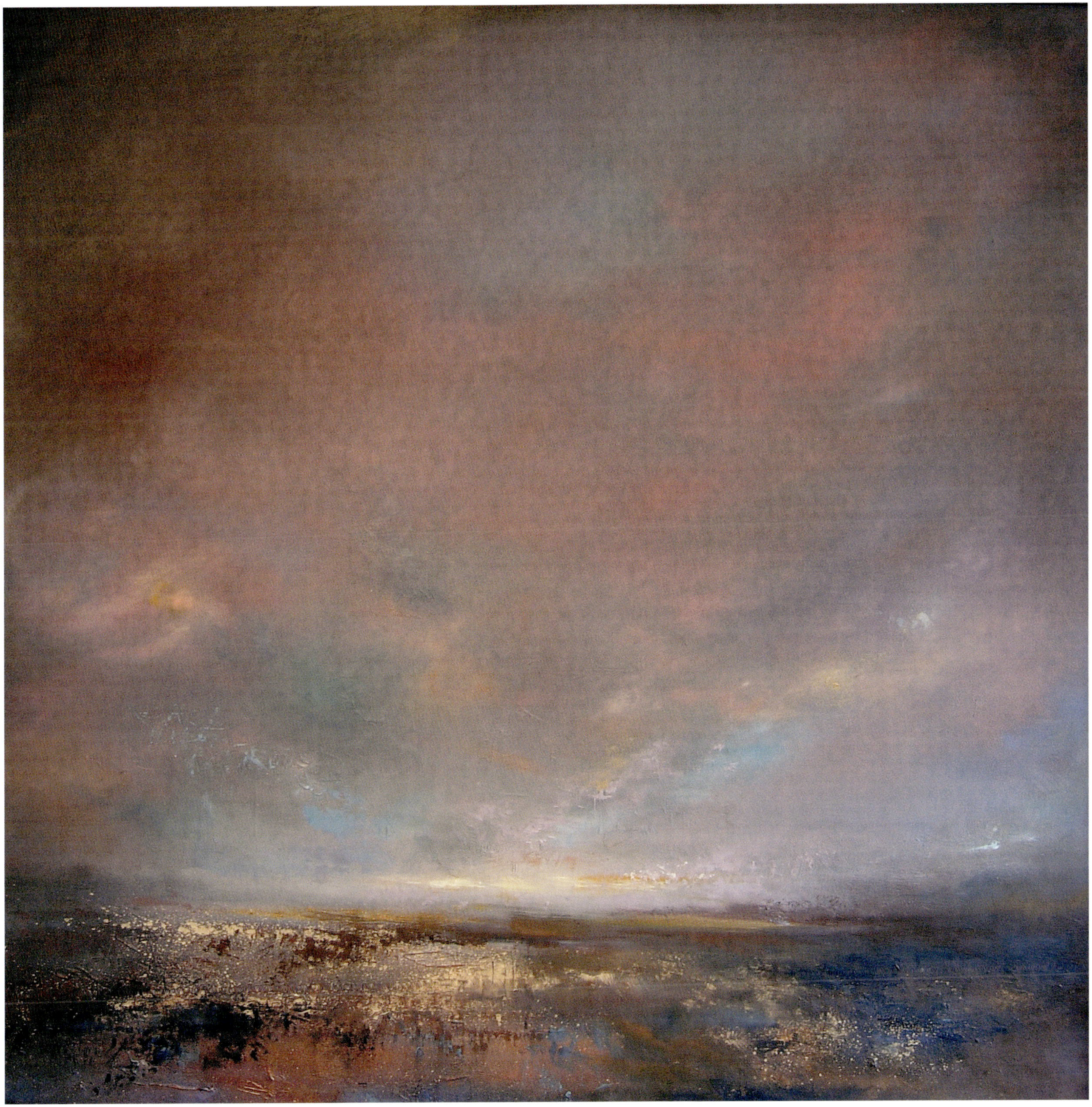

Holkham Sands
oils on canvas
100x100 cm

5 November

I found it difficult to wake up this morning, even though the sparrows were noisily chirping outside my window and laughter from the women from Picnic Fayre Deli made me smile to myself. But eventually my conscience began to nag that the day had begun and that I should get up and brave the freezing cold.

My friend and fellow artist Dan Cole was due to arrive late morning, he'd driven through the night from Cornwall. His wife Helen had packed him a boxful of flying saucers and fizzy cola sweets, so by the time he arrived he had no need for sleep! After forcing him to have a big breakfast and a large mug of tea, we got to grips with the busy day ahead of us. We had to hang our joint exhibition, which was opening the next day. It always takes longer than you imagine but finally by 4.30pm we were finished. I was amazed that Dan then suggested we walk down to Cley beach – the man just doesn't sleep! It was a bitter wind that blew in from the sea and after looking out for a minute or two, we decided to head back. When we reached the water pools on the west side of the path, an egret made us stop. It was a striking bright white against the darkening marsh; silently it picked its way around the edges of the pools but didn't hang around for long. Then mist began to rise from the surface of the water and transfixed us further. We were mezmerised and stood silently, both taking it all in, painting imaginary pictures in our minds. I think forty minutes went by before our eyes could no longer see through the dark, only then did we realize how freezing cold we were. There was only one thing for it – warming whiskies in The George.

I painted this picture from my memories of that evening using a bit of extra reference for the cloud. I can still remember the cold as I look at it now – and the whisky.

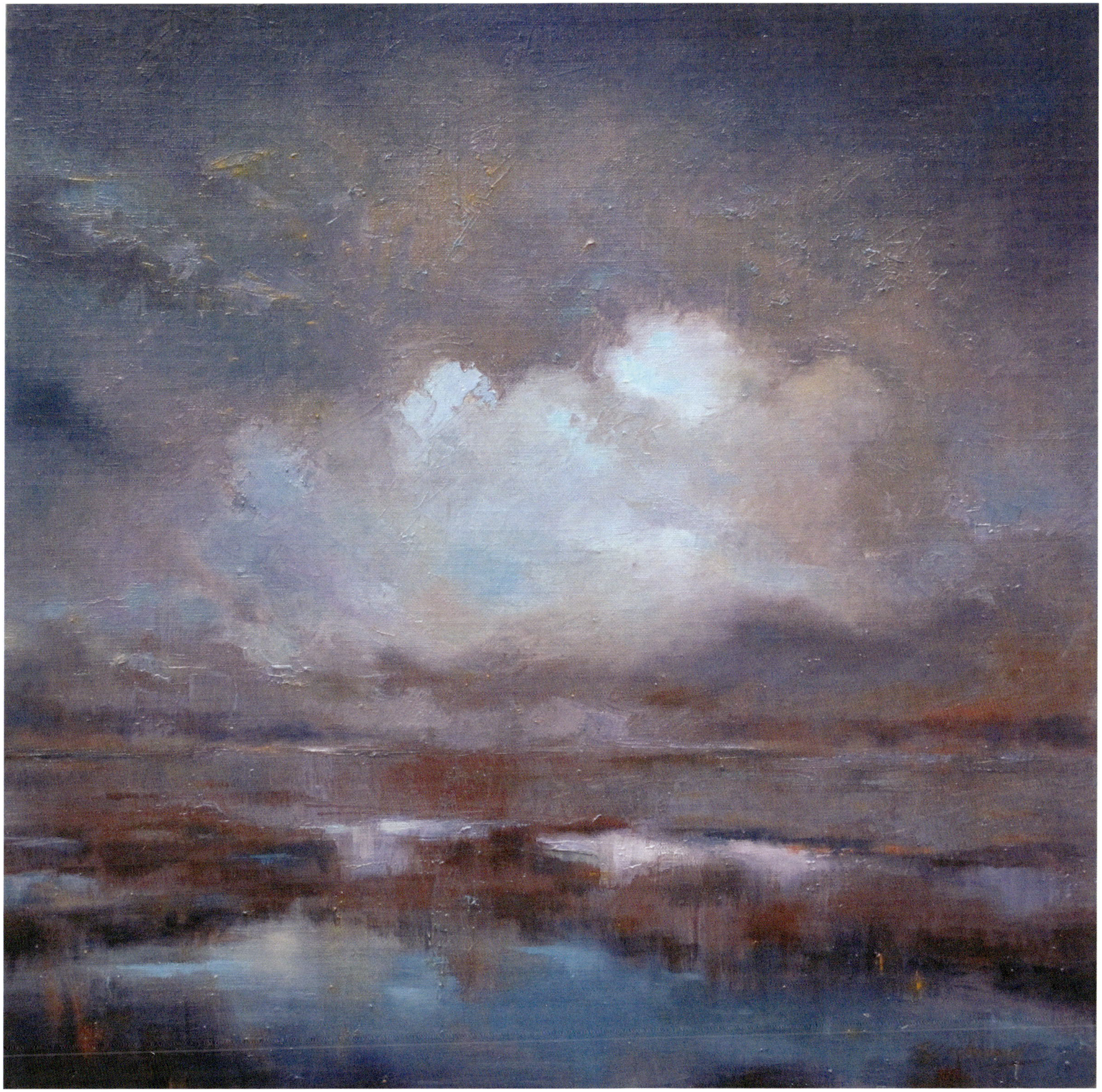

Night Marsh Pools, Cley
oils on linen
60x60 cm

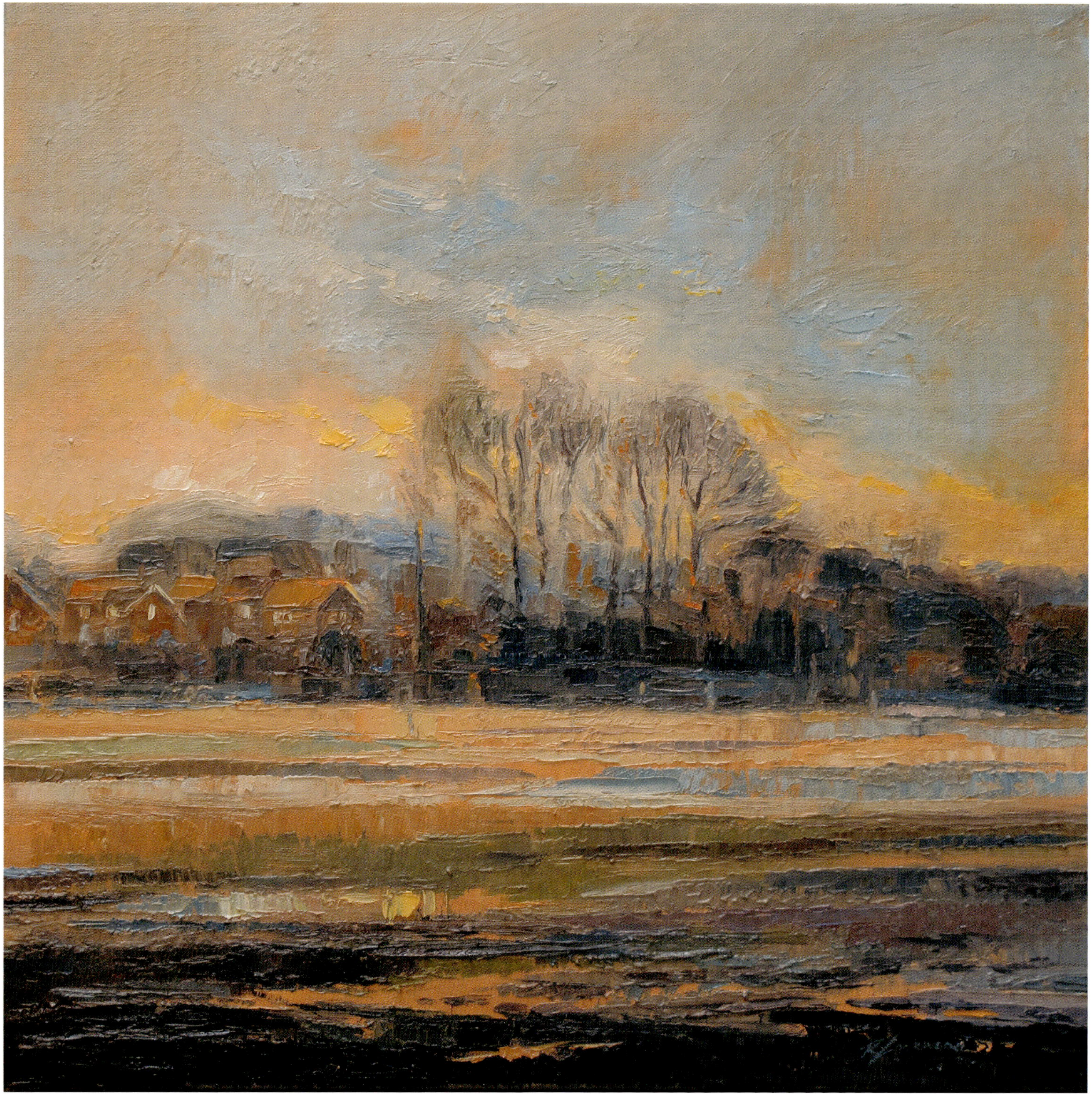

Winter Meadow, Cley
oils on canvas
50x50 cm

9 November

Even when I'm taking an evening run around my home patch, I'm always looking out for possible scenes to paint. The landscape is constantly changing throughout the year and I'm determined not to miss a thing. Most of the scenes I come across I find by accident, simply from constantly being out there. On the days I actually go out in search of a potential painting, invariably I come home disappointed. So over the years I've come to realise never to take an opportunity for granted; they're usually just fleeting moments where the light or weather change so quickly and then disappear.

Summer is probably the easiest time to paint as the light is more constant, even though the landscape tends to be flatter because of it. But one of the things I love about winter is the shadows, albeit they are more transient.

I saw the view on the left while out jogging. It's from a gate just before you reach the bridge at Wiveton. I couldn't stop when I was running for fear of seizing up, so I made a note to come back later. After several visits the perfect evening came – ice on the marsh combined with an amazing evening light.

To make the most of this evening, I walked out on the marshes. It was the smallest of details that inspired me to paint this picture on the right, just one solitary streak of light on the horizon, it brought the whole landscape to life.

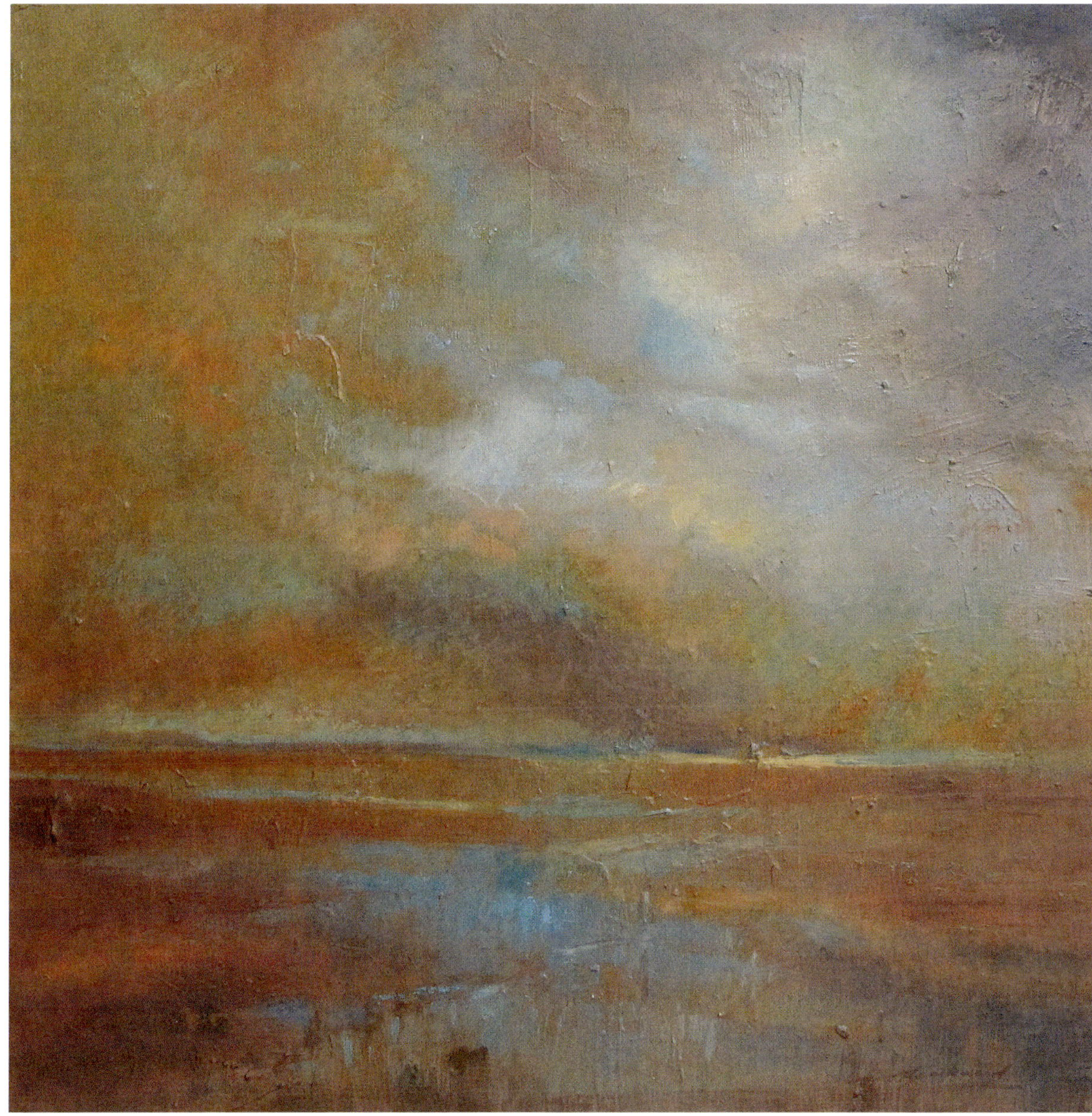

Light On Horizon
oils on canvas 50x50 cm

15 November

The frost this morning made the landscape the colour of boiled bones – chalky and pale, but with rich colours remaining in the protective folds of marsh plants. It's a challenge looking for colour in this landscape but the longer you stare, the more you begin to see. Pale greys become pinks and yellows, grey mauves and faded limes.

I love this building on the Point as it's so incongruous, a dazzling bright blue building rising from the empty marsh set in a National Trust nature reserve. It used to be a Lifeboat station but now it's a visitor centre, a welcome respite after the arduous walk from Cley Beach car park, or a boat trip if you don't fancy the long trek. I don't think I'll ever tire of painting this scene. This and the Watch House (I call it Halfway House) further along the Point are my two favourite landmarks for painting.

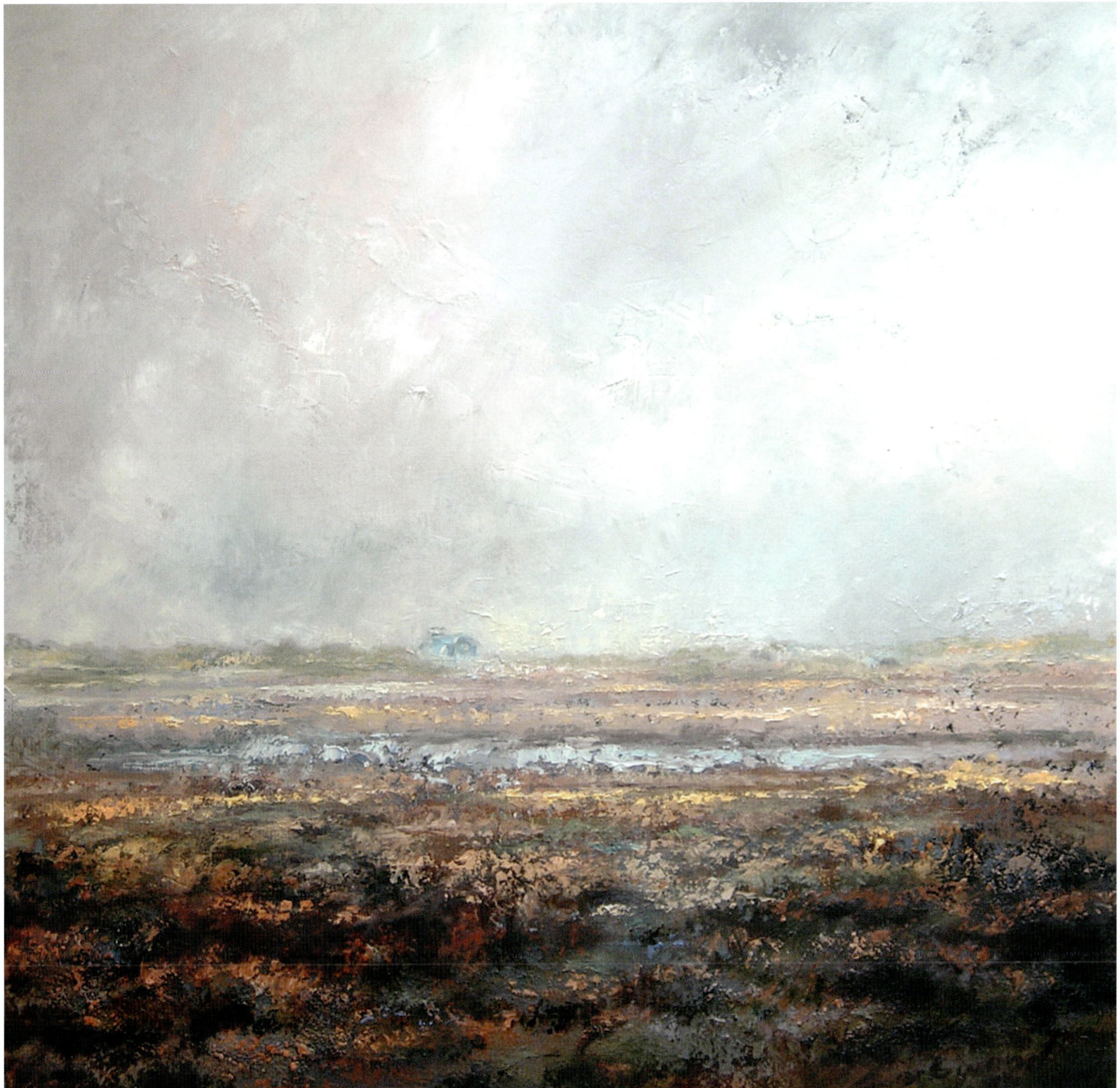

Old Life Boat Station,
Blakeney Point
oils on canvas
60x60 cm

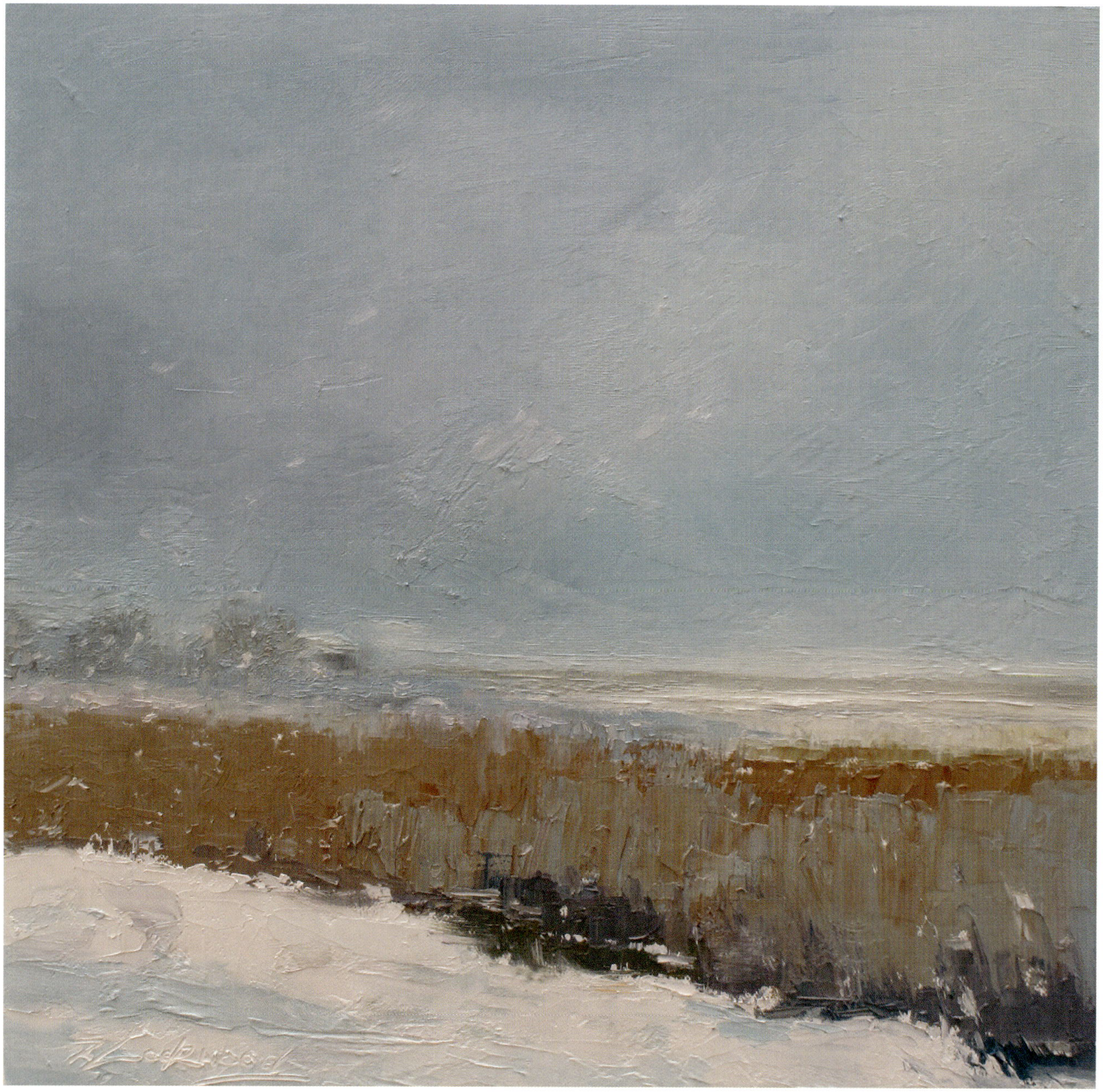

Snow on the Reserve, Cley
oils on canvas 40x40 cm

2 December

Somehow I knew even before I pulled the curtains back this morning that it had been snowing. The sounds are different, still and muffled. I walked the long way to the studio this morning as I wanted to see the reeds in the snow. The moorhens didn't seem impressed by this rude blanket of cold invading their home; many were calling, as if in complaint, constantly flicking their tails as they strutted past me.

As there was hardly any wind, snow still clung to the seaward side of the reed mace heads. It must have come in from the north or north-east and it looked like more was on its way; I walked quickly to the studio to light my woodburner. This was a quick painting, done pretty much as soon as I'd finished with the fire. It's more of a memory for me than a finished oil painting. But I'm happy with it and leave it propped up against the wall in my studio.

18 December

I don't always paint from my doorstep; I saw this landscape while driving back from a visit to my family in Sheffield. It was so unassuming and yet so striking, I had to pull over. It was just a field of freshly turned earth, a typical rural fenland scene but the line of sunlight stretching across it turned a mundane scene into something extraordinary. As the sunlight panned across the fields and into the distance, it lit up a wind farm just visible on the horizon - what a contrast.

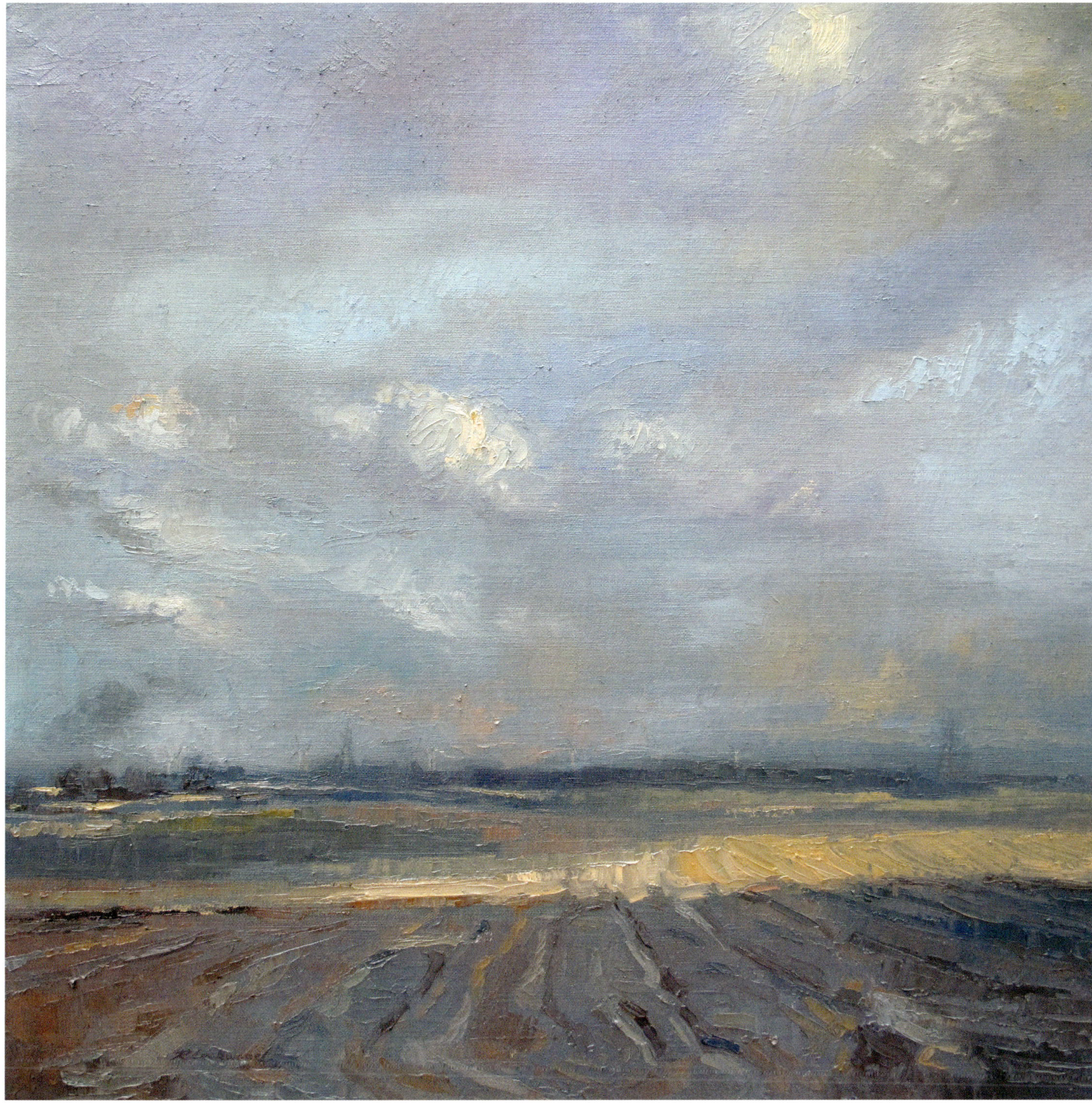

Ploughed Field
oils on canvas 60x60 cm

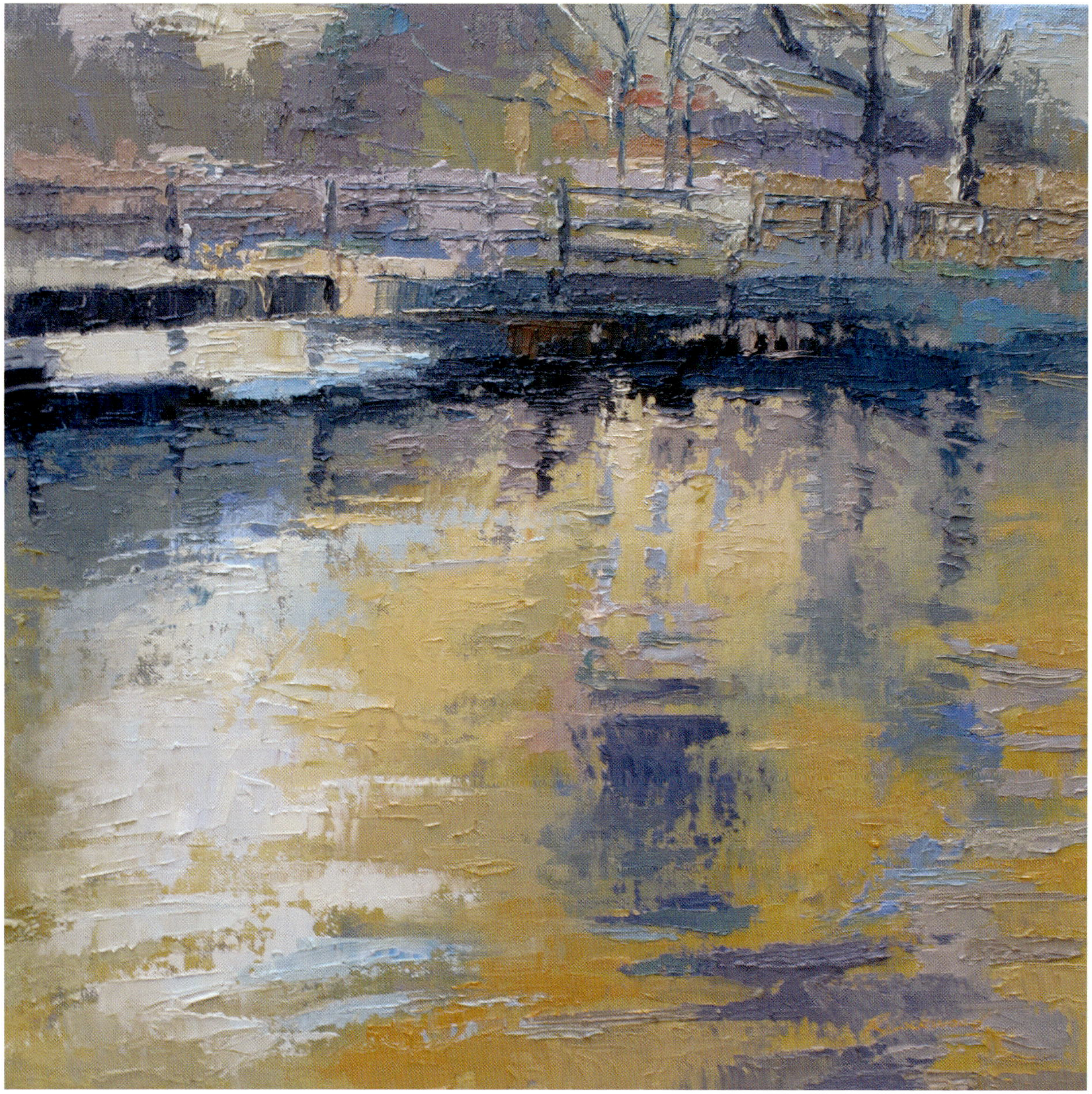

Letheringsett Ford
oils on canvas board
35x35 cm

29 November

I have a big appetite for colour – I'm drawn to it and will try to squeeze it out of the palest thing. I've tried painting simpler, more muted images but I can't – colour just wants to come out. I start with an olive-grey and before I know it, oranges and turquoises have found their way through. So when I come across a view that is unusual in colour, I have to stop and take it all in. And it is amazing, in my eyes anyway, how much colour there is out there.

After a regular visit to the mill at Letheringsett to get my flour, I made a detour to check out the ford. It's a beautiful spot and recently I'd noticed some Highland Cows standing in the stream – surely a future painting. I wanted to see if they were there again, but they were way off in the distance, camouflaged like haystacks. There had been a few storms over the previous days, leaving the water levels high in the ford. This particular afternoon the sky looked sulphurous and brooding, which created strange reflections on the water. It was such an unusual colour, I knew it had to become a painting.

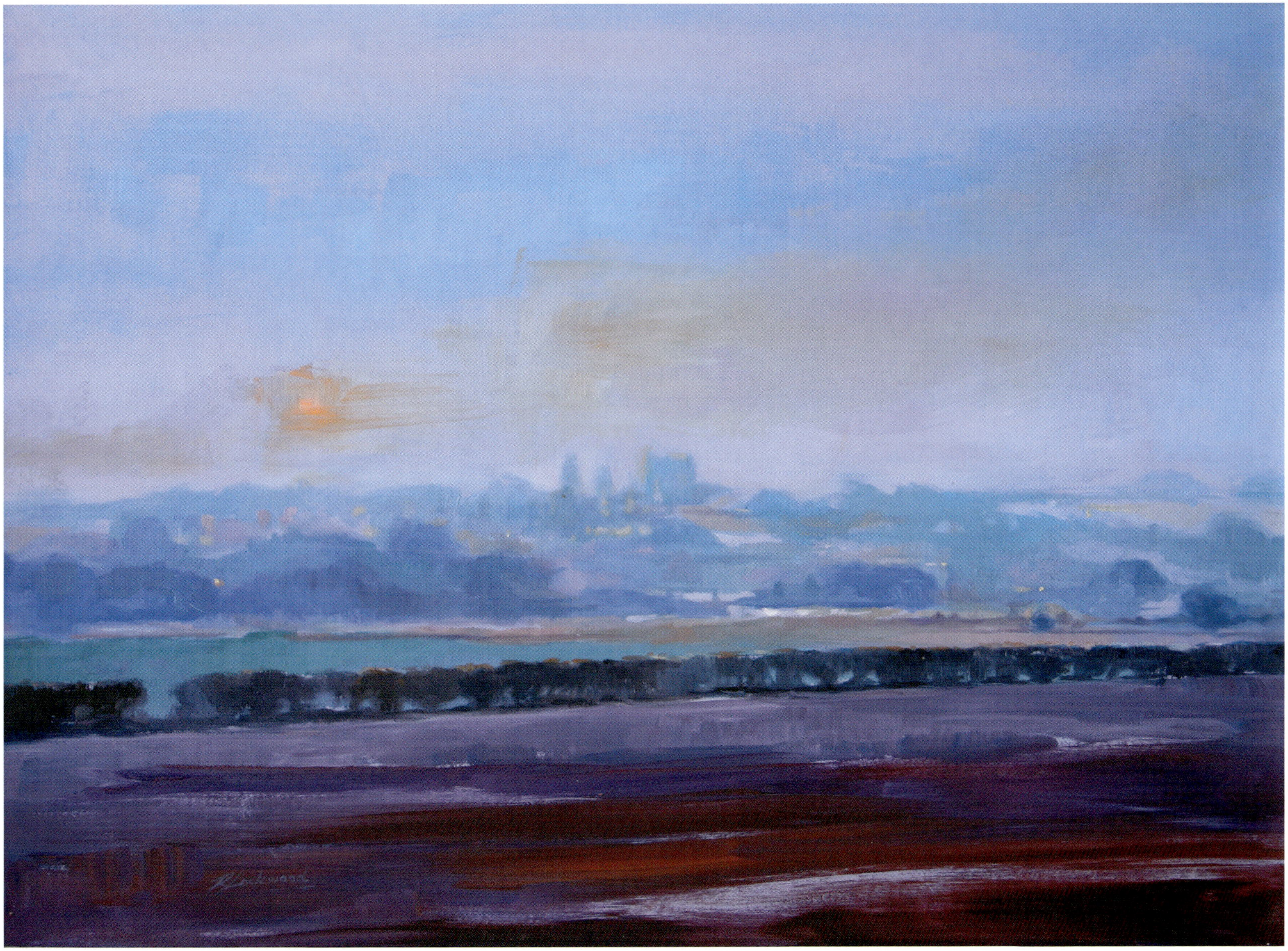

Late Light, Fakenham
oils on canvas 40x50 cm

15 December

I started this painting some time ago of a view over towards Fakenham. It's not my usual area for painting, but I was driving back from the framers when I looked across the fields and saw this vivid landscape. My eyes were probably still getting used to the fading light but this was how I saw it. I didn't hold back when it came to using the mauves and purples and the orange on the turquoise sky – being allowed to add that - well it's like the cherry on the cake…hmm cake.

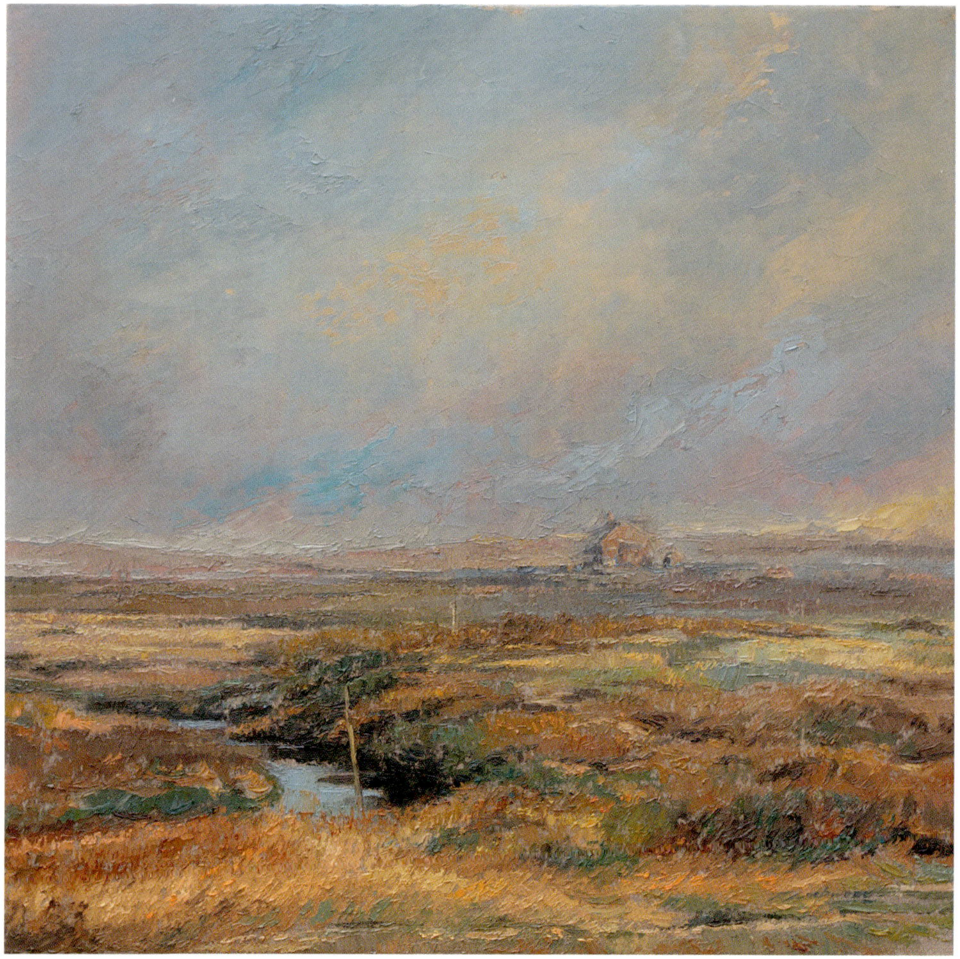

Halfway House, Cley
oils on canvas 60x60 cm

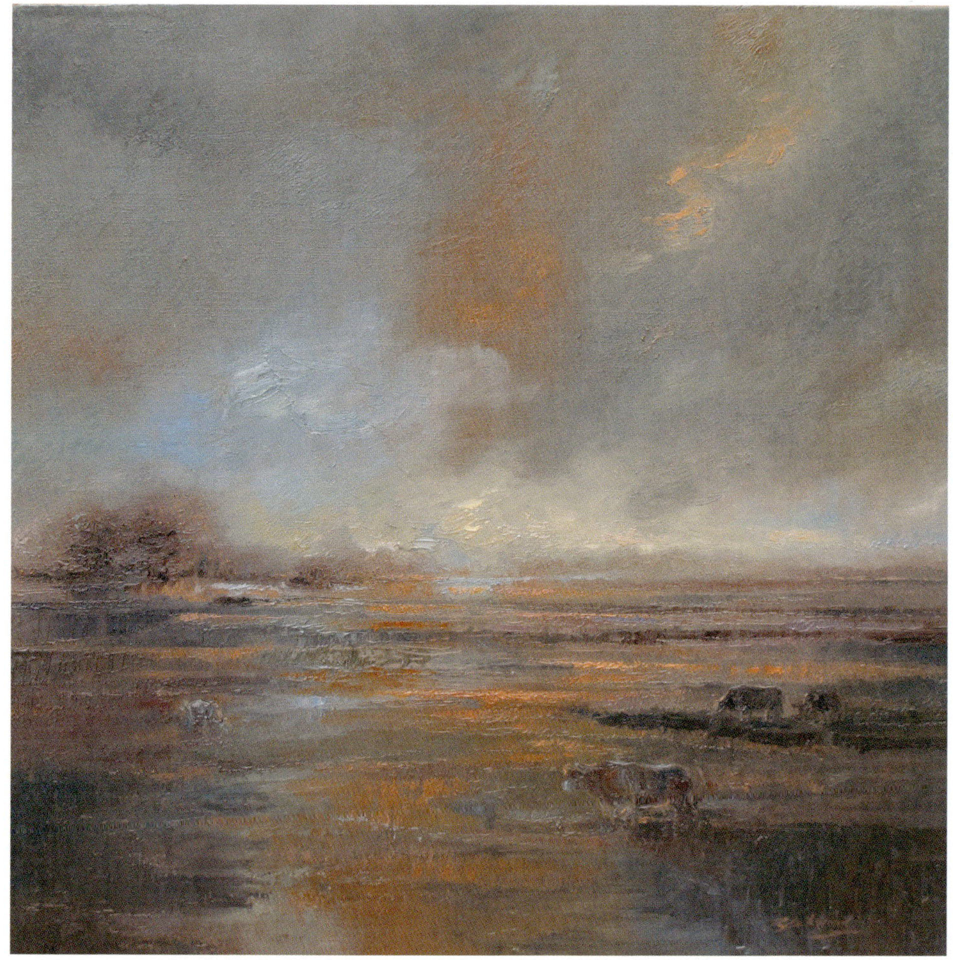

Evening Over the Freshes, Cley
oils on canvas 60x60 cm

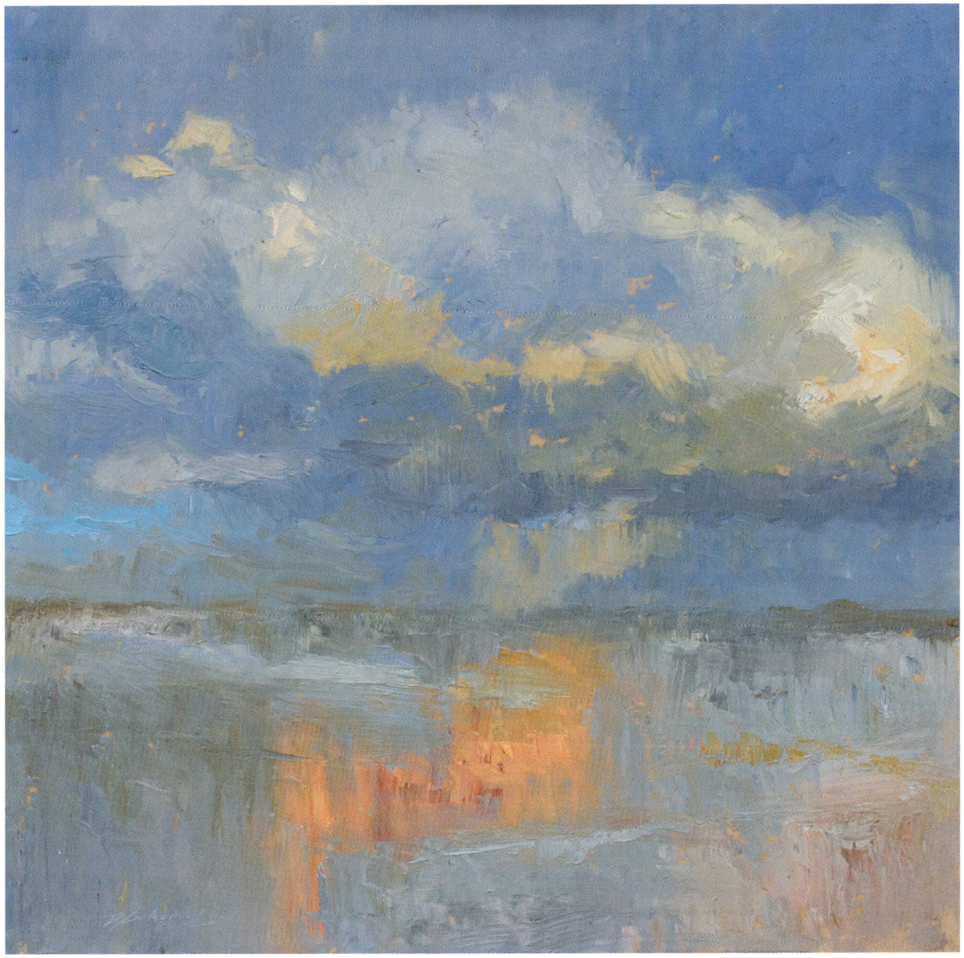

Pale Light Over The Freshes, Cley
oils on board 60x60 cm

....and finally, at the time of putting this book together we've been spoilt by some glorious summer weather. In the last week alone we've had strong winds, thunder storms, torrential rain, blistering sunshine, high tides and a full moon - all of which make great painting conditions out on the marsh. I couldn't help but add my most recent paintings of my favourite place. The beauty of painting here is knowing that tomorrow morning the light out on the marsh will be completely different again.

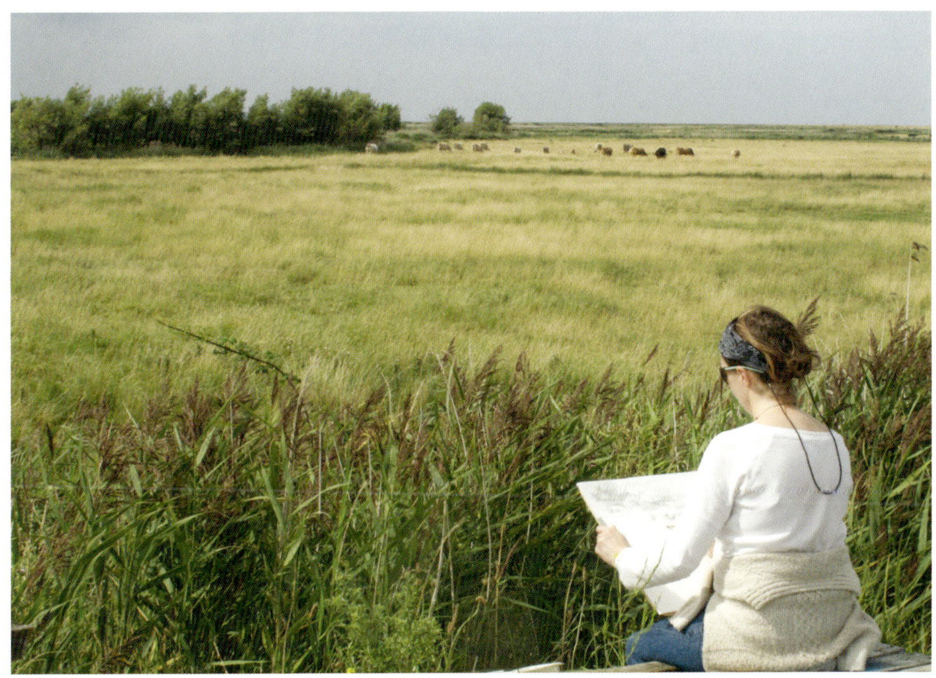

One of my favourite places to paint is just behind the gallery on the coastal path to Blakeney. Here I can see cows, marsh, water and of course the big skies.

My Studio

Although my inspiration comes from outside, some of my painting is done from my studio, so it seemed only fair to give this wonderful space a bit of credit too. I moved my studio from Sheringham to be closer to home, luckily we found three acres of grazing land for sale on the edge of Cley. We converted the stable into my studio and decided to convert the land into a mini nature reserve. To date we've planted over 400 trees and shrubs, and there's more to follow. I know it's going to take a long time to revert the land back to a natural state, but amazingly within two months of erecting a Barn Owl box, a pair moved in and went on to raise two chicks. Also, within a few months of building a natural pond, frogs, newts, dragonflies and many other creatures took up residence. As well as the natural pond, I've built a deeper pond for fish and lilies. This I use to some extent as a stage set. By moving certain potted plants around, I can create scenes to paint. It may sound a little contrived but there's no substitute to painting from the real thing.

Another of my favourite painting subjects is mice. Apart from Sophie's and Amy's cats bringing them in by the bucket-load, it's hard to get up close to them. So I've got various areas around the studio where I encourage them to visit. Luckily we have Harvest Mice in the fields as well as my favourite Wood Mice. I like the idea of seeing the land around the studio as another canvas. Gradually I want to add layer upon layer to the landscape, wildflowers, shrubs and trees, and if I could, I'd create my own personal marsh - but that's a pipe dream!

Thank Yous

Finally I'd like to say thank you to Red Hare Publishing for giving me the support and opportunity to produce this book. And especially Sarah who has helped me with the text and created the book. And many thanks to Mike Dawson and Danny from Crowes for all their help and support, especially Mike's proof-reading expertise! And of course to Virginia McKenna (bornfree.org.uk) my childhood hero, for writing my foreword.

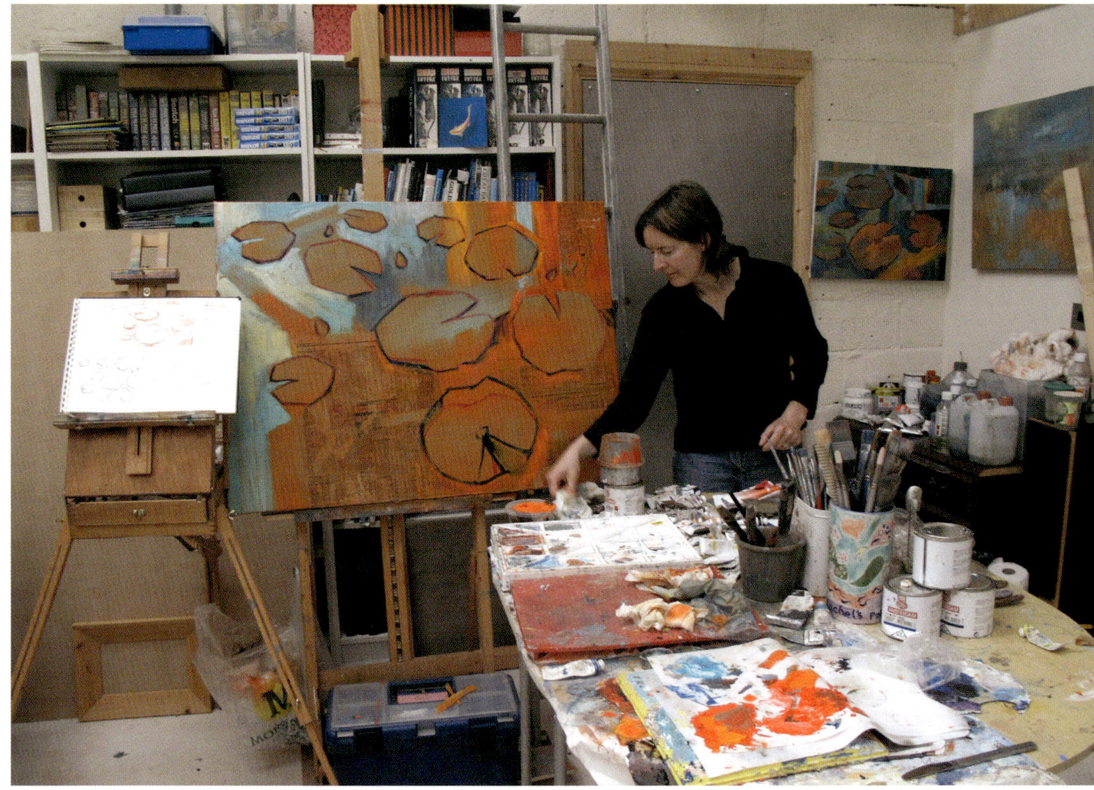

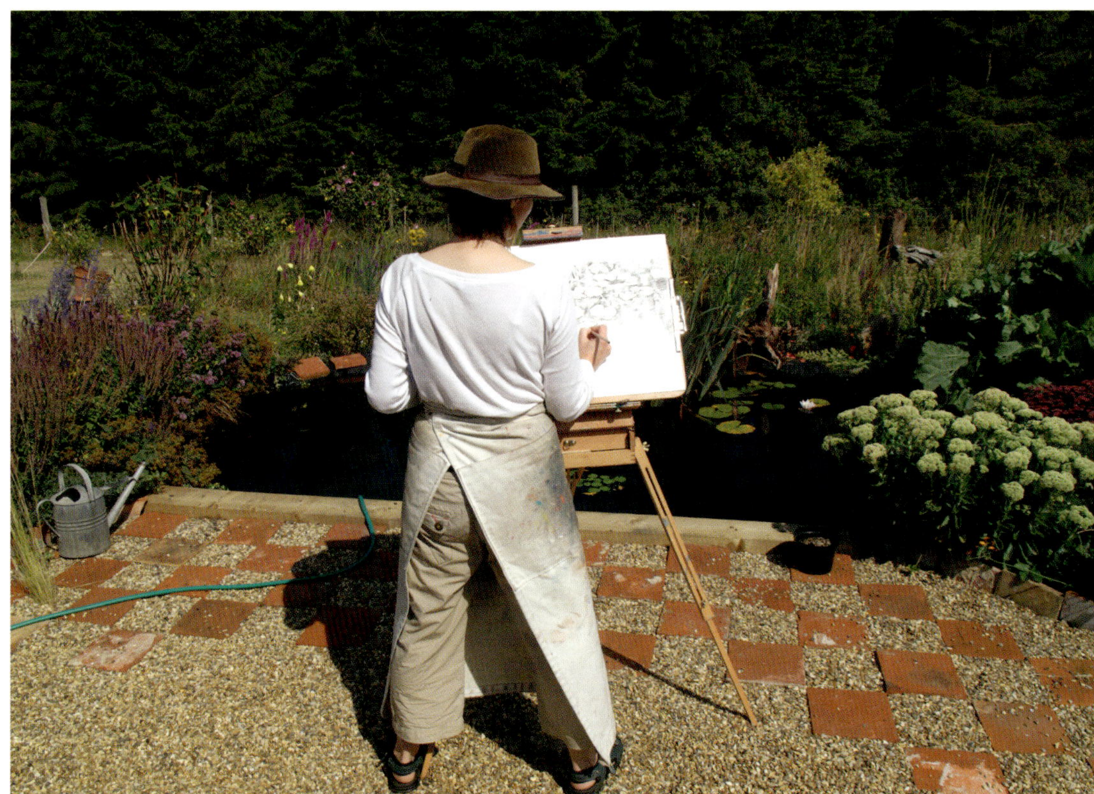

Top: me in my studio
Below: sketching the lilies in my pond.

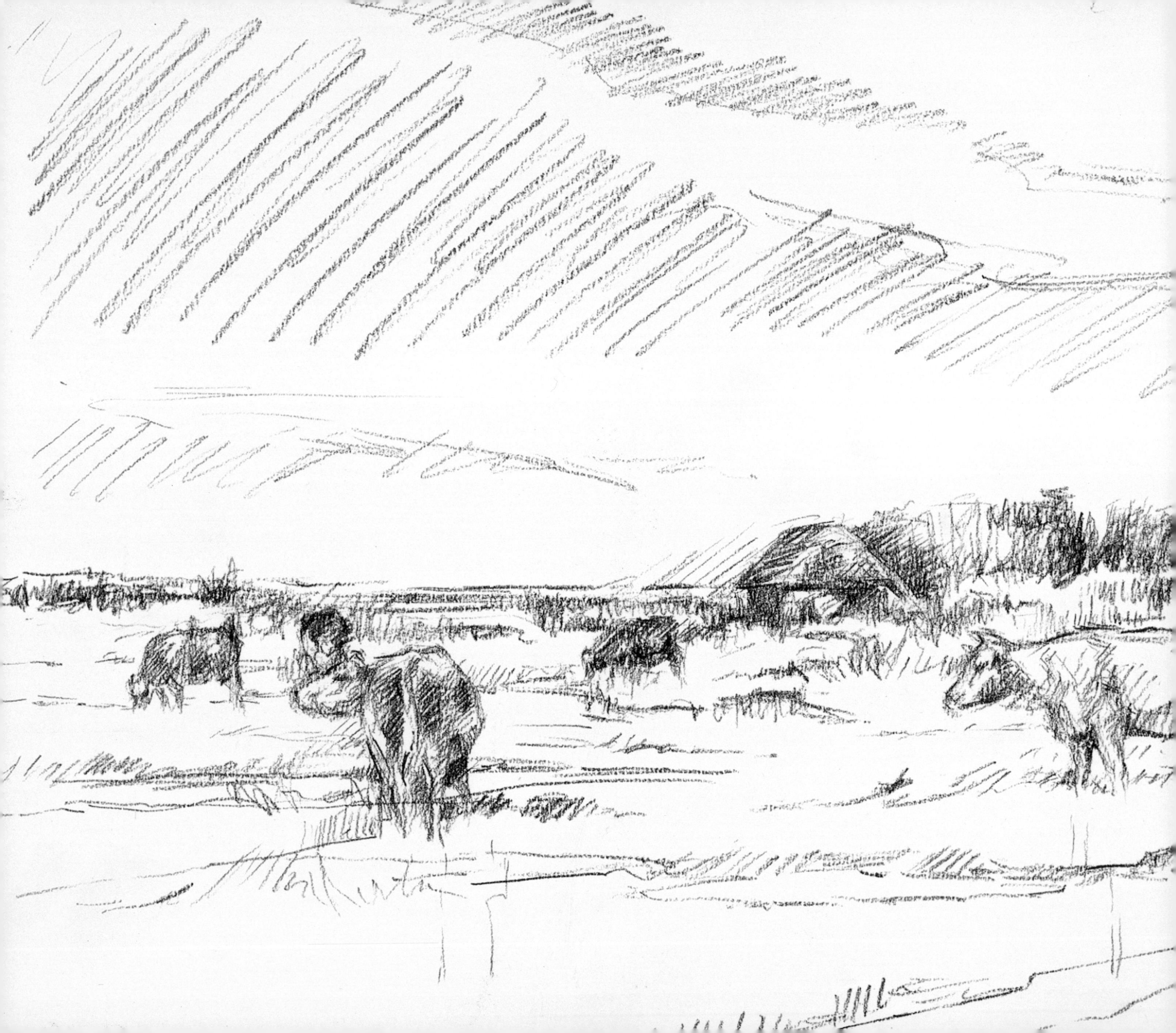